TRAUMATIC DEFEAT

TRAUMATIC DEFEAT

POWs, MIAs, *and* NATIONAL MYTHMAKING

Patrick Gallagher

University Press of Kansas

Published by the University Press of Kansas (Lawrence, Kansas
66045), which was organized by the Kansas Board of Regents and
is operated and funded by Emporia State University, Fort Hays State
University, Kansas State University, Pittsburg State University, the
University of Kansas, and Wichita State University

Library of Congress Cataloging-in-Publication Data

Names: Gallagher, Patrick, 1979– author.
Title: Traumatic defeat : POWs, MIAs, and national mythmaking
/ Patrick Gallagher.
Description: Lawrence, Kansas : University Press of Kansas,
[2018] | Includes bibliographical references and index.
Identifiers: LCCN 2018004670
ISBN 9780700626441 (cloth : alk. paper)
ISBN 9780700626458 (ebook)
Subjects: LCSH: Prisoners of war—Germany—History—20th
century. | Loss (Psychology)—Political aspects—Case studies. |
War—Psychological aspects—Case studies. | Conspiracy theories—
Case studies. | Collective memory—Case studies. | World War,
1939–1945—Missing in action—Germany. | World War, 1939–
1945—Prisoners and prisons, Russian. | Prisoners of war—United
States—History—20th century. | Vietnam War, 1961–1975—
Prisoners and prisons, North Vietnamese. | Vietnam War, 1961–
1975—Missing in action—United States.
Classification: LCC D805.G3 G319 2018
DDC 940.54/7208931—dc23.
LC record available at https://lccn.loc.gov/2018004670.

British Library Cataloguing-in-Publication Data is available.

Printed in the United States of America

10 9 8 7 6 5 4 3 2 1

The paper used in this publication is recycled and contains 30
percent postconsumer waste. It is acid free and meets the minimum
requirements of the American National Standard for Permanence of
Paper for Printed Library Materials Z39.48-1992.

Contents

Acknowledgments

This book was many years in the making, and I can scarce begin to thank all the people who assisted me in writing it. I got the very earliest idea that grew into it while studying for my comprehensive exams as a graduate student in the History Department at the State University of New York at Albany, and great thanks go to Professors Dan White, Richard Fogarty, and Carl Bon Tempo, who helped guide my research and writing. The department also assisted me generally with travel grants, and with general support and assistance in my program overall. The Communications Workers of America, of which I was a member as a unionized graduate student, also helped me finance travel to various archives with its Graduate Student Employees Union Professional Development Awards program.

Considerable primary research went into the writing of this book, and many were the weeks I spent sitting in archives, frantically poring over material as quickly as I could. I am indebted to the assistance of many archivists in finding all that I did. I am exceptionally grateful for the assistance given by the staff of the National Archives in Washington, DC. Similarly, the staff at the Richard Nixon Presidential Library were very helpful—particularly Jason Schultz, who helped me coordinate my research at that facility. I also owe Annagret Neupert at the Bundesarchiv-Koblenz a great deal of thanks for her assistance in my research in Germany, as well as answering any number of questions I had regarding use of the material I found there for this book.

I should not fail to mention the support I received from my family both in the initial decision to finally go to graduate school and become a professional historian, and in writing on this topic. My parents, both of whom are part of the Vietnam generation, have always encouraged my love of history and have my thanks for that. Finally, I cannot thank my wife, Marcia, enough for her love, support, and—especially—patience as I worked through the long years of writing this book.

Introduction

Wars breed myths, and each war shapes its attendant mythology through its course and conclusion. One of the biggest determining factors to shape war myths is whether a given nation is among the victors or the vanquished. For the former, wartime mythology tends toward triumphant validation of whatever national virtues presumably led to victory, while the latter often tell stories and invent myths to explain their defeat, or find some way to cushion its impact. In some cases, defeated nations take this further and create myths centered on prisoners of war (POWs) and those missing in action (MIAs) to justify the lost struggle, mute national guilt for wartime crimes, and in extreme cases reject the very verdict of defeat itself. Born from POW/MIA activism, such myths hold that some MIAs survive in secret, undisclosed camps during and after the war, kept there by the enemy for various reasons.

Secret camp myths evolve from two parallel needs within defeated nations, each of which serves to reinforce the other. The first is born from the hopes of relatives of the missing, who often find themselves unable to mourn in the absence of a corpse or other conclusive proof of death. Trapped in a no-man's land of grief, these family members cling to the idea that their missing men cannot be dead but rather must survive in secret enemy prison camps. Believers in secret camps can become so personally invested that seemingly no amount of evidence against the existence of such camps is sufficient to change their minds, nor is any length of time without the return of the missing. The second is the need many feel to find something redemptive from the larger war experience. In particular, morally ambiguous wars make the celebration of traditional war heroes difficult, and so those searching for substitutes seize upon the figures of POWs and MIAs as acceptable replacements. By so doing, advocates of the alleged secret camps in which MIAs supposedly survive emphasize the suffering of those missing men as a way to highlight the real or imagined victimization of the nation at large. In this way, such advocates create a social space in which those who want to imagine themselves as victims-by-proxy of their own wars can do so. This process creates something redemptive for a defeated nation and also appropriates the suffering of the victims of that nation's wartime atrocities, while simultaneously downplaying whatever responsibility the nation had for the war to begin with. Therefore, the construction of secret camp myths necessarily involves distorting the truth about the wars that spawn them, and it entails a retreat from reality both on a personal and national level.

This book presents two case studies of the secret camp myth: West Germany in the aftermath of World War II, and the United States after the Vietnam War. In the former instance, the myth was directed specifically at the Eastern Front and men missing in the Soviet Union, rather than those captured by the Western Allies. The American secret camp myth focuses on all US servicemen missing from war in Southeast Asia. Though both are predated by a French secret camp myth from World War I, these two instances have enough in common to be useful for the student of war and its aftermath. Specifically, both nations suffered extreme trauma by losing their respective wars, and both had a difficult time finding redemptive elements from their wartime experiences, in particular uncompromised war heroes.[1] Lacking such heroes, both settled on POWs and MIAs as suitable substitutes; by focusing on them West Germany and the United States minimized their own feelings of war guilt and recast themselves as victims of wars they had started.

Though the cases are similar there are also differences, particularly with regard to the longevity of the American myth compared with the relatively short life of the German one. Indeed, German calls to bring the captives home had concluded by the mid-1950s at the latest, while to this day no self-respecting VFW or American Legion post is without its black POW/MIA flag.[2] The likelihood of American MIA survival was considerably less plausible than in the German instance, particularly because the Soviet Union did in fact retain large numbers of German prisoners following World War II and was at times inconsistent in reporting just how many and which prisoners it still held. Contrarily, there is no credible evidence that Vietnam covertly kept any American prisoners following the end of that war, and yet that version of the myth survives. It is a striking inversion: in the case where it was more plausible to believe in secret camps, such a belief did not last long, whereas in the instance where continued captivity was not all that likely, people adhered to such a belief for decades. This dissimilarity becomes all the starker when one considers the actual numbers of missing for each nation. Germany's missing and unaccounted for numbered just over 2 million, the vast majority of whom disappeared somewhere on the Eastern Front.[3] America's missing in Southeast Asia reached only 2,255 in total. Even this number is a bit misleading, since just under half of these, 1,095, were never truly MIA or POW, but were instead known KIAs whose bodies were never recovered. Official reports on these men "Killed in Action—Bodies not Recovered" sometimes included them alongside actual MIAs, and sometimes not, further muddying waters already made murky by political demands for this or that man's status to be shifted from the KIA to MIA category.[4] By examining the secret camp myth as a larger phenomenon rather than as something specific to either Germany or the United States, this study will cast light on why the one concluded, and the other persisted, despite these disparities.

Germany fought a particularly atrocious war in all theaters, and especially on the Eastern Front. The United States, similarly though not equivalently, compromised its own image by the behavior and official policies of its military in Southeast Asia throughout the long Vietnam conflict. Though never a planned war of extermination like Germany's war in Eastern Europe, America's war in Southeast Asia included routine atrocity and massacre, despite a sort of collective amnesia that has since confined memories of such behavior to only well-publicized events like My Lai.[5] Each nation's respective civilian populations thus found their returning veterans to be less than ideal figures for national canonization, albeit not for exactly the same reasons. By the end of America's direct involvement in Vietnam in 1973 popular support had turned decisively against the war and those who had fought it, though never as contemptuously as is still commonly believed.[6] German veterans existed under the pervasive shadow of the Third Reich's atrocities, despite efforts to whitewash the actions of the regular army. In both cases, regular veterans served as unpleasant reminders of things better forgotten. Contrarily, activist groups and concerned individuals elevated POWs and MIAs to hero status by emphasizing how their heroism lay in their passive endurance of enemy captivity, the barbarities of which helped to downplay any involvement those men may have had in war crimes.

Germany's partition into East and West following World War II led to two very different attitudes toward veterans. In East Germany, Soviet pressure, political ideology, and antifascism as founding state doctrine all contributed to clamp down on any major idolization of POW returnees and impeded the creation of a social space in which they could be recast as heroes. By contrast, West Germans found POWs in Soviet camps much more appealing since West Germans could identify with their suffering and thus reimagine themselves through those prisoners as fellow victims of the war. When substantial numbers of West German prisoners continued to suffer in communist hands after the end of regular repatriations, civilians at home called for their return using language and images that borrowed significantly from Germany's own wartime camp victims. In East Germany, the official line was that such men were justly convicted war criminals who did not deserve any such veneration. As a result, only West Germany had the political and social space for such a myth to develop, as well as no countervailing wartime narrative that might impede such development.

However, returning POWs at times proved to be less than ideal figures for such a transformation. Because they had firsthand knowledge of the realities of both the war and captivity, they could disrupt the careful construction of new national mythology via unwanted contradiction. POW/MIA activists found MIAs to be more compelling figures for national canonization. Conceptually, they were prisoners who never returned and archetypal soldier-victims, sublimely silent heroes-at-a-distance of uncomfortable wars that produced very little else worthy of pride or praise.

Americans and West Germans thus found the idea of secret camps attractive in more than one way. On a personal level, those trapped in the no-man's land of grief could hold out hope that their missing man was somehow still alive in the secret camps and would come home someday, despite the increasing improbability of that ever occurring. On a larger level, those determined to wrest something useful from painful defeats could point to the alleged suffering of the men in the secret camps as evidence of how the enemy really was the villain of the war, and in some cases even how the aggressor nation was victimized by the war it started. Examining the ways these phenomena came about requires entering into the historiography of wartime suffering and loss, with a particular eye toward the progressing totality of victimization of soldiers through the twentieth century.[7]

The historiography of the German secret camp myth is bound to the larger story of the German experience of World War II. More specifically, most work done on the subject has been part of larger studies on POWs and prisoner experiences, or just of the war experience generally. The missing do not seem to have warranted much study in their own right, so they often appear as a subordinate part of the prisoner/returning veteran story. Erich Maschke and Kurt W. Böhme's massive fifteen-volume *Zur Geschichte der deutschen Kriegsgefangenen des Zweiten Weltkrieges* remains a core work to which virtually all other writings on the subject refer, and it established the pattern of treating MIAs as an adjunct to the more-important POW story, itself a minority aspect of the larger narrative of the war. Subsequent works have largely adhered to this formula, as in James Diehl's *The Thanks of the Fatherland: German Veterans after the Second World War*, which focuses on how West Germany struggled to incorporate returning POWs. Of specific interest here is how Diehl details the evolution of POW/MIA advocacy groups such as the Verband der Heimkehrer, one of the early voices that called for diplomatic pressure on the Soviets to return their remaining prisoners, both real and suspected.[8]

Nevertheless, within this qualified context there are some works that examine the German secret camp myth. Frank Biess's *Homecomings: Returning POWs and the Legacies of Defeat in Postwar Germany* explicitly mentions the concept—that hundreds of thousands of German soldiers remained in clandestine captivity following the purported release by the Soviets of all nonconvicted POWs—as one of the convenient fictions of the early Cold War. Biess describes how many people in West Germany embraced the idea of secret prison camps, bolstered in this belief by discrepancies in Soviet reporting on numbers of prisoners held as well as by opportunistic politicians and advocates who knowingly inflamed hopes for MIA survival. Above and beyond any personal reasons for needing the myth to be true, adherents also found the myth easy to accept because of the way it facilitated coming to grips with Germany's catastrophic wartime losses by recasting the narrative into language of German victimization at the hands of its cruel conquerors. By advocating for the return of both real and imagined prisoners in Soviet custody, West Germans were able to transform those men, and by extension themselves, into co-equal victims of the war itself, while simultaneously deemphasizing their own role in perpetrating that war and its atrocities.[9] Of equal importance, Biess discusses how popular agitation on the POW/MIA issue influenced Chancellor Konrad Adenauer's 1955 trip to Moscow, and how that pressure shaped the policies of his government, particularly in the realm of foreign relations.[10]

More recently, Nicholas Stargardt's *The German War: A Nation under Arms 1939–1945* also includes mention of the German secret camp myth. While Stargardt's focus is primarily on why German society invested itself as totally as it did in fighting the war, he does also examine the manner in which wartime victimization was convenient for redemptive reimaginings of the war after it was over. Moreover, he cites firsthand accounts of Germans during the last years of the war openly drawing equivalences between their own suffering and that inflicted by Germans upon their various victims.[11] He also examines the impact of Germans missing in the East on the home front, and how increasing casualty rates coupled with decreasing reliability of official reports led many to speculate about potential MIA survival in Soviet captivity.

Biess and Stargardt, however, are virtually the only authors to address the German secret camp myth directly, and those few others who do mention it tend to refer to Biess's work.[12] What is more, both authors treat it as a component part of the larger study of West Germany and World War II rather than a subject worthy of examination in its own right. Examining the secret camp myth as an international phenomenon helps to better uncover those common elements in both cases that contribute to its creation.

The American example has a more established historiography for POW/MIA issues and also the secret camp myth itself. H. Bruce Franklin's *MIA, or, Mythmaking in America* and *Vietnam and Other American Fantasies* explore how the myth came into existence during the war in Vietnam and grew to become what he calls a virtual "national religion."[13] Franklin argues that however well-intentioned the original proponents of the myth were, driven by their need for the war dead miraculously to be alive, belief in MIA survival has ballooned far beyond the boundaries of plausibility, and indeed good taste. He finds less excusable how opportunists, both in government and elsewhere, took advantage of the emotional resonance inherent in POW/MIA activism for their own ends.[14] The distinction between true believers in the secret camp myth and opportunists is best understood via the two mutually reinforcing needs that drive such a belief. In his understandable eagerness to address the many scoundrels who do exist within secret camp advocacy, Franklin sometimes downplays those whose belief was painfully genuine, due to being trapped in the no-man's land of grief.

More recently, Michael Allen's *Until the Last Man Comes Home: POWs, MIAs, and the Unending Vietnam War* builds upon Franklin's analysis of the politicization of the myth, arguing that much of the myth's durability came from the manner in which then president Richard Nixon co-opted basic concern over POW return in an effort to channel interest in that issue into support for his administration's policies, and indeed literally created the term POW/MIA out of formerly distinct and separate categories of POW and MIA. Like Franklin, Allen contends that the myth survives in the American popular consciousness due to a mix of politics and genuine popular belief. If anything, he goes further than Franklin in asserting the primacy of politics in keeping POW/MIA issues alive, though unlike Franklin he argues that earlier studies have overemphasized Nixon's role.[15] Both authors examine how cultural objects such as movies and video games reinforce popular acceptance of the core premise of the secret camp myth and indeed owe their existence and popularity to the common understanding of the basic structure of the myth. Here, one is unavoidably reminded of the existence of an entire category of action movies produced in the 1980s, the "Vietnam POW rescue" subgenre, including *Rambo: First Blood, Part II* starring Sylvester Stallone, and *Missing in Action* starring Chuck Norris, to which both Franklin and Allen refer.

Franklin's and Allen's works exist as part of the larger historiography of the Vietnam War, and both are primarily concerned with telling an American story within the context of America's experience of that war and its aftermath, though Allen does briefly compare American proponents of the secret camp myth with the earlier German mythmakers.[16] As a result, in both cases the myth comes across as a distinctly American episode born in the jungles of Southeast Asia, rather than a variant of an older international phenomenon. To be sure, Allen and Franklin are both chiefly concerned with writing American histories of that war and its aftermath, and neither is particularly weakened by this lack of focus on non-American examples. However, by focusing only on the American phenomenon they do ignore that those who created and developed the American secret camp myth were not breaking new ground so much as reacting to similar pressures that drove the creators of the earlier German myth. The secret camp myth is not unique to American cultural history, and it should therefore be examined in a broader context, which no author has yet done substantially.

The story of the secret camp myth is also a part of the existing historiography of warfare, loss, and mourning. Regardless of how cynics have manipulated the two variants of the myth for their own ends, the mainstay proponents of each were for the most part true believers. Their adherence to the myth is rooted in the difficulties they encounter in mourning, a broader subject that historians have examined in a variety of wartime and postwar contexts. Jean-Yves Le Naour examines a French example of this problem at the end of World War I that he refers to as a "refusal to mourn," which so often plagues families of the missing.[17] Indeed, Le Naour even mentions a French precursor to the secret camp myth dating from 1918, though he does not expand upon it.[18] Going back further, Drew Gilpin Faust's *This Republic of Suffering: Death and the American Civil War* argues that that war was the forerunner of the nightmares of the twentieth century.[19] Of much closer interest, Faust describes how even in that earlier war, "the unknown fate of missing kin left a 'dread void of uncertainty' that knowledge would never fill."[20] Jay Winter's *Sites of Memory, Sites of Mourning* similarly examines how Europeans faced loss following World War I. Winter argues that the modernist interpretation of mourning following that war fails to consider adequately the traditional means of coping with grief.[21] Like Faust, he does not fail to mention those relatives who were unable to mourn properly, due to the ambiguous status of their missing men.[22] However, these stories remain secondary to his analysis of those who were, eventually, able to find ways to mourn loss. Focusing more directly on the case of the missing and the secret camp myth their status spawned delves more deeply into an important and little-explored facet of the larger story of postwar mourning: those who could not find a way to mourn at all.

Chapter 1 examines Germany's war on the Eastern Front, from the 1941 invasion of the Soviet Union to the fall of Berlin in 1945. It details the frequency and manner by which German soldiers became casualties over time, in particular how casualty rates rose while simultaneously reporting and records on casualty type and status grew increasingly unreliable. Lacking such information, many Germans had no real knowledge of whether their relatives were dead or alive, in captivity or not. This chapter also covers who exactly made up the ranks of Germany's prisoners and missing, as well as where they came from within German military and society. Finally, it considers how Nazi ideology and indoctrination impeded the flow of what little information did exist concerning German POWs in the East, as well as how the Nazi state's casualty propaganda actively misled the civilian population and distorted the realities of Eastern Front losses.

Chapter 2 examines the aftermath of defeat in the western occupied zones and subsequently in the Federal German Republic. It covers the slow, inconsistent way prisoners returned from Soviet captivity, and how rumors of MIA survival in so-called silent camps appeared in West German media. It also examines how German POW/MIA activism arose following the war—especially how use of iconography that borrowed more than a little from the images of the Holocaust recast German POWs in the USSR solely as victims of communist barbarity. By portraying POWs and MIAs in that light, such efforts thus served as an avenue for all West Germans to reimagine themselves as victims of the war rather than as its perpetrators. The chapter also considers why this was so specifically a West German phenomenon, and why nothing equivalent arose in the German Democratic Republic. Most important, it details how West German POW/MIA activism peaked and subsided in the mid-1950s, unlike the much longer-lived American equivalent.

Chapter 3 details how US involvement in Vietnam led to its own men going missing, and how these men came from a narrow section of mostly middle-class professional officers in the air services, unlike the broader social origins of German POWs. Unlike the draftee masses who fought the ground war in Southeast Asia, the men around whom the American secret camp myth centers were mostly elites. The chapter also examines the loss statistics of the major US air campaigns, as well as how unlikely unaided MIA survival was considering the terrain over which several of those campaigns took place. In addition, it examines how American POW/MIA activism emerged during the war from a constituency of wives of the missing, who organized initially simply to try to obtain reliable information about the status of their men. The chapter then proceeds to show how self-interested parties within the Nixon administration actively worked to fold these activists into their own base of support and by so doing hijacked POW/MIA advocacy and used it in the service of prolonging the war itself. This politicization served to validate activist concerns initially, but the cynical manipulation of officials artificially raised hopes for POW survival far beyond what was plausible or even possible. This all but guaranteed that POW/MIA activism would continue after the 1973 repatriation of actual prisoners, since activists believed so many more were still alive, somewhere in Southeast Asia.

Chapter 4 explains how Watergate and the downfall of President Nixon helped to solidify the paranoid streak already present within American POW/MIA activism and led to the radicalization of those who remained active after 1973. Repatriation led to the departure of more reasonably minded activists and the ascension of the more militant, who were determined to find live MIAs. These activists would be satisfied by nothing short of the resurrection of the missing they believed were still alive in covert Vietnamese captivity, despite all evidence to the contrary. When a much hoped-for 1970s congressional inquiry into the POW/MIA issue failed to validate these beliefs and hopes, POW/MIA activism entrenched itself and helped set the stage for the revival of POW/MIA hysteria in the 1980s.

Chapter 5 shows how various elements brought the POW/MIA issue back to the forefront, most prominently via the popular and redemptive Hollywood retellings of the war in general and the POW/MIA aspects of it in particular. It also demonstrates how opportunistic private actors got involved in POW/MIA activism to bilk hundreds of thousands of dollars from desperate family members, telling false tales of secret prison camps and claiming to search for live prisoners, not one of whom ever emerged from Southeast Asia. With the not-insubstantial encouragement of President Ronald Reagan, popular belief in MIA survival grew, led to a second set of congressional hearings in the early 1990s, and even played a minor part in the fringe aspects of the 1992 presidential election.[23] Congress again concluded that there were no live POWs in Southeast Asia after 1973 and likely never had been. American POW/MIA advocacy survived this second repudiation and against all odds continues to play a role, albeit diminished, in the national conversation concerning memories of Vietnam and related veterans' affairs.

This study concludes with a final comparison of the two examples of the secret camp phenomenon. Through careful analysis of what they have in common, as well as where they diverge, it demonstrates how that phenomenon is a logical outcome of the desire to find some nationally redemptive element of lost, controversial wars. It also shows how such idolization of POWs and MIAs masks a refusal to accept the realities of war and can threaten to distort the honest telling of the history of such wars.

ONE

✧

Germany's War on the Eastern Front and the Origins of Its Secret Camp Myth

Germany suffered staggering casualties in the war it inaugurated in Europe in 1939. Its genocidal war of conquest in the East resulted in millions of dead, wounded, and missing men. Among that latter category, substantial numbers became prisoners of the Soviet Union or simply vanished along the shifting battle lines. The German secret camp myth contended that many of these unaccounted-for missing men were, in reality, covertly retained by the Soviet Union in undisclosed camps. The key factor in transforming this idea from a fringe belief to a more mainstream one was the disparity in the number of POWs returning from captivity versus those expected, which was compounded by the Soviets openly retaining some POWs as war criminals well into the 1950s. Due to a combination of wartime obfuscation by their own government and the collapse of Germany as a state after the war, civilians had a difficult time determining the status of their missing, and they often clung to rumors spread by returned POWs and others about the existence of secret camps in which MIAs might still survive.

German civilians found the secret camp myth attractive since it satisfied two interconnected needs. First, for the relatives of the missing trapped in the no-man's land of grief, the myth gave a plausible reason for hoping their missing man was still alive, despite the lack of information pointing in that direction. Relatives often found the ambiguity of these men's status maddening, for while they could hope for survival—as there was no definitive proof of death—neither did they have any evidence that their men were still alive. If secret camps existed, in which German prisoners anonymously languished, then family members could believe any missing man might survive so long as there was nothing to prove otherwise. Second, the myth offered a way around the criminal legacy of the Nazi state by creating an alternative war hero archetype from the POWs and MIAs. While Germans could neither fully memorialize their war dead nor celebrate their veterans due to wartime atrocities, they could decently venerate live Germans still suffering the barbarities of secret Soviet prison camps. Moreover, by overemphasizing that victimization, Germans found ways to appropriate the very suffering their own camps inflicted, and so recast themselves as victims of the war Germany had started.

However, despite these attractive elements, and despite most MIAs never reappearing from the East, German secret camp advocacy did not achieve the longevity of its American counterpart. By the mid-1950s, German activism on the subject had reached its logical conclusion and subsided, never to revive. Why such a difference? The German argument that living POWs remained in enemy captivity long past the end of hostilities was upon initial inspection much more plausible given the nature of the war in the East and that of Stalinist Russia after the war. Far more Germans went missing in the East than Americans did in Southeast Asia, and those missing came from a much broader swath of larger German society. Despite all of this, the German secret camp myth and POW/MIA activism generally never took on a life of their own, and neither became dominant elements of national mythology related to that war. To understand the reasons behind the short-lived German secret camp myth, it is important to understand why Germans fought the war they did on the Eastern Front, and how and where Germans were captured and went missing on that front. Similarly, POW/MIA activism after the war was unavoidably shaped by the war itself, and that activism consequently existed in the shadow of Germany's war crimes.

Sowing the Wind: Hitler's War of Extermination

World War II laid the foundation for the secret camp myth, and the myth could not have existed in the form it did had Germany not fought the war as it did. Nazi Germany's primary motivation was expansion eastward and the establishment of a settler empire in lands conquered from the Poles and Soviets. German expansionists had long looked in that direction, and

Germany's Nazi rulers' mad dream of *Lebensraum* was that *Drang nach Osten* ("thrust toward the East") desire taken to its logical extreme.[1] Adolf Hitler declared as early as 1925 that "we National Socialists must hold unflinchingly to our aim in foreign policy, namely, *to secure for the German people the land and soil to which they are entitled on this earth*"[2] (emphasis original). Russia was the ideal target both for practical and racial reasons, in Hitler's understanding. He argued that the Bolshevik Revolution had robbed the old Russian Empire of the one element that allowed a state populated by an "inferior" Slavic race to exist as a power in Europe: an elite intelligentsia made up of ethnic Germans. With those leadership positions now filled by the sinister-yet-feckless Jewish conspirators Hitler saw lurking behind the Russian Revolution, he could not imagine the Soviet successor state as capable of long surviving on its own. "The giant empire in the east," he concluded, "is ripe for collapse."[3] This decision by the Nazi leadership to plunge headlong into the Soviet Union guaranteed huge amounts of POWs and MIAs, whose ambiguous statuses fed the secret camp myth. Those leaders had not expected such a result, both due to ideological blindness to the Soviet will and capacity to resist and because of the deceptively quick and cheap victories German armed forces had so far won in Poland and in the West.

Hitler had planned the invasion of that empire not only as a campaign of conquest but also as one of explicit extermination, which led Germany's military to fight that war with unprecedented brutality and caused a ripple effect in prisoner policy and treatment on both sides, albeit far more murderously in the German case than the Soviet. As Supreme High Command of the Army (Oberkommando des Heeres, or OKH) Chief of Staff Franz Halder recorded in his private diary,

We must get away from this standpoint of soldierly comradeship. The communist is no comrade, before or after. It is a war of extermination. . . . We do not wage war in order to preserve the enemy. . . . Extermination of the Bolshevik commissars and communist intelligentsia. . . . The leaders must know what is involved. They must lead in this struggle! The troops must defend themselves with the methods with which they are attacked. Commissars and secret service personnel are criminals and must be treated as such. The troops need not get out of their leader's control. The leader must give his orders in accordance with the feelings of the troops. The leader must make sacrifices and overcome their [*sic*] scruples.[4]

While Halder's sentiments on first inspection seem to promise harshness narrowly focused on those political enemies found in Russia, in practice they came to apply to the bulk of the Red Army and Russian population generally. Commanders throughout the military communicated this message to the common German soldiers in the *Guidelines for the Behavior of the Fighting Force in Russia* to give only one example, distributed throughout the Wehrmacht in May 1941. It contained the following passage:

> The struggle demands ruthless and energetic action against *Bolshevik agitators, guerrillas, saboteurs, Jews* and the complete liquidation of any active or passive resistance.
>
> Extreme reserve and most alert vigilance are called for towards all members of the *Red Army*—even prisoners—as treacherous methods of fighting are to be expected. The *Asiatic* soldiers of the Red Army in particular are inscrutable, unpredictable, insidious, and unfeeling.[5] (emphasis original)

High Command made the barbaric implications of this guideline even more explicit in the June 1941 "Commissar Decree," which stated that Soviet political officers were to be shot out of hand whenever captured. Generals passed this decree down to their subordinate units in various subsequent orders, all of which contained euphemisms allowing for an ever-wider latitude and indeed encouragement for German troops to treat captured Red Army soldiers and the captive civilian population with murderous harshness. It is therefore hardly surprising that the Wehrmacht fought its war in the East with savage, indiscriminate violence directed against not only the Soviet military but also the people of the East, with only infrequent exceptions.

Such behavior contributed to the development of the German secret camp myth in two ways. First, the atrocious way the German Army treated the vast number of enemy prisoners it took reinforced the brutal exterminatory nature of warfare on the Eastern Front and thus helped to solidify the Nazi trope that ultimate victory or total destruction were the only two possible outcomes of that fight. Early on, this encouraged enthusiastic support of the expected imminent victory; later in the war it caused Germans to be mortally terrified of the Red Army and fear capture at least as much as death, if not more so. As a result, soldiers increasingly preferred desertion and flight to fighting to the death, or risking capture, which helped contribute to rising numbers of MIAs as the front collapsed and the end approached for the Thousand-Year Reich.[6] Second, Germans were in touch with their fighting men in the East despite the best efforts of official censors and propagandists, and they were generally aware of the atrocities being committed in their names—notwithstanding their claims of innocence and ignorance after the war. Accordingly, their fears of vengeful Red Army hordes during the war translated to fears of a vindictive Soviet occupation after that war, with some justification. These fears, combined with widely felt but seldom expressed guilt over Germany's war crimes, gave Germans every reason to embrace the role of war victim in order to avoid facing the root of that guilt.[7] In an attempt to deal with these uncomfortable legacies of the war, many Germans popularized the POW and MIA as symbols of Germany's victimization at communist hands, and what better symbol of such victimization could there be than POWs who remained in Soviet custody after the end of regular repatriations, as well as the unaccounted-for MIAs who might well survive alongside them?

Given Germany's eastward focus, it should come as no surprise that the overwhelming bulk of Germany's armed forces fought on the Eastern Front throughout the war, and it was that front that generated the POWs/MIAs about whom the German secret camp myth eventually concerned itself. Because the war they fought was a large-scale conventional conflict, the majority of Germany's missing came not from any one, discrete segment of German society but rather from across a much broader social spectrum. Conscription, banned following World War I but reintroduced in 1935, guaranteed that young men from all ranks and stations would spend time in the military even if they did not go on to make a career of it.[8] Furthermore, over the course of the war Germany's increasing desperation for manpower led to a loosening of conscription standards and a lowering of the age of induction, which ensured that men who had been passed over previously and teenagers of ever-younger ages would serve as well.[9] Similarly, the Volkssturm "people's militia," formed in late 1944, incorporated those older men who had avoided conscription thus far, armed them with whatever weapons remained, and marched them East to face the oncoming Soviet tanks.[10]

Breaking down the statistics further, official accounting efforts following the war confirmed that the majority of POWs and MIAs in particular had come from the German working class, with a survey of the US occupation zone conducted in 1947 revealing that 86.9 percent of POWs and 82.2 percent of MIAs living in that zone after the war came from such a background.[11] In terms of age, most fell within 20 to 40 years old (79.1 percent for POWs, 78.2 percent for MIAs).[12] While these men returned, or settled, in parts of Germany occupied by the Western Allies after the war, it is important to remember that the vast majority of the German military fought in the East, and correspondingly the results of this survey are applicable to German POWs and MIAs on the Eastern Front more generally. Throughout the course of the war, about 20 million German men served in one capacity or another, and of those 20 million, most were conscripts.[13]

This was, then, a people's army, drawn from a society that by the time of the invasion of Soviet Russia in 1941 had been thoroughly militarized by the Nazi Party and state. State-mandated conditioning started early, with mandatory participation in youth organizations such as Hitlerjugend (Hitler Youth) and its female auxiliary, the Bund Deutscher Mädel (the League of German Girls, or BDM), from 1933 on.[14] Working adults, whether or not they were party members or even politically active, soon discovered Nazism had entered the workplace after the banning and assimilation of independent trade unions into the Deutsche Arbeitsfront (German Labor Front, or DAF), membership in which was mandatory for virtually all industrial and commercial work.[15] These various measures and others like them bound all elements of German society to the Nazi Party and, through the party, to its scheme of conquest in the East, thus further ensuring that the impact of that attempt at conquest would be felt across virtually every level of German society. The Nazi state had tapped almost every conceivable manpower resource at its disposal and sent most of those men to fight the Red Army, and so the populations of the alleged secret camps necessarily came from almost every corner of German society.

Admittedly, information on the men in the ranks is harder to come by than that of officers, and especially generals. Individual memoirs do exist, but comparatively little has been done to write a comprehensive "ground-level" social history of the Wehrmacht from the perspective of the common *Landser*.[16] Holes in the historical record aggravate this problem: the Bundesarchiv/Militärarchiv, Germany's modern national archive of military records, reports that it lost a substantial proportion of its collection during the war, in particular those records from units below the divisional level.[17] However, enough records remain to sketch at least a rough outline of the makeup of the German military that fought in the East. As an army of conscripts, the Wehrmacht operated under the principle that it was preferable to keep young men from the same conscription district together throughout their term of service. This was organizationally inefficient but heavily advantageous from the perspective of unit morale, since it kindled a sense of familiarity and family among the men. It also meant that at the platoon and company levels, Wehrmacht units often took on a geographical flavor due to the relative homogeneity of their recruits.[18] This practice would break down due to skyrocketing manpower needs across the army in early 1941, however.[19]

With the weakening of regional and personal ties, unit cohesion from 1941 onward was increasingly based on ideology, specifically the virulent Nazi racial ideology that had progressively infested every arm of the German military and had decreed the war in the East to be a fight to the death against the racial enemies of the German *Volk*. Under such circumstances, it is unsurprising that, in proclamation at least, Germany's fighting men mostly held to the party position that death was preferable to surrender when fighting such a vile, subhuman enemy. This indoctrination only grew more pronounced as the war's fortunes turned against the Wehrmacht, with a growing emphasis on "political education" from 1943 onward.[20]

Given the scope and breadth of Germany's war in the East, it is important to consider how, when, and where these men were captured or went missing. Four rough chronological categories best illustrate how this all took place: from the initiation of Operation Barbarossa on 21 June 1941 to spring 1942; Operation Blue in June 1942 to the surrender of the Sixth Army at Stalingrad in February 1943; Operation Citadel of July–August 1943 and its aftermath; and, finally, the progressive disintegration of the front following the defeat at Kursk in August 1943 to the fall of Berlin. German armed forces progressively suffered ever-greater casualties in the East, culminating in the near-complete collapse of organized resistance in Berlin in the spring of 1945, and not only did this result in ever-rising numbers of men captured, but many men simply vanished during these titanic battles and movements of men across the vast spaces of the East. Equally important to the construction of a secret camp myth was that these casualties increased at the very moment when casualty reporting broke down and news about soldiers' fates became increasingly unreliable.

The World Will Hold Its Breath: Germany's Invasion of the USSR

The Wehrmacht general staff had planned Operation Barbarossa as another of the rapid blitzkrieg campaigns by which they had won such stunning victories in Poland and Western Europe. Some of these men were nevertheless apprehensive about their ability to repeat those earlier successes. Hitler did his best to convince his generals. To those who balked at the size of this new opponent, he could rightly point out that they had been outnumbered in France as well, and that was against an army that was not primarily made up of "subhumans." He also argued that the purges of the 1930s, during which Soviet dictator Josef Stalin had massacred significant numbers of his own senior commanders, had rendered the Red Army a paper tiger, a weakness that the Finnish debacle supposedly confirmed.[21] This, he concluded, was compounded by what he saw as the incoherencies and racial weaknesses inherent in the Soviet system overall, which could never stand against the might of the German master race and was on the brink of collapse in any case. Hitler had declared to the chief of operations of the Armed Forces High Command (Oberkommando der Wehrmacht, OKW), Alfred Jodl, shortly before the onset of Barbarossa that "You only have to kick in the door and the whole rotten structure will come crashing down."[22]

Despite spectacular early victories and German conquest of huge amounts of Soviet territory, the Soviet system did not come crashing down even with the door kicked in. The Führer's constant interference contributed to Barbarossa's failure, as did his frequent alteration of plans. Fundamental material inadequacies were more significant than such shortsighted micromanaging, however. Equipped for another blitzkrieg, the Wehrmacht was increasingly unable to replace its losses and sustain its efforts as the fighting wore on. Attrition of its panzers in particular, which could not quickly be replaced, led to what historian Omer Bartov has described as the "demodernization" of the front, with Wehrmacht troops increasingly reverting to premechanized forms of warfare.[23] These problems had been surmountable in the earlier Western campaigns due to the speed of German triumph and comparatively smaller spaces to be conquered. However, in Russia the incomplete mechanization of the Wehrmacht and vast distances its forces had to cover proved fatal to dreams of another swift victory.[24] This failure, and the degradation of Germany's armed forces that followed, not only contributed to the rising casualty count but also made it increasingly harder for the German military as a whole to keep track of just who had become a casualty, as such logistical strain both deprioritized record keeping and made it more difficult to accomplish generally. As a result, Barbarossa helped lay the groundwork for the later birth of the secret camp myth, by plunging the German military into an extended, bloody conflict it could not win while simultaneously making it that much harder for the Wehrmacht to account for its missing men.

In total, Germany suffered over 800,000 casualties throughout Operation Barbarossa. Of these, about 120,000 were either POWs or MIAs. This is necessarily an approximation due to the sheer size of forces involved. The remoteness of many of the Soviet POW camps made accounting for individual Germans captured or missing extremely difficult under the best of circumstances.[25] What is more, ideological presumptions about Germany's fighting men and the war in the East inhibited officialdom from making honest efforts at casualty reporting. The aforementioned casualty figures come primarily from Soviet sources, which is less surprising than it might initially appear. The Nazi state constantly projected the need for heroism and sacrifice both domestically and within its armed forces. That state expected its soldiers to triumph or fall defiantly rather than surrender. During earlier campaigns, the speed of German victories muted this enforced fanaticism to a degree, as did the comparative lack of racial animus toward the Western Allies. Against the "subhuman" Russians and their scheming Jewish masters, the Nazi state considered its brave heroes surrendering to be unthinkable—and potentially poisonous to its hero-cult and desired heroic narrative of victory, struggle, and sacrifice.[26] Thus, the Wehrmacht Casualty Office (the Wehrmachtsauskunftstelle für Kriegerverluste und Kriegsgefangene, or WASt) actively suppressed the publication of statistics on German POWs and regularly reclassified POWs as MIA, or even KIA.[27] It did so under the guidance of both the Propaganda Ministry and the Reich Security Main Office (Reichssicherheitshauptamt, or RSHA), which acted directly to throttle the trickle of information that emerged from the Soviet camp system by intercepting and withholding what little mail POWs were able to send, without even notifying family members that anything had been received.[28] A subordinate agency within the hierarchy of the infamous SS (Schutzstaffel, literally "Protection Squadron"), the RSHA coordinated the operation of Germany's various police and internal security agencies, the feared Gestapo in particular, and had broad, almost arbitrary authority over what was or was not permissible behavior within the Reich.[29] Therefore, WASt's RSHA-influenced obfuscation of casualty statistics, downplaying of actual casualty numbers, and stonewalling family members of the missing contributed to the lack of information that laid the foundation for the secret camp myth after the war.

Civilians had to contend with other obstacles as well when it came to discovering the fate of their missing men. First, attempts to lobby for changes in POW policy or even to seek further information on the missing risked accusations of defeatism or antistate activities. It is not surprising therefore to learn that family members resorted instead to informal, occasionally covert, activities to try to learn more about the fate of the missing. Such actions at times skirted the boundaries of acceptable behavior, when they did not overstep them entirely, and risked drawing the baleful eye of the Gestapo. After all, the main alternate source of information concerning men missing in the East was the enemy who may have taken them prisoner. Soviet propagandists did from time to time broadcast information on and publish flyers about prisoners they had taken, but listening to foreign broadcasts was illegal from 1939 on.[30] Even seeking out informal gossip and rumors concerning one's missing relatives could be dangerous, as such behavior was prohibited on the grounds of encouraging defeatism, and one could never quite be sure that today's source of conversation might not become tomorrow's informer.[31]

On a more pragmatic level, the exterminatory nature of the war in the East inhibited the usual transmission vector for POW/MIA information between belligerents: the International Red Cross. The Soviet Union was not a signatory of the 1929 Geneva Convention and had repudiated any legacy obligations held over from Imperial Russia's signing of the 1907 Hague Convention, though the Soviets had claimed they would honor that older convention's provisions despite the illegitimacy of the Tsarist state.[32] For its part, Germany made virtually no effort to honor its Geneva Convention obligations with regard to Soviet prisoners outside of the occasional propaganda effort staged for the Red Cross and international press.[33] In practice, neither side observed these conventions regarding treatment of prisoners and notification through neutral bodies of prisoner numbers and status. Overall, the war in the East was fought almost entirely without the international oversight that warring powers had come to expect as the norm since the early twentieth century, and without any reliable means for those men to communicate back to their families that they had survived capture. Under such circumstances, German record keepers could not necessarily distinguish between a man killed in action and one who had either gone missing or been captured, even had they wished so to do. Such a desire was itself unlikely since they labored under the ideological presupposition that missing men were more likely to have died fighting than to have surrendered. Therefore, German civilians were at a double disadvantage when it came to tracking their missing men and determining whether they were alive, as their own government falsified what information it had on the missing for ideological grounds, and it had only incomplete data to begin with.

German civilians had to contend with more than just legal and ideological restrictions on their search for information on the missing. As the war worsened, the Reich was increasingly under direct attack from its various enemies, and as a result civilian life was progressively disrupted. Allied strategic bombing directly affected civilians, particularly after 1943, and by war's end these attacks reduced many Germans' horizon to the most basic, immediate survival concerns. Even if relatives of the missing could muster the courage to risk police censure and arrest, their more immediate concerns necessarily devolved to acquiring food, water, and shelter secure enough to make it through one more night.[34] Even more than just the aerial attacks, they had to contend with the approach of and occupation by foreign armies as the Red Army thundered onward following its great victory at Kursk, as also the Western Allies did following their Normandy landings in 1944. Between invading armies, the relentless destruction of logistics networks and German infrastructure, particularly the rail network, German civilians lacked the luxury of time and resources to organize and agitate for information on their missing during the war, even if they had had the political liberty so to do.[35]

Death of an Army: Stalingrad and the Growing Number of Germany's Missing

Despite its substantial losses in men and material during and after Barbarossa, the Wehrmacht was prepared for a new offensive in spring 1942. This new offensive, named Operation Blue, envisioned a two-pronged southern drive across the Caucasus to seize the Soviets' main oil reserves and capture the city of Stalingrad on the Volga River. The speed of their advance, and the refusal of the Red Army to stand and fight, convinced many German commanders that they had finally broken the Red Army's ability to resist.[36] In reality, the Soviet leadership, including Stalin himself, had learned at least partial lessons from the mayhem of 1941 and refused to play into the hands of the oncoming Germans. Indeed, the Soviet dictator had at last grasped that his refusal to allow for tactical withdrawals in 1941 had contributed greatly to the destruction of his frontier armies, and for the moment he allowed his commanders the flexibility to fall back whenever German pincers threatened.[37] Ignorant of this, General Friedrich Paulus's Sixth Army pushed ever deeper into Soviet territory, toward Stalingrad.

Not only did Germany lose the entire Sixth Army at Stalingrad, it also lost the largest number of prisoners in a single incident in the war so far. Although Barbarossa resulted in slightly more POWs and MIAs overall, those casualties occurred over the course of the months-long operation, rather than from a single surrender. Simultaneously, though Barbarossa had failed in its ultimate objective, in early 1942 Germans could plausibly believe that the war was going well for them. Therefore, Stalingrad not only served as one of the war's turning points but also helped to create the German secret camp myth both by contributing so singularly to the German POW/MIA population and also by shaking German confidence.

Ignorant of the doom waiting for them, elements of Army Group B, including the Sixth Army as well as detachments from the Fourth Panzer Army and non-German auxiliaries, advanced on Stalingrad, making good progress by late July 1942. Though the Sixth Army was able to push into the bombed-out city, the battle then devolved into anarchic city fighting as the Germans attempted to crush the remaining Soviet resistance and the Red Army tried to hold on long enough for the massive reinforcements building on the eastern bank of the Volga to assemble for their planned counterattack. To this end, General Georgi Zhukov used the summer and autumn of 1942 to build up massive reinforcements against the flanks of the Sixth Army. The poorly equipped Romanian Army guarded these flanks and could not long resist the Soviet onslaught. So fast did the two prongs of the Red Army's attack advance, indeed, that by 22 November, merely three days after the inauguration of Operation Uranus, they had surrounded the Sixth Army.[38]

This encirclement spelled the beginning of the end for those Axis troops now trapped in the Stalingrad pocket. Hitler forbade them from staging any breakout and retreat, permission for which General Paulus had requested in the immediate aftermath of the Soviet encirclement, and so battle casualties, privation, and disease slowly wore down these trapped soldiers.[39] Hitler insisted that they fight on to the bitter end, both for the pragmatic reason that "every day and every hour won in this way the other fronts will become stronger" and also from ideological conviction stemming from the Nazi cult of heroism and sacrifice.[40] This latter apocalyptic belief was epitomized when Hitler promoted the despairing Paulus to field marshal in response to Paulus's 24 January 1943 request to surrender. Paulus understood Hitler's subtext here, that no German of that rank had ever been taken alive, and Hitler none-too-subtly reminded Paulus of that fact in the same message.[41] Hitler was shocked when the newly minted field marshal capitulated to the Soviets, instead of killing himself as Hitler had expected. Incensed, the Führer angrily proclaimed,

How can one be so cowardly? I don't understand it. . . . What is life? Life is the Nation. The individual must die anyway. Beyond the life of the individual is the life of the Nation. . . . So many people have to die, and then a man like that besmirches the heroism of so many others at the last minute. He could have freed himself from all sorrow and ascended into eternity and national immortality, but he prefers to go to Moscow![42]

Inconvenient Survival: POWs, Propaganda, and the Nazi Cult of the Hero

Paulus's personal surrender serves as a prominent example of the problem POWs caused for the Nazi state in two specific ways. First, they threatened the Nazi assumption that, with sufficient will, any effort would necessarily succeed regardless of practical considerations. Second, POWs served as unwanted counterexamples to the Nazi cult of heroic sacrifice. For both reasons, official reports downplayed and misrepresented POW numbers and statistics, which gave the German population further reason to distrust earlier claims after the war.[43] After all, Germans had been told prior to Stalingrad that they were winning the war, and that their armies were everywhere undefeated. Afterward, they learned only that the Sixth Army had died fighting, without reference to the specific casualty count. When they discovered just how baldly their government had concealed the truth from them, many necessarily began to doubt the official account not only of casualty numbers but also casualty status. Who was to say that every man whom the Nazi state had declared a dead hero of the *Herrenvolk* was not potentially a prisoner somewhere in the Soviet camp system? Knowledge of Germany's own vast and brutal system of concentration camps likely also contributed to fears for men potentially lost in the Soviet equivalent.

In the end, the combined count of German POWs and MIAs at Stalingrad was greater than anything seen prior to that point. Of the approximately 100,000 captured, only about 6,000 would ever see Germany again. As with most other battles on the Eastern Front, there is a significant discrepancy between German and Soviet records as to casualty numbers, and indeed among Soviet sources themselves. The reports of Paulus and Soviet field marshal Konstantin Rokossovsky both place the prisoner count at close to 100,000, but NKVD (Narodnyy Komissariat Vnutrennikh Del, or People's Commissariat for Internal Affairs) records estimate as many as 130,000 Germans were captured, though the count may well have been intentionally inflated for propaganda purposes.[44] Regardless of which source is most accurate, that so few German soldiers eventually returned demonstrated that most had disappeared either en route to or after reaching the Soviet prison camps. These POW deaths were not necessarily the result of active mistreatment but rather of the weakened health of the men who had survived the horrible conditions long enough to surrender in February 1943. Unsurprisingly, many of the approximately 91,000 who surrendered with Paulus were emaciated, weak, and often already sick and/or suffering from frostbite. Considerable numbers of these men subsequently died on their way to prison camps, which often were many weeks of hard travel from the Stalingrad battle area.[45] The fate of these missing was all the more ambiguous to the German public after the war since many did not appear on official Soviet lists of men known to have died in captivity or indeed to have ever been captured at all. Such incomplete and fragmentary information further fueled the concerns and anxieties of German civilians, many of whom were thus predisposed to believe rumors of secret camps after the war.

Even had the Soviets kept better records, the German home front would still not have known how many men survived Stalingrad as POWs since German propaganda worked furiously to insinuate they had all died rather than surrender. Such an answer might have satisfied Nazi fanatics, but even among party faithful there was the widespread, understandably understated sentiment that though it was generally better for men to fight to the end against the Judeo-Bolshevik barbarians, perhaps it would not be that bad if one's own husband or son had surrendered and thus retained at least a chance of staying alive.[46] This belief was tempered by fears of what the prisoner experience might be, and it contains the beginnings of an important inversion so critical to secret camp myth mentality and attendant reimagining of the POW/MIA as a war hero. German civilians quite naturally feared the conditions of the Soviet prison camps, whose reputation was well known outside the USSR ever since the purges of the 1930s, and the RSHA and Propaganda Ministry preyed upon those fears with its exaggerated reports of possible deportation to Siberia in unheated cattle cars, starvation, torture, and mass shootings.[47] In other words, Germans worried that the Soviets might be inflicting upon their missing men those atrocities that Germany's armed forces were actively inflicting upon the captive peoples of the East, and especially upon Jews everywhere the Reich now commanded.

There was some justification to such fears, but nothing equal to what Red Army men and others faced in German captivity. While the conditions of imprisonment in the Soviet camp network rarely rose above the level of primitive, and German POWs did frequently suffer and die at alarming rates, Soviet desire for vengeance was tempered to a large degree by the desperate need for war labor, and it lacked any equivalent racial hatred to that of the Nazis. Soviet captivity policy could be harsh and deprived German prisoners of necessities but lacked the exterminatory extremism of the German concentration camp system. That the Soviets made no conscious or systematic effort to murder them was admittedly scant comfort to those German POWs who suffered from disease, overwork, and lack of food and adequate shelter in Soviet prisons.[48] These deprivations resulted instead from overarching, chronic wartime shortages throughout the Soviet Union, making German prisoners authors of their own misfortune.

The catastrophe at Stalingrad was of such a magnitude that even the best German propaganda efforts could not conceal or adequately spin it, though not for lack of trying. Following the surrender there was a news blackout on Stalingrad of over a week, before at last German radio announced, on 3 February 1943, that "The battle of Stalingrad has ended. True to their oath to fight to the last breath, the Sixth Army under the exemplary leadership of Field-Marshal Paulus has been overcome by the superiority of the enemy and by the unfavorable circumstances confronting our forces."[49] This broadcast made no mention of casualty figures and used additional language that heavily implied that the entire Sixth Army had gone down fighting, thus further concealing the unpleasant reality of a mass capitulation.[50] Propaganda Minister Josef Goebbels rallied the faithful in reaction to Stalingrad with his memorable 18 February 1943 Sportpalast speech, during which he whipped the crowd into a total war-glorifying frenzy in perhaps the crowning moment of his long career in audience manipulation. Tellingly, when he referred to Stalingrad in that speech he rhetorically folded that disaster into the larger narrative of tragic-yet-noble sacrifice freely made by the Aryan heroes of the Reich, thus reinforcing the heroic narrative that loomed so large within Nazi ideology and fed into the secret camp myth.[51] The German home front had thus already absorbed the concept of their missing men being dead heroes of the eternal Reich, so after the war they had merely to reconsider the terms of that heroism to reimagine them as living, though absent, heroes of a beaten and victimized Germany.

Apocalypse: Kursk and the Acceleration of German Casualty Rates

The Wehrmacht was not yet a beaten force despite the loss of the Sixth Army, and its leadership contemplated returning to the offensive after Stalingrad. Subsequent German successes lent reassurance that they could soldier on and gain victory despite that defeat, and the apparent vulnerability of the new Soviet position tempted their offensive planning with the hopes that the panzers might once more manage one of the massive double-envelopments that had so marked the glory days of Barbarossa.[52] All of this led to the most titanic conflagration of the war in the East, the largest armored clash in military history, and the beginning of the end for German ambitions of living space in the East. So too, the Battle of Kursk resulted in casualties almost twice those of Stalingrad, albeit with a less lopsided ratio of POWs/ MIAs to other categories. Germany's defeat at Kursk thus contributed to the secret camp myth by adding to the count of missing men and also because it signaled the point after which German armies were progressively in retreat, and even less capable of accounting for missing men than previously.

Kursk's casualty toll was numerically worse than that of Stalingrad, though it may have been psychologically easier to deal with since no entire army capitulated to the enemy. Throughout the Kursk campaign, including Operation Citadel and the two subsequent Soviet counteroffensives, the Wehrmacht suffered 111,132 casualties, of which 20,233 were MIAs.[53] Taken together, the Germans thus lost at least 160,000 total casualties throughout the campaign, of whom over 20,000 were unaccounted for. The count grows even higher if one includes ancillary actions and skirmishes. Though the Red Army captured fewer Germans during these battles than at the earlier calamity on the Volga, Germany suffered more casualties overall. Of greater consequence to the Reich was that by failing in this last great attempt to recover the initiative in the East, the German military would thenceforth fight and slowly lose a strictly defensive war against the resurgent Red Army. As the Wehrmacht retreated westward and unit cohesion grew increasingly frayed, men went missing with greater frequency—without there being any official record of whether they had been killed, taken prisoner, or deserted. Accordingly, this period helped to feed the secret camp myth by providing a bulk of missing men who might conceivably still be alive in secret captivity after the war.

That final defeat did not occur overnight, of course. Kursk took place in mid-1943, just under two years before Germany's final surrender. Accordingly, just how and where Germans were taken prisoner or went missing during this final phase of the war in the East is of crucial importance. Determining these specifics is hampered by a new complication to the already questionable nature of official German casualty records. In addition to the problem of the murky, at times nonexistent delineation between POWs and MIAs in Wehrmacht casualty reports, accurate bookkeeping took on a much lower priority for units fighting for their lives in increasingly improvised formations as the situation at the front got worse. The Nazi government compounded this problem by further obfuscating what little information did reach Berlin for the sake of morale. Even worse, those official accounts the regime did make public for propaganda purposes share only a passing resemblance to reality under the most charitable reading. Due to these in-accuracies and official distortions, Germans had conflicting and incomplete information about their missing men before attempting to balance those reports against what they might have learned from Soviet claims.[54] Soviet sources suffer from a different though related problem: inflation of casual-ties inflicted and prisoners taken, done for propaganda purposes. Red Army and NKVD records almost invariably report having killed and captured more Germans than the Wehrmacht admitted losing. Both sides were likely spinning the numbers in a way calculated to make each look as best they could, so it is prudent to treat each set of records provisionally.

Disintegration: Collapse of the Unified Front and Subsequent Encirclements

While it is outside the scope of this study to examine every battle and campaign of the remainder of the war in the East, there are many specific situations that help to highlight the increasingly destabilized position of Germany's armies following Kursk. In particular, there were a number of subsequent encirclements in which tens of thousands of German troops eventually capituled to the Soviets and went into captivity, specifically at Sevastopol, Minsk, in the Courland pocket, and at Budapest. The German military suffered these defeats at the same time that its record keeping dete-riorated, and indeed as German territory shrunk on an almost daily basis. Therefore, it is unsurprising that German civilians had progressively worse and worse ideas of the status of men caught in these encirclements. As a result, they cannot but have helped contribute to the growth of the German secret camp myth after the war.

In April 1944, the 4th Ukrainian Front cut the Wehrmacht's Army Group A off in the Crimea.[55] Outnumbered and outmatched, the Germans fell back on Sevastopol to await rescue. Hitler initially forbade any evacuation and only grudgingly authorized a sea lift in late April, after much desperate per-suasion.[56] The Red Air Force made repeated attacks on the rescue ships and sunk several with their full complement, most notably the *Totila* and *Teja*, carrying approximately ten thousand German soldiers between them. These two ships in particular are important to later proponents of the secret camp myth, since their escorts only rescued a very few of the soldiers they carried.[57] German forces had no opportunity to recover the bodies of the remainder, which fueled rumors that, perhaps, some of them might have survived and improbably swam to shore. Overall, of 150,000 men in Crimea, fewer than 40,000 made it out.[58] Of the rest, 61,000 became POWs, including 26,000 "left on the beach" by the final rescue ships after the Red Army broke into Sevastopol itself.[59] German records estimated that the Soviets captured 29,000 Germans and 7,000 of their Romanian allies, whereas the Soviets claimed a higher total of 61,580 prisoners.[60] These losses contributed to the secret camp myth both by adding to Germany's missing masses and also as they had gone missing under even more ambiguous circumstances than had been the case previously.

Sevastopol was only a prelude to the disasters facing the Wehrmacht in the East throughout the rest of 1944, as in late June of that year the Soviets launched Operation Bagration, a large campaign that contained numerous smaller offensives and battles. All contributed to the secret camp myth to some degree, but most notable among them was the assault on Minsk. Hitler had declared the city a "*Feste Platz*," or fortified point to be held at all costs, as he had most other cities still under Wehrmacht control. As a result, the Red Army was able to encircle the Fourth Army and most of what remained of the Ninth.[61] The Soviets caught over a hundred thousand Germans in the Minsk pocket, and only 15,000 of those managed to escape. When the Fourth Army surrendered in July 1944, it only had 57,000 men left.[62] This loss also heralded the collapse of Army Group Center, though the Wehrmacht did subsequently assign its name to other, smaller formations for morale reasons. The Red Army managed a second mass encirclement at Vilnius shortly after Minsk, capturing approximately five thousand men from the Third Panzer Army. This haul of prisoners included much of the Fourth Army remnant that had only just escaped from the Minsk pocket.[63]

Operation Bagration was a stunning defeat of the already reeling German forces in the East. The Soviets claimed to have inflicted over half a million losses, including taking just under 160,000 prisoners.[64] German estimates put the total number lower, at approximately 300,000 losses, of whom 262,929 were unaccounted for in one way or another. Though this latter account is lower than the Soviet claim overall, it does report a higher proportion of missing men and was far more than the flagging Wehrmacht could easily bear in any case.[65] Barring the discovery of new records, the exact number of German casualties will likely remain uncertain, as will the percentage of those casualties who were POWs. This uncertainty helps to illustrate the emotionally corrosive effect such losses had on family members back home. The problem of not knowing left many trapped in the no-man's land of grief on which the secret camp myth depended.

Though the Wehrmacht did reestablish a defensive front following Bagration, it was fragile and nowhere near capable of withstanding subsequent Soviet offensives for any length of time. In September 1944 a Soviet autumn offensive against Army Group North drove between it and the shattered remnants of Army Group Center to the south, reestablishing Soviet rule over the Baltic states and pinning Army Group North in Latvia's Courland Peninsula.[66] The Red Army trapped over 200,000 Germans, primarily from the Sixteenth and Eighteenth Armies, in that isthmus.[67] Despite being thus cut off, Army Group Courland—as Hitler had renamed what was left of Army Group North—held out until two days after the general German surrender in 1945 due to communications difficulties. According to Soviet official sources, fewer than 190,000 members of Army Group Courland survived to go into Soviet captivity after that final surrender.[68]

By cutting Army Group Courland off in its namesake peninsula, the Red Army had removed the last major obstacle to its drive westward into East Prussia and Germany proper. This is important to the creation of the secret camp myth since these territories contained considerable numbers of German civilians and naval personnel. Admiral Karl Dönitz ordered the evacuation of these Germans by sealift in January 1945, which included use of the massive ocean liner and Nazi Party showpiece *Wilhelm Gustloff*. Soviet submarine S-13 sank that ship on 30 January 1945 in what is generally considered the worst loss of life of any single maritime disaster, with perhaps as many as 9,400 passengers disappearing in the frigid Baltic Sea. There is a major problem with accounting for the missing of the *Gustloff*: the panicked nature of the evacuations in question. Civilian refugees fleeing the Red Army poured into any port that offered a chance of escape, and it is certain many more passengers were on board than were listed on the ship's official manifest. Total crew and passengers of the *Gustloff*, then, may have been as high as 10,000, but as with so much else this remains an estimation and approximation.[69] The *Gustloff* passengers therefore added to the total number of Germans missing under unconfirmable circumstances in the East, potentially alive in the secret camps. The German Navy collectively named the sealifts from the East "Operation Hannibal," and it experienced similar tragedies to that of the *Gustloff,* such as the sinking of the *Goya*, from whose complement of approximately 7,000 only 175 survived.[70] Of more specific importance to the developing German secret camp myth was that these lives were lost in such a way no recovery of most of the bodies was possible. Coupled with the incomplete knowledge of who exactly was on board these ships, the victims of the *Gustloff* and *Goya* sinking belong in the category of the ambiguous lost.

Endkampf und Untergang: Germany's Losses and Impending Defeat

Elsewhere through late 1944 into 1945 the ragged line established after the conclusion of Operation Bagration frayed and disintegrated. The last active formations participated in the climactic Battle of Berlin, but by that time they were more "paper" forces than anything else. By 1945 German units rarely had the actual numbers of men and equipment that official German records report. As an example, General Walther Wenck's Twelfth Army, which was among the last operational forces in the Berlin area, was significantly understrength and composed largely of scratch formations of Volkssturm militia and other irregulars grafted onto what remained of the withered original Wehrmacht divisions.[71] It should come as no surprise that these units only infrequently and incompletely kept track of their actual strength, adding to the difficulty in tracking POWs and MIAs during the war's final act.

Outside of Berlin, the Soviets managed further mass encirclements of German forces, particularly those attempting to hold back the red flood in Germany's satellite allies. In Budapest, the Soviets trapped some 33,000 German and 37,000 Hungarian members of the city's garrison, as well as well over 80,000 civilians. Three joint German-Hungarian relief efforts failed in January 1945, and only 700 or so German soldiers managed to escape the encirclement.[72] The remaining 60,000 Germans and Hungarians surrendered on 13 February.[73]

The fall of Budapest heralded the accelerating collapse of any sort of organized German defensive front. Though German armies fought on in the East, they increasingly did so as disorganized, independent forces more concerned with holding the Red Army at bay long enough for civilians to flee westward, or to buy themselves enough time to surrender to the Anglo-Americans. Many German soldiers felt considerably less stigma in surrendering to the Western Allies, which Nazi propaganda had not labeled as racial enemies per se. More practically, Germans rightly feared Soviet retaliation for Nazi war crimes and thus had every practical reason to prefer to surrender to the Western Allies. Finally, soldiers were not alone in the East as the Red Army pressed ever closer. By continuing to fight on, they consciously bought time for the flood of civilian refugees to flee westward toward a hoped-for refuge behind British and American lines.[74] This hectic, uncoordinated mass movement of both military and civilian groups guaranteed that many people among these often disorganized masses vanished from any official accounting, disappearing somewhere in the confusion of collapsing fronts, evacuation attempts, and the oncoming Red Army. The problem of records once more complicates determining exactly how many soldiers and civilians vanished in this fashion. The Nazi state was no longer even nominally in control of the territory of Germany itself by early 1945 and was unable to properly keep track of the hundreds of thousands of Germans, military and civilian, in movement across Central and Eastern Europe as the end approached. In some regions communities even reverted to traditional authorities and entirely ignored scattered, unrealistic last-ditch orders, despite the risk of retaliation by roving SS drumhead tribunals and other Nazi fanatics.[75] Due to this breakdown, German civilians had even less opportunity to keep in touch with those outside their immediate communities, to say nothing of finding information about their missing relatives.

Finally, there was Berlin. British and American strategic bombing had already pummeled much of the city into rubble by spring 1945, as the Red Army closed in on the doomed Nazi capital. German troops within the ring consisted of a motley mix of about 45,000 Wehrmacht and Waffen-SS troops, which were supplemented by some 40,000 members of the Volkssturm militia, as well as substantial numbers of armed police and Hitler Youth units. Their levels of quality varied considerably, for while many of the Wehrmacht and Waffen-SS regulars were battle-hardened veterans, few others had much if any combat experience, save those members of the Volkssturm old enough to have served in the trenches of World War I. What they all did have in common, however, was a lack of adequate equipment and ammunition.[76] So too, they rarely if ever bothered to keep accurate records of their unit strength or casualty figures, which made later accounting for losses all but impossible outside of very broad strokes, feeding the uncertainty at the heart of the secret camp myth.

Opposing them were over a million and a half Red Army veterans, many of them with considerable urban warfare experience gained at Stalingrad and the other city fights of the long march westward. The sole hope the city's defenders had was that Wenck's Twelfth Army, one of the last operational Wehrmacht formations operating outside the Berlin encirclement, might yet achieve a break-in. This last ragged hope died unfulfilled, for though the Twelfth Army managed to fight its way into the suburb of Potsdam, it there ran up against Soviet resistance that its exhausted, outnumbered, and underequipped men were incapable of fighting further.[77] Oblivious to the macabre melodrama playing out in the Führer bunker, the Red Army pushed on toward the Reichstag, and Generals Helmuth Weidling and Hans Krebs opened surrender negotiations with Soviet General Vasily Chuikov on 1 May, delaying the actual capitulation until the next day to allow a breakout attempt by the strongest elements of what remained of Berlin's garrison.[78]

As Hitler's nominal successor, Admiral Dönitz initially stalled for time from his headquarters at Flensburg but on 7 May bowed to undeniable reality and accepted the unconditional surrender terms being offered by the Allies.[79] Though remnants of Army Group Center refused to capitulate for an additional few days, 8 May was the effective end of the war in Europe and has been recognized as VE Day ever since. All across the shattered continent, defeated Germans began to slowly filter back into a Germany now divided into occupation zones. In the East, the Soviets began to expel German populations from places they had lived for centuries in accordance with terms set at the Yalta Conference in 1944. These displaced persons joined the masses of other refugees and expellees trying to find their way home, or to a new home, and it is hardly surprising that any number of them went missing in the confusion. This displacement contributed to the secret camp myth in two ways. First, it added to the overall number of missing people who might survive in the secret camps. More important, Germans felt the forced migration was deliberately punitive, a case of unwarranted Soviet aggression against its defeated enemy.[80] This sense of victimization laid the foundation for the second aspect of the secret camp myth, by predisposing Germans to see themselves as victims of the war.

The end of hostilities brought any number of new priorities for both conquerors and conquered, among them the identification and return of those millions of POWs and civilian internees in Soviet captivity. The quantity of prisoners and missing men alone was intimidating, and as with so much else, official accounts differ. German estimates range from as low as 541,505 men unaccounted for to just under 1.3 million, while the Soviets claim to have taken about 3.4 million German prisoners.[81] The problem of resolving just whom the Soviets held or could confirm were dead was staggering in its magnitude. In addition to the problem of records, Germans lacked any mechanism by which they could compel or induce the Soviets to share their own POW/MIA information. The nation lay devastated, occupied, and faced division at its conquerors' hands. Moreover, those conquerors were not inclined to do Germans all that many favors, especially once they discovered just how black Germany's crimes really were. How then were Germans to discover the fate of men who never returned from the Eastern Front? The methods they devised, and activism in which they engaged, helps illustrate both key aspects of secret camp mythology. Those trapped in the no-man's land of grief found in the concept of secret camps a lifeline to which they could cling, while those who wanted to construct something useful from the war discovered that POWs and MIAs could be recast as a new, redemptive type of war hero. Interestingly, the rise and fall of the German secret camp myth also demonstrates how despite having far more missing people to account for under circumstances that made secret captivity much more believable, Germans did manage to resolve satisfactorily their trauma over the missing in a way concerned Americans still have not.

⟁

TWO

The Short-Lived German
Secret Camp Myth

World War II left in its aftermath two key elements that led Germans to articulate the secret camp myth. First, that so many Germans had disappeared under ambiguous circumstances all but guaranteed a substantial number of civilians found themselves in the no-man's land of grief. Unable to mourn losses they could not confirm, such individuals were often eager believers in the existence of rumored secret Soviet prison camps in which the missing might yet survive. Second, Germans found it difficult to salvage anything nationally useful from the war experience due to their devastating defeat and Germany's many war crimes. Those who sought to at least dilute such opprobrium used the suffering of German POWs in Soviet captivity as symbols of the larger victimization of conquered Germany itself, and to symbolically place their own nation on the list of the war's victims. The Soviet decision to retain substantial numbers of POWs as convicted war criminals following the end of regular prisoner repatriation made such a reconceptualization that much more appealing, as did continuing confusion about just who was still alive in Soviet custody.

Germany lay shattered following the formal surrender in May 1945. All across the devastated map of Europe, people of virtually all nationalities were on the move. Not just former POWs, but also displaced civilians of all sorts attempted to make their way home, and to find families with whom they had had little if any recent contact. Against this backdrop, German POWs returned from Allied captivity, and family members tried to ascertain the fate of those who remained missing following repatriation. Prisoners returning from Anglo-American detention generally found that process to be a straightforward one, in part since Germany had observed international POW conventions regarding the Western Allies and received similar consideration in turn. Such was emphatically not the case between the belligerents on the Eastern Front, and while Soviet treatment of German POWs was not as explicitly and avowedly murderous as the Nazi equivalent, nevertheless the nonobservance of various convention rights, most importantly Red Cross camp inspections, left many in Germany in the dark concerning whether their missing man was even alive, let alone what prison camp he might be in. What is more, repatriation from the USSR did not include a substantial minority of Germans whom the Soviets held as convicted war criminals sentenced to various terms of imprisonment. This all created the social environment where West Germans found it plausible to argue that other MIAs might still be alive in secret camps and advocate for the return of these presumed survivors from their ongoing Soviet captivity.

However, although the West German political establishment engaged with this constituency, the German secret camp myth did not long survive, and it was functionally dead a mere decade after war's end. With so many missing, why was German POW/MIA activism not a long-term affair? Importantly, though that activism did for a time become part of the national political conversation in West Germany after World War II, it was able to reach a satisfactory conclusion after which secret camp advocates were for the most part willing to cease their agitation and admit that any remaining MIAs were almost certainly dead. Specifically, German social and political actors were able to satisfy this constituency by connecting that activism to larger redemptive themes of heroism and victimization and also by effecting the return of substantial numbers of live prisoners in the 1950s.

Not Knowing: The German Home Front and Lack of POW/MIA Information

The nature of Germany's defeat made it that much more difficult to ascertain just what had happened to the MIAs. Civilians no longer had to worry about their own government's restrictions on asking questions, or deal with the physical dangers of wartime, but peacetime brought similar complications. The occupying powers discouraged POW/MIA activism, as they believed it was a reincarnation of the militarism that enabled Nazism in the first place and that had so destabilized Germany following World War I.

Having marched home in 1918 "undefeated on the battlefield," veterans of the Western Front contributed greatly to the instability of the early Weimar government.[1] Subsequently, veterans' organizations like the Stahlhelm and Reichsbanner were active participants in the rowdy street brawls that became part and parcel of parliamentary politics during the troubled life of the Weimar Republic, to the point where they took on the mantle of "political combat leagues" (politische Kampfbünde).[2] The brown-shirted storm troopers of the Nazi SA (Sturmabteilung) represented this blending of militaristic violence with politics taken to its logical extreme, and following World War II the Allies were determined to not let that particular part of the recent past repeat itself.

From the Allied perspective, militarism and Nazism were inescapably linked, and the latter would surely resurface were the former not suppressed.[3] The Western powers were suspicious of any thematically similar organizations that arose in the aftermath of 1945, given their role in destabilizing the only previous German attempt at democracy, and saw to it that those that did limited themselves to domestic concerns, such as arguing for the restoration of military pensions and similar issues. The occupation and partition of Germany into separate zones initially with a direct Allied military presence also contributed to keeping membership in such groups smaller than it might otherwise have been, as did the lack of a postwar narrative by which veterans could recast themselves as anything other than unequivocally defeated.[4]

In the Soviet zone, ideology continued to play a role in suppressing POW/MIA activism, though from a different direction. The Soviets quite understandably viewed German POWs as criminal invaders of the USSR, and they supported the German Communist line that the only "good" Germans had been the comparatively tiny number of antifascist partisans.[5] This emphasis did not mesh with the reconceptualization of POWs and MIAs as redemptive hero-victims inherent in secret camp mythology.

Because of these limitations German POW/MIA activism was slow to coalesce immediately following the war, as was the secret camp myth itself. Individual family members of the missing instead acted independently. Some tried to contact Soviet authorities directly to gain information about the missing, though they rarely met with much success. During the removal of the surviving remnants of Field Marshal Ferdinand Schörner's army group in May 1945, German prisoners noticed women attempting to reach their

CHAPTER TWO

train when it was passing through Romania. They learned that these women were also German, and they were ostensibly trying to pass on food and supplies to the POWs despite the hostility of Soviet guards. This, those prisoners learned, was subterfuge, as the women's real motive was just to speak with as many prisoners en route to Soviet prison camps as possible. By so doing, these women sought to pass messages along and learn what they could about their own missing relatives from these men. They then promulgated what little they had learned outward through a growing ad hoc web of contacts among families of the missing. This informal network of personal relationships and word-of-mouth communications became the first conduit for information on the missing within the German civilian population.[6] However, much of the information available was incomplete, and at times it barely rose above the level of gossip and rumor, little of which dissuaded the hopes of those trapped in the no-man's land of grief. Undeterred, they continued to expect joyous reunions when the POWs came home.

Heimkehrer: The Incomplete Return of German POWs from the USSR

From internment camps as distant as North America and the reaches of Siberia, Germany's POWs straggled their way back to the Fatherland. This mass movement was hindered by Europe's devastated transportation infrastructure and further complicated and slowed by ongoing efforts to locate alleged war criminals among the service arms. This included those uniformed men who had participated in wartime atrocities as well as others who attempted to hide from the Nazi hunters among the anonymous masses of men in bedraggled field gray uniforms, of whom Reichsführer-SS Heinrich Himmler was only the most notorious example.[7] German family members of MIAs held out hope that their man would be among those slowly returning, particularly from the Eastern Front where information about who was a POW versus being truly unaccounted for was even more fragmentary than elsewhere. On balance, the Western Allies were fairly quick in returning their prisoners, though the French temporarily retained considerable numbers of POWs for reconstruction labor purposes.[8] Despite this complication and others, German POWs from the West were more or less all home again by 1948, at the latest.[9]

By contrast, German prisoners were still returning from the Soviet Union in early 1949, which unlike the West included substantial numbers of civilian internees.[10] Indeed, such were their numbers that in 1948 the emerging administration of West Germany established the Office for Displaced Persons (Amt für Heimatvertriebene) to centralize information and resources for issues pertaining to the missing and displaced.[11] This office in turn became the Federal Ministry of Displaced Persons, Refugees, and War Victims (Bundesministerium für Vertriebene, Flüchtlinge, und Kriegsgeschädigte, or BMVT) following the parliamentary elections of 1949.[12] In both incarnations, this agency faced a considerable initial difficulty: finding out just how many POWs the Soviets even held, and who those men actually were. The BMVT determined that by late 1947, the Soviets had consolidated most German POWs in five major clusters of POW camps, located near the cities of Chelyabinsk, Leningrad, Ufa, Moscow, and Riga. What they did not know was how many camps specifically existed, how many prisoners were in each camp, or even specifically who the known POWs all were.[13] Such uncertainties fed German anxieties and stoked fears about Soviet treatment of German POWs.

The BMVT turned to the German population at large for assistance in cutting through the wartime obfuscation of who among all the men unaccounted for were known prisoners. Specifically, BMVT officials asked family members of the missing to fill out registration cards with information that could help identify their missing man, such as his last known location, battle, or date when he had gone missing. This process had already worked with some success for POWs in the West, where mail contact mediated by the Red Cross between prisoners and their families had by and large been the rule. Understandably, the same process resulted in far less useful information when applied to missing Germans on the Eastern Front, where there was no comparable arrangement.[14]

Given the comparative lack of concrete information about men missing in the East, Germans speculated widely about their missing men in the first years after the war. They worked with information from many different, mostly informal, sources. Many considered the testimony of POWs who had returned to be the most compelling, though it was not always particularly accurate. Many POW returnees claimed to have heard of special "silent camps" (*Schweigelager*) that held unknown additional numbers of German prisoners. Supposedly, the Soviets maintained these silent camps separate from their conventional prison camps, to conceal prisoners whom they did not intend to return. Such rumors led to the first explicit articulation of the German secret camp myth when the *Stuttgarter Zeitung* published the following in July 1949:

Former members of the German-Romanian army, who arrived on Tuesday and Wednesday in Russian transports at a Hessian returnee camp, stated that former German soldiers of the Romanian Army were detained in huge "silent camps" in Donets at Kharkov and at Dnjepropetowsk. None of the occupants of these camps have been allowed to write.

The camps were constructed by the Soviets using special lists of an estimated four million missing Germans since war's end and in addition to POWs, civilians, mostly women and children from the former German eastern territories are reported among the returnees still retained in the Soviet Union.[15]

This story was hardly alone in playing up the "silent" part of these camps. Once established, the West German government intentionally emphasized the enforced silence of prisoners to rationalize their unreasonably high estimates of how many POWs might still be alive in Soviet prison camps.[16] After all, if there were at least *some* known prisoners whom the Soviets had prevented contacting their families prior to their repatriation, then who could say how many more men listed as MIA might still survive in these silent camps? This rationale appeared all the more reasonable given the official casualty narrative that hugely inflated the numbers of potentially surviving POWs in the East. So too, the very uncertainty of the entire situation encouraged West Germans to expect survival in the absence of positive proof of death rather than vice versa, given the presumed masses of unidentified men in these silent camps.

While West Germans believed that the overwhelming majority of their remaining missing men were in Soviet silent camps, they had a difficult time getting information about their missing men from other Eastern European nations as well, in particular Yugoslavia. Interestingly, despite being a non-Soviet-aligned communist nation, Yugoslavia was similarly reticent in providing information about the German POWs it also retained much longer than the Western Allies. As late as July 1949, according to *Der Tagesspiegel*:

On Thursday the West German Chancellor—for the first time as "the Chancellor of the Federal Republic of Germany"—sent a telegram addressed to the western military governors to the 20 June Conference of Foreign Ministers in Paris as a protest note on the POW question. This step was taken as the German authorities had not received any answer to their appeal to the foreign ministers. They asked the military governors to transmit the text of that note to the foreign ministers. The Chancellor, we are also informed, also appealed to the occupation forces to encourage the governments of Yugoslavia and Albania to release their detained POWs and "ethnic Germans." According to investigation Yugoslavia has repatriated a total of 74,354 of the 85,453 prisoners so far. Approximately 3900 have been sentenced to forced labor and more than 1300 are believed still in pre-trial custody. The rest have reportedly died in captivity without any official news from Yugoslavia.[17]

These men were admittedly incidental when compared to the much-larger number of Germans believed to be potentially still alive in Soviet custody, but this example demonstrates how the international politics of POWs loomed large for West Germans and West Germany years after the end of World War II.

An important and complementary aspect of the larger POW question was the experience of those men who returned to Germany from the USSR shortly after the war, versus that minority of POWs who languished in the so-called silent camps well into the 1950s. Regardless of which set of prison camps they had come from, the early returnees universally encountered little in the way of official reception or assistance in reintegration. This is hardly surprising, for two interconnected reasons: first, Germany was under foreign occupation immediately following the war and had no official government that might enact such policies. Second, even had that not been the case, Germany was economically and physically devastated, and dependent on its conquerors for most of its basic resources. Consequently, early returnees received only a minimum of support following their formal processing out of service, compared with later returnees whom West Germany was more than able and willing to help reintegrate by the prosperous 1950s.[18]

Reintegration of early returnees would have been difficult enough had their only problem been the economic and physical devastation of their homeland. However, they also experienced considerable social upheaval. German men returning from POW camps often found startling changes in domestic gender relations and a considerable blurring of formerly distinct male and female spheres of activity. Wartime manpower and labor demands were the two primary drivers behind this upheaval, as Germany had had to call upon its female population increasingly as the conflict went against it. Even if wartime labor needs had not pushed women workers into Germany's arms factories and elsewhere, the simple absence of men away at the fronts was more than sufficient to cause no small amount of social reordering as women assumed domestic responsibilities traditionally held by fathers and husbands. For men who had often sustained themselves in Soviet prison camps with dreams of a return to a settled home life, the shock of these changes could be as profound as anything else they experienced upon their return.[19]

It is important to note that such potential difficulties with shifting gender roles was not a trivial matter; it had ramifications specific to those worries and fears that motivated the West German POW/MIA activism behind the German secret camp myth. Many Germans feared that time spent behind the wire had led to the degradation not only of the physical health of the POWs but also of their very masculinity and sexuality. Those Germans believed that prolonged confinement in Soviet camps led to "dystrophy," and they pointed to the perceived derangement of sexual impulses and urges of many returnees as proof of its danger. Germans believed such afflicted individuals suffered from a "retardation of the sexual constitution, which may pervert the undirected sexual impulse."[20] As time passed and men continued to languish in Soviet camps, both real and imagined, Germans increasingly worried about what sort of men might finally come home. After all, if the early returnees potentially suffered from physical and sexual disorders, how much worse would it be for those who still lingered in secret Soviet camps?

Germans also feared their men would suffer from political contamination at the hands of their sinister Bolshevik captors. Though most of these fears were baseless, there was some small justification for such concerns since the Soviets had attempted to recruit German POWs into antifascist organizations during the war, albeit inconsistently. Indeed, several prominent captive generals, most notably the former commander of the doomed Sixth Army, Field Marshal Friedrich Paulus, had joined the Soviet-sponsored National Committee for a Free Germany (Nationalkomitee Freies Deutschland, or NKFD) in late 1944, into which the Soviets had merged the earlier collaborationist League of German Officers (Bund Deutscher Offiziere, or BDO).[21] Germans worried that the mere existence of these Soviet-sponsored organizations demonstrated communist contamination of German POWs, and knowledge that those groups actively propagandized not only to the masses of German POWs in Soviet prison camps but also via radio only made such fears worse.

Importantly, this was not the first time Germans had faced fears of politically contaminated POW returnees. Following the Russian Revolution of 1917, approximately 2 million German and Austro-Hungarian POWs originally held by Tsarist Russia fell into the custody of the nascent Soviet state, which propagandized extensively among them.[22] The Soviets hoped to turn the POWs into agents of international revolution, and also make them sympathetic to the Red cause in the ongoing Russian Civil War, starved as the Bolsheviks were for experienced fighting men in their efforts to repel the White counter-revolutionaries and other factions fighting in the remains of the former Tsarist state.[23] It is difficult to estimate just how successful were these Soviet efforts, particularly as there were pragmatic incentives to at least claim to sympathize with socialist propaganda, but it is certain that at least a hardcore minority of German POW returnees from World War I came home determined to foment revolution. Indeed, many of the founding members of the German Communist party (Kommunistischepartei Deutschlands, or KPD) had been POWs on the Eastern Front and were active participants in the abortive German Revolution of 1918.[24]

It is not surprising therefore that West German civilians feared that their returning POWs might be infected with the political ideology they had spent the war years despising and which, as embodied by the Red Army, most directly represented the utter devastation of their homeland. To be sure, those POWs who had collaborated with the Soviets represented a tiny minority of the overall prisoner population, but German civilians nevertheless feared that imprisonment led to collaboration. One of the West German government's first acts was to create a new category of civil and criminal law for those suspected of such improper behavior. West Germany held a few hundred of these *Kameradenschinder* ("torturers of their comrades") trials in the late 1940s, on the strength of POW accusations of perceived disloyalty by their comrades. Such accusations invariably included some collaborationist element and focused almost exclusively on German POWs from the Eastern Front, demonstrating the persistence of anti-Soviet ideology even after the downfall of the Nazi regime.[25]

Despite these trials, there was no great turmoil in accepting most POWs back with open arms. Kameradenschinder trials invariably portrayed the accused as exceptions to the POW norm of passive-yet-noble resistance, a standard that helped add to the growing secret camp myth. In any case, Germans reserved the bulk of their loathing for those collaborators in high places, such as Paulus and General Walter von Seydlitz.[26] It was not in West Germans' best interests to find too many of that sort of traitor anyway, or to dwell too deeply on what, exactly, those traitors had done that was so reprehensible. They were, after all, not eager to discover any wartime complicity of the Wehrmacht with the various atrocities of the Nazi state, particularly if returning POWs were to be successfully reimagined in something approaching a heroic light.

Kriegsverurteilte: German Prisoners in the USSR after Repatriation's End

The year 1949 marked a major turning point for the German secret camp myth, for early that year the Soviets announced the end of regular repatriations, having by then released approximately 1.9 million German POWs. However, the end of repatriations did not mean the Soviets had returned all their German prisoners. Shortly after announcing the end of repatriations, Radio Moscow (TASS) stated that the Soviet Union would retain some 13,536 other prisoners, both military and civilian. TASS declared that Soviet courts had convicted these prisoners of war crimes and sentenced them to terms as long as twenty-five years in some cases.[27] Crucially for the emerging German secret camp myth, the mathematics of the missing did not add up. By German estimates, there were 2.7 million German POWs and MIAs on the Eastern Front at war's end. Even allowing for the substantial number of POWs who had died in captivity, this left tens if not hundreds of thousands of Germans unaccounted for on the Eastern Front. What is more, the official Soviet claim of how many war criminals they planned to retain significantly understated the actual number of such prisoners. More recent examinations of Soviet court records place that number closer to 34,000.[28] Though West Germans did not know exactly how many survived, and generally were not willing to take the Soviets at their word, they did know that there were live prisoners in the USSR. Here then was the German secret camp myth defined: live MIAs survived alongside those convicted POWs whom the Soviets admitted to holding, and they did so in undisclosed silent camps somewhere in the Soviet Union.

The way West Germans thought and spoke about these remaining prisoners—and the MIAs they hoped might survive alongside them in the silent camps—is illustrative of a key aspect of the secret camp phenomenon: that of postwar reconceptualization of the wartime hero figure. West Germans found it difficult to salvage much that was symbolically useful from those who had served under the swastika, and what little they did find was unavoidably tainted. However, unlike other veterans, the heroic suffering of German POWs washed away at least some national guilt via their victimization at the hands of the "barbarous" enemy. West Germans considered the prisoners who remained in Soviet custody after 1949 even more useful in this regard since those men stood as persistent symbols of German victimization. Tellingly, West Germans much more frequently used the term *Kriegsverurteilte* to refer to German POWs convicted of war crimes by Soviet courts. That they preferred that word, which translates best as "war convicted" or "war condemned," as opposed to *Kriegsverbrecher* ("war criminal"), reflects a broadly felt if perhaps not as widely stated public opinion.[29] West Germans could rationalize that while these prisoners might have been *convicted* of some charge, were they actually *criminals*, given the circumstances of those convictions? Even when the West German press used the phrase *war criminal,* by the 1950s it almost invariably qualified that term with "alleged" or "so-called," thus to heavily imply that such allegations were suspect, save when a genuine Nazi bigwig was the subject of discussion.[30]

This larger sentiment is itself a key element of why the German secret camp myth was explicitly a *West* German phenomenon rather than a more broadly German one. In the Soviet occupation zone, the KPD predecessors of what became East Germany's ruling Socialist Unity Party (Sozialistische Einheitspartei Deutschlands, or SED) were initially quite suspicious of returnees from the Soviet Union. Karl Lewke reported to the party that those men constituted

One million anti-Bolshevists heading our way. . . . Every day, between 1,000 and 2,000 prisoners of war pass through the camp gates of Frankfurt/Oder to freedom. Tired, broken, and ragged, they disperse across Germany. Each one an agitator, each one an instigator against "communist" conditions. Each one, on account of his external appearance, a living demonstration of these very "communist" conditions. All things are twisted, appear in a bad light—if civilians and released prisoners of war meet.

What about acknowledging the shared responsibility of the German people—what about an objective, political discussion? Who in these chance group meetings speaks of reconstruction, collaboration, and the like? No, there is never any talk of that. Here, the consequences of a total war, the effects of a total defeat are merely the evil intentions of the even more evil Bolshevism. Forgotten is Hitler, forgotten Nazism. Indeed, even the awful terrors of the battlefield, the fears, the horror of the thundering bombing nights of biting smoke—all this seems pushed into the distant past. They see only today, all their anger, their hatred is directed against this. They eagerly indulge in the hope of an imminent military confrontation between Russia and England-America. All Nazi insinuations fall on willing ears. The German legion set up by the English is already marching in the English zone. In fact, people know precisely: for four weeks the starved men are first nursed back, six weeks of home vacation makes them ready for new military training.[31]

In Lewke's opinion, returning POWs were by definition suspect to party plans to establish a new state built explicitly on an antifascist foundation.[32] Although the SED initially shared this sentiment, in practice it tended toward pragmatism with regard to the early returnees. While not discounting that these men were politically suspect, the party prioritized the need for their labor and economic contributions in rebuilding and for the most part ignored low-level complicity in war crimes in the East.[33] After the end of Soviet repatriations, however, the SED hardened its line against the war convicts, whose sentences it held were legitimate.[34] This official stance helped undercut the possibility of there being any sort of equivalent secret camp myth in East Germany since those men were considered politically unreliable and because the SED rejected any state sanction for their conversion into convenient hero-victims of unwarranted Soviet barbarity.

West Germans reacted to the official end of repatriations with almost universal disbelief and outrage. Chancellor Konrad Adenauer interrupted debate on the floor of the Bundestag in May 1949 to proclaim that TASS's statement had "left unclear the fate of 1.5 million POWs."[35] He was hardly alone in expressing such sentiments. That same month, *Die Zeit* ran a front-page article on the subject, proclaiming that the Soviets' proclamation was effectively a "death sentence for half a million German POWs."[36] Just over a month later, the Information Service for POW Questions of the Länderrat of the American occupation zone published a declaration on POWs, which was picked up by the United Press. That agency claimed, "The Soviet Government continues to hold over 100,000 POWs. By some German estimates, they could even amount to 600,000. [Soviet Foreign Minister Vyacheslav] Molotov's March 1947 statement of 890,532 German POWs could in no way be reconciled with Soviet wartime communiques that spoke of 3,730,995 POWs."[37] The *Stuttgarter Nachrichten* followed suit in July, arguing there might be over 2 million POWs still alive in the USSR.[38]

Every one of these claims took it as given that substantial numbers of MIAs survived alongside that much smaller body of POWs, though perhaps not for long. Almost without exception, they estimated much higher numbers of potential POWs than could possibly exist even under the best of circumstances. German POW/MIA advocates were working with faulty data, whether they knew it or not. They had at hand only Soviet reports, which were unreliable and mistrusted, and leftover wartime records, which WASt had intentionally misrepresented for the sake of propaganda and ideology. While some activists were honestly misled by these faulty sources of information, others were more cynically willing to accept WASt figures at face value for their own reasons. Most prominently, Chancellor Adenauer and Evangelical Relief Association chief and Christian Democratic Union (CDU) delegate Eugen Gerstenmaier knew perfectly well that the idea of hundreds of thousands of surviving POWs after the end of regular reparations was entirely absurd, but they perpetuated such claims regardless.[39]

Such statements also exist in the larger context of the emerging Cold War, and West German individuals and entities did not fail to capitalize on the Soviet declaration. The Social Democrats (Sozialdemokratische Partei Deutschlands, or SPD) published a poster calling for the release of the "5,000,000 who are missing" not long after the end of Soviet repatriations. This poster contains a symbolic element crucial to understanding the evolution of the German secret camp myth and its iconography: men behind barbed wire. In this early depiction of Germans in a silent camp, the figures do not appear as emaciated wrecks, as they do in later images. They seem more bored than anything else, patiently waiting for someone to recognize their plight and set them free, but not noticeably suffering beyond their enforced absence. Nevertheless, barbed wire menaces the foreground, demonstrating the involuntary nature of their confinement and implying how that confinement is enforced by violence.[40] This SPD poster also served as a prototype for later secret camp appeals, particularly after other groups and parties took the image of the POW/MIA to its logical conclusion, creating the vision of the German hero-victim so necessary for the redemptive aspect of the secret camp myth. More important, the focus here on barbed wire demonstrates the beginnings of an inversion of guilt and appropriation of suffering by using one of the most potent symbols of the Holocaust to recast German POWs in a role like that of Germany's own victims.

Ordinary Germans did not take long to react to the Soviet declaration on the end of repatriations, and, given the numbers of men unaccounted for in the East, it is surprising there was not a stronger public reaction. Their early appeals tended to be for information rather than direct action. Consider the following response sent by the BMVT to one Frau Wurst:

It's not easy to comply with your request for a "clear answer" on the silent camps in Russia, as there is hardly anyone in Germany who knows every detail concerning the actual conditions in Russia. As you well know the Russian authorities themselves claim to not be aware of any information about these POW camps, so we have to rely on the statements of the returning POWs. Returnee descriptions have developed the following depiction of the silent camps: There should be no doubt that there actually are a number of camps in Russia, from which no [prisoners] have written. Prisoners of War are moved to these camps to be punished for whatever reason (political liabilities, alleged lack of work ethic and similar causes). Their stay in such camps can, it seems, last for up to several years. On the other hand there are, in our experience with prisoners of war in Russia, hardly a case where the person concerned has not already had the opportunity to notify his kin in Germany. So far despite many loud rumors, there are entirely no proved cases of a prisoner of war spending his entire captivity in one of these silent camps. To our knowledge the official bodies invariably claim that any prisoners of war held in any way in Russia since the war has been allowed to send his family a message, and if they have no news of him, it must be admitted that he is dead. Are you also in contact with the Search Service for Prisoners of War and the Missing in Stuttgart, Charlottenplatz 17? That service can in most cases provide addresses of homecomers, as well as last known Postnumber to families of the missing, and it is often able to provide information or at least clues about the fate of missing persons.

We regret that we cannot give you more satisfying information. It is extraordinarily oppressive for all parties involved that, four years after the war, there remains considerable ambiguity about the prisoners of war still in Russia, or dead in Russian captivity. Negotiations on these matters will continue with the occupying powers and we hope that they succeed, and one day induce the Soviet Union to provide clear information.[41]

Frau Wurst was not alone in her search for information on the missing, nor was she the only one having difficulty determining the proper place to begin such a search. Repeatedly, they found themselves up against two fundamental obstacles: the unreliability of German records, and the inaccessibility of Soviet authorities:

In reply to your letter of 7 January 1949 I inform you that according to the documents presented by the Department on POWs questions, POWs are often sentenced for the smallest of offenses to significant penalties and transported to prison camps. During this time the convicts do not have the opportunity to contact their families. In many cases, however, it was found that after a certain time these convicts are released prior to having completed their sentence in the prison camp and are assigned to a normal POW camp. However, since this release from prison depends on many contingencies, I'm unable to tell you with certainty whether and to what extent your son must serve this punishment. Given the insignificance of his offence, however, it is likely he did not serve the full seven years of his sentence. Unfortunately, there is little opportunity to learn more about your son, as the Russian authorities provide no information about such prisoners.[42]

In this response, the BMVT cast clear responsibility for any lack of information entirely on the Soviet government and suggested that the former enemy knew more about the missing than he was saying. The BMVT here also implied that the Soviets had it in their power to help, but had chosen not so to do. In reality, Soviet inability to answer West German inquiries about the unaccounted for owed more to practical and logistical complications than it did to any intentional malice on the part of Moscow. The Soviets had had a hard time even keeping track of their own casualties during the war, so vast was the scale of fighting and carnage on the Eastern Front. To this day, body recovery continues in Russia, with teams uncovering a mass burial site on the Neva near the old Leningrad siege lines as recently as the summer of 2013.[43] Since the USSR had been so devastated by the German invasion and subsequent liberation, that state can hardly be blamed for not prioritizing record keeping on German prisoners and casualties.

Das Kriegsgefangeneproblem: The Politics of POW/MIA Advocacy

German POW/MIA activism took on more concrete forms following the end of regular repatriations, with distinct organizations assuming prominent roles in the ongoing search for West Germany's missing. Two groups, the German Red Cross (Deutsche Rotekreuz, or DRK) and the Association of Returnees (Verband der Heimkehrer, or VdH), played significant roles in that search. The DRK in particular interacted closely with the government of Chancellor Adenauer in what was admittedly a complicated and occasionally critical relationship.

DRK president Heinrich Weitz was more than just professionally interested in determining the fate of Germany's missing. His son was among those unaccounted for in the USSR.[44] Unsurprisingly, he had campaigned to make POW/MIA accounting a priority within the DRK even before winning election as president of that organization in 1952. After his election, he was instrumental in shifting the lion's share of DRK activities toward locating remaining prisoners and accounting for the missing. Indeed, he was the driving force behind the DRK proposing a resolution at the 1952 International Conference of the Red Cross to complete the accounting process, and also to gain the release of the "war convicted" still in Soviet custody.[45]

A key moment in the evolution of the DRK's strategy toward gaining the release of those remaining German POWs came in 1952 at the 18th International Conference of the Red Cross in Toronto. At that conference, the DRK found concrete reasons to be hopeful but also experienced a setback. Specifically, the DRK delegation drew considerable encouragement from an agreement between the People's Republic of China and Japan for the former to return approximately 63,000 Japanese POWs still held in China, with each nation's Red Cross Society acting as intermediaries.[46] Despite this, the DRK itself experienced precious little sympathy from other delegations when lobbying on behalf of the war-convicted Germans and any live MIAs who might be with them in the silent camps. Weitz put this hostility down to the persistent taint of Nazism, which limited international sympathies for those Germans convicted of war crimes. As the DRK delegation had well learned at the 1952 Toronto conference, it could "expect little from general proclamations, as these always amount to moral indictments, which only further reinforce the negative attitudes of detaining countries."[47] Put more plainly, DRK attempts to win outside sympathy by painting German POWs as victims of the war failed since no one had any doubts about just why those men had been in Soviet Russia in the first place.

Weitz therefore concluded that the DRK needed to focus on reconstructing the image of the missing, as well as to try to develop some manner of direct line of communication with the Soviets, whether through the Soviet Red Cross or government directly. He hoped that by focusing on the humanity of the POWs he could thus tug at heartstrings while downplaying the inconvenient aspects of those men, hopefully without having to consciously remind anyone just why, exactly, they were still held prisoner. He also hoped this approach would avoid directly pointing an accusatory finger at the USSR.[48] In addition to the problem of war crimes, the DRK and West German POW/MIA advocates also had to grapple with their comparative lack of leverage. Even ignoring the moral ambiguity surrounding the entire issue of German POWs, these advocates were citizens of a nation that was still recovering from the war, despite the "economic miracle" already underway by the early 1950s. Even were they able to open direct talks with the Soviets about the war-convicted and missing men, how could they induce them to release those men? The politics of the early Cold War also played a part here, for the more West Germany became a solid member of the West, the less likely were its POW/MIA activists to find a cooperative partner in Moscow.

Weitz's second chief goal was to develop contacts with the Soviet Union in the hopes of achieving some manner of direct talks about the war-convicted Germans. Such an aim risked further entangling German POW/MIA activism in the national politics of West Germany, however, since it threatened to trespass on territory that the most prominent statesman in the new nation, Chancellor Adenauer, considered his personal preserve. Adenauer had already made repatriation of those remaining POWs part of his foreign policy toward the Soviet Union, which included any missing men supposedly in the silent camps. Unlike Weitz, and potentially at cross-purposes with the DRK president, Adenauer thought POW/MIA matters a secondary concern to his larger plan of gaining increased recognition and legitimacy for West Germany.[49] He also hoped that developing diplomatic and economic ties to the USSR would help marginalize the rival East German state, which required a delicate balancing act between repairing West Germany's relationship with the rest of the West generally, and the United States in particular, while not overly alienating the Soviets.[50] West Germany was, after all, a new country just emerging from occupation and seeking to rediscover its place within a European order that was itself changing and shifting due to decolonization struggles and the rising dominance of the two superpowers.

Though whether Adenauer personally believed in the existence of the silent camps is unclear, what is certain is that he considered activism on the issue to be subordinate to his larger policy goals. He embraced it when it served his ends, and he distanced himself from it when it did not. In particular, Adenauer was determined not to allow independent action by activists and secret camp advocates to get out of control, or to upstage him personally. He repeatedly discouraged attempts by the DRK to send a delegation to Moscow to negotiate directly with the Soviet Red Cross and government after 1949. Writing to Weitz in early 1953, Adenauer informed him that a visit Weitz had been discussing with State Secretary Walter Hallstein would only serve to raise false hopes in the families of the missing. Since Adenauer believed there was no chance the DRK would be able to wrest any concessions from the Soviets, he did not approve the visit. Further, Adenauer argued that appealing to the Western powers was a more effective way to win the return of Germany's missing, and he feared those powers would see ulterior political motives in the DRK's planned visit.[51] Weitz attempted to answer such worries, but Adenauer's interference effectively blocked DRK efforts to negotiate directly with the Soviets, and nothing came of that planned delegation to Moscow.

Adenauer was not the only politician to attempt to harness the potential of the secret camp myth for his own ends, though he was the most effective one so to do. SPD chairman Kurt Schumacher tried to make the return of prisoners from the USSR a campaign issue during the 1947 state elections in the British occupation zone.[52] This effort appears to be the sole attempt by the SPD to wrest the issue away from the Christian Democratic Union (Adenauer's party), and though individual SPD members were active in subsequent secret camp advocacy, they presented no further collective challenge to CDU leadership on that issue. Similarly, West Germany's right-wing parties, such as the National Democratic Party (Nationaldemokratische Partei Deutschlands, or NPD), were content to leave well enough alone, perhaps as reimaging prisoners as passively redemptive hero-victims clashed with the older, inherited Nazi hero cult conception of the glorious dead.

Appropriated Suffering: POWs and MIAs as Redemptive Figures

The second major group to advocate on behalf of missing Germans was the Association of Returnees (Verband der Heimkehrer, or VdH), which grew out of the 1950 merger of two state-level organizations that had developed incrementally after the war.[53] Though the VdH did advocate for the return of the war-convicted and those missing men whom it believed alive in the silent camps, it did not focus exclusively on the secret camp issue. Rather, the VdH's larger concern was returnee issues generally, and while it prioritized POW/MIA concerns, it had many other attendant ones given the scope of displaced Germans across Europe.

The VdH's advocacy heavily emphasized the redemptive nature of POW suffering and victimization in explicitly religious and Christian fashion, intended both to portray missing and imprisoned Germans in as sympathetic a light as possible and also to contrast with the atheistic Soviet Union. The VdH made publicizing the fate of unreleased POWs its primary mission after 1949 by targeting its appeals via mass media. The association flooded daily newspapers across West Germany with horror stories about the Soviet camps as told by POW returnees, with the heavy implication that those

Germans who remained imprisoned by the Soviets were experiencing even worse treatment. The VdH also used returnee testimony to confirm the popular belief that POW war crimes convictions were nothing more than the result of communist vindictiveness and harsh victor's justice.[54]

Such a focus on German suffering in Soviet hands reflected the sentiments of the VdH's membership. Its monthly newspaper, *Der Heimkehrer*, regularly contained articles and letters from individual members arguing that no one adequately acknowledged German suffering and victimization from the war, particularly that of the men in Soviet custody. Most VdH members admitted that Germany's war crimes were horrific and deserved some degree of punishment, but they argued that the Allies overstated their scope, and that German suffering in the silent camps was actually the worse of the two.[55]

VdH publicity efforts culminated in two exhibitions that toured West Germany in the early 1950s and that attracted record numbers of visitors, including Bundestag deputies: "Prisoners of War Speak," and "We Admonish," both of which were underwritten by the West German government.[56] Much like earlier news media appeals, both of these exhibitions invariably emphasized the imagined brutality of the silent camps, with gaunt, shaved-headed Germans silently enduring communist barbarity behind the wire.[57] By using such specific imagery, the VdH symbolically transformed German POWs from war criminals into hero-victims. Such representations take the reconceptualization of POWs and appropriation of others' suffering that first appeared in the SPD's "5000000 fehlen" poster to its logical conclusion. As before, barbed wire dominates the image, but now the prisoner is reduced from an anonymous crowd to a single, solitary individual, emaciated and suffering but nevertheless retaining a degree of passive defiance and dignity. [58] A key, powerful message lay beneath these images and reinforced a growing sentiment in West Germany in the late 1940s: for all the horrors of World War II and the Nazi state, the people of Germany were as much victims of that war as anyone else.

The use of such potent symbols and depictions demonstrates a remarkable attempt at inverting the realities of the war. The gaunt, bedraggled figures of these images cannot help but call to mind images of gaunt victims of Nazi concentration camps, as too did the emphasis on barbed wire. By using such similar imagery and thus implying similar victimization of German POWs at Soviet hands, the proponents of the German secret camp myth were appropriating the suffering of Germany's own victims. Moreover, they were using that appropriated suffering in service of rehabilitating and elevating men who had inflicted that original suffering upon the victims of Germany's own camps. There is a deep irony at play here as well, as having collectively been aware of and, often, active perpetrators of Nazi crimes against humanity, Germans were already familiar with the meaning and impact of such images as they now used to emphasize the plight of their own missing men. Though himself a victim of the Nazi state, Chancellor Adenauer demonstrated a mastery of this language of borrowed victimization and appropriated suffering when he spoke at a POW commemoration event in 1950. He used terms many West Germans had already internalized when he asked if "ever before in history millions of people have been sentenced with such heartlessness to misery and misfortune?"[59] This recasting of West Germany's missing as hero-victims of Soviet barbarity thus also acted to manufacture an equivalence of suffering between Germans and their own victims, where it did not seek to mute the voices of the latter entirely.

This reconceptualization is also important in order to understand another aspect of why the secret camp myth was so specifically a West German social phenomenon rather than a pan-German one. Not only was the POW not a suitable figure for canonization in East Germany for political reasons, there also was no comparable empty social space into which he might step. The SED had already established the partisan and the resistance fighter as the only "good" Germans of the war, to bolster both its own legitimacy as ruling party and its larger plan to establish antifascism as the raison d'être for East Germany more generally.[60] With such a hero figure already in place, it is hardly surprising that the SED had no room for any other, particularly one as antagonistic to the party line as West Germany's hero-victim POW/MIA would have been.

More than just a particular inversion of victimization, the VdH's campaign also played to the parallel "Clean Hands" myth by which surviving Wehrmacht leadership were rewriting and whitewashing the history of the regular army on the Eastern Front. By arguing that "war criminal" POWs were merely the unfortunate victims of Soviet vindictiveness, the VdH was indirectly arguing against the very existence of war criminals within the ranks of the Wehrmacht. After all, if these men's convictions were just the result of Stalinist show trials, then it was much easier to believe that other allegations of war crimes—perhaps *all* allegations of war crimes supposedly committed by the ordinary men on the Eastern Front—were similarly fabricated. This thought process transferred any remaining war guilt onto the shoulders of the Nazi Party elites and their SS cronies, leaving behind common soldiers innocent of any particular wrongdoing. Unbelievable as it may seem, there was a minority presence within the VdH that even attempted to apply this redemptive counter-narrative to the Waffen-SS as well. Specifically, at the first VdH meeting to include former SS members, which took place in October 1952, former SS paratrooper General Herman Bernhard Ramcke gave a fiery speech about how the only real war criminals were the Western Allies. This caused considerable embarrassment for the VdH as an organization, which the rousing applause he received from his immediate audience made all the worse.[61]

This process conceptually transformed the soldiers of the Wehrmacht into apolitical men who did their duty to the Fatherland, only to be punished by the vengeful communist enemy after the war. More tellingly, the Clean Hands myth also reinforced the secret camp myth by portraying all soldiers of the Wehrmacht as men who had been tricked, and victimized, by the illegitimate Nazi state, with the men trapped in the silent camps thus experiencing a subsequent victimization by the vengeance-maddened communists.[62] Though German POW/MIA activism and belief in secret camps did eventually subside, it nevertheless helped reinforce that larger false narrative, which persisted for decades.

Taken together, then, the DRK and VdH represented the respectable portion of German secret camp advocacy. Both organizations had complicated relationships with official government policy and were at times frustrated by that government's inability or refusal to act more strenuously on behalf of the men the Soviets retained after 1949, which included both those POWs known to exist and the hoped-for surviving MIAs in the silent camps. The membership of both were intimately connected with West Germany's missing men, and given the total mobilization of German society for the war effort it would have been surprising if it were not.

Delayed Homecomings: Late Returnees and Decline of the Secret Camp Myth

Despite the number of men West Germans believed potentially still alive in the silent camps, and the plausibility of Stalinist Russia potentially concealing how many live prisoners it held, the secret camp myth was remarkably short-lived. Two key moments that help explain the briefness of this phenomenon: the years 1953–1954 and 1955–1956. First, early in 1953 Josef Stalin died, allowing less hardline and doctrinaire figures within the Soviet political leadership to moderate certain elements of state policy, POW retention among them. At the same time, a failed uprising in East Germany necessitated some sort of action on the part of Moscow to bolster the legitimacy of its SED clients, which took the form of the release of approximately 10,000 POWs and 2,000 civilian internees.[63]

One could be forgiven for thinking that the emergence of live POWs from Soviet captivity in 1953 would embolden German POW/MIA activism, and to a point that is correct. However, a mere handful of years later the secret camp myth was functionally dead, its advocacy groups mostly disbanded or redirected to other concerns, and its adherents more or less demobilized. The 1955 visit of Chancellor Adenauer to Moscow and subsequent release of the remaining war convicted was crucial to this remarkable reversal, and built upon the earlier 1953–1954 release. Though neither Adenauer nor anyone else in West Germany was aware of it, the Soviet leadership had been looking for an excuse to get rid of these prisoners, who had become a political embarrassment as well as a roadblock to the reengagement with the West that the Soviets had been maneuvering toward ever since the death of Stalin. The Kremlin presented this final prisoner release as a "goodwill gesture," demonstrating once more how the entire drama of POW politics played out against the backdrop of the Cold War.[64]

Regardless of their feelings on Soviet motives behind the 1953 release, West Germans had high expectations for the late returnees, which demonstrates their acceptance of the new hero narrative that activists had applied to those men. Specifically, West Germans hoped that these men could re-insert the moral character, which presumably allowed them to resist communist contamination for so long, back into West German society, and so prevent any moral degradation created by the "economic miracle" of the early 1950s. Given how high the country had risen from the rubble of the war, some West Germans worried, "We've allowed ourselves to be seduced by the exhilarating feeling of growing prosperity that has long drowned out anything unpleasant and disconcerting."[65] Like the earlier returnees, these men would likely require a fair amount of assistance to overcome the deprivations of their captivity and to reintegrate into a German society so markedly different than that which they had last experienced prior to their wartime capture. Many West Germans hoped that these men would, despite often being physically frail, bring back into that society a sense of authentic German-ness that would add a moral dimension to the process of national rebuilding, and thus neuter the dangers of looming capitalist decadence.[66] This sentiment carried within it two important aspects of the secret camp myth. First, returning POWs could hardly be potential wellsprings of moral regeneration if West Germans did not broadly consider these men to be clean, or at least cleansed, of any war guilt. Second, as with the earlier re-turnees, whether these men had any particular inclination to act as national moral saviors seems to have mattered little to those determined to see them as such.

Unlike the lack of assistance it had given to the early returnees, West Germany followed through for the men who came home after 1953. The economic and physical situation was, after all, markedly different, in large part due to the "economic miracle" by which West Germany had so rapidly rebuilt itself. Much to the resentment of men who came home earlier, the government went out of its way to help the late returnees, in particular via the passage of the 1950 Returned Prisoner of War Law (also called the Re-turnee Law, or Heimkehrergesetz), which not only granted economic assis-tance to late returnees but also gave them preferential treatment to access to housing, and whenever possible guaranteed them the return of their prewar jobs or their equivalent.[67] The VdH had lobbied heavily for the passage of this measure, and it continued to press for additional compensation that had not been included in the original law. Its argument was that the late returnees had demonstrated that they were the "best citizens" of West Ger-many, having "conquered new moral ground" and "elevated the reputation of the German people" by surviving Soviet captivity without being contam-inated by communism. Such arguments demonstrated once more how West German POW/MIA advocates assigned morally redemptive character to the suffering of their missing men.[68]

Despite a few initial problems, the final repatriation went off without much difficulty. Following Adenauer's historic visit to Moscow in 1955 an-other 9,626 German POWs came home, and by early 1956 all remaining German POWs had returned.[69] With those symbolic resurrections, West Germans apparently were able to as a whole accept that the remaining miss-ing were, in fact, dead and gone. The end of the last round of repatriations in 1956 marked the effective end of popular German POW/MIA activism. The idea of the silent camps lingered for some time during the decade in the popular consciousness, and even served as a backdrop for a short-lived subgenre of cult movies, but commanded no further major political action.[70] Despite Adenauer's interference with regard to dealing directly with the So-viets on the behalf of remaining German prisoners, Weitz and the DRK gen-erally regarded that repatriation as victory enough, particularly since it led several years later to engagement with the Soviet Red Cross.[71] For his part, Adenauer had largely used POW/MIA activism as a way to attract support from those interested parties for his larger policies designed to rehabilitate

West Germany and secure German sovereignty once more, at least in the West. Having achieved that, he had no further reason to be particularly concerned with future agitation on the POW/MIA issue.[72] West Germans, for the most part, were more than satisfied with his efforts to rescue the men from the silent camps. Surveys taken in the late 1960s showed that 75 percent of all West Germans polled ranked POW repatriation from the silent camps as the greatest accomplishment of Adenauer's government, a sentiment that persisted well into the 1970s.[73] The VdH, largest of the advocacy groups, was itself satisfied that it had gotten back all the live POWs, and through the rest of the 1950s it transformed its mission into locating and accounting for the MIAs it was then willing to admit likely were dead somewhere in the East.[74]

Despite the vast number of men missing, and initial plausibility of MIA survival in the murkily detailed Soviet camp system, the German secret camp myth lasted just over a decade. On first inspection, this would appear to be the natural conclusion for such a phenomenon: considering the scale, scope, and racially charged nature of warfare on the Eastern Front, one would expect that there would be a significant number of men unaccounted for after the war. So too, with poor and at times intentionally inaccurate wartime casualty reporting combined with the lingering ideological suspicion of the victorious enemy, it is unsurprising that some West Germans suspected that enemy had secretly retained live prisoners. For West Germans, the question was never one of the existence of prison camps after the end of regular repatriations, for the Soviets had openly admitted to them. Rather, they did not know how many of their men were among the war convicted, or the specific camp locations where they might be found. Given the number of Germans unaccounted for, it similarly makes sense that some of the missing might well eventually resurface among those camps' populations. With the final return of living POWs, then, West Germans were for the most part able to accept that their remaining MIAs were dead. However true all of this was for the West German instance of the secret camp myth, there is a comparable myth birthed from a later war in another part of the world that set such expectations on their heads, and persisted far longer, for far less believable reasons.

THREE

⟡

Missing Americans in
Southeast Asia and the Origins
of POW/MIA Activism

The origins of the American secret camp myth can only be understood via
the larger context of the war in Vietnam and the way America fought that
war. The majority of America's missing men came from the air services,
and the high professional and technical requirements of those assignments
meant the American POW/MIA population was disproportionately filled
by career officers, mostly white, and mostly middle-class or higher. The
American military concentrated much of its airpower on the Ho Chi Minh
Trail and other supply routes, which led to great difficulty keeping track
of downed airmen since they so often went down over sparsely populated
jungles that were often under enemy control. Relatives of the missing were
frustrated in gaining information about their missing men's status, due to
both this general uncertainty and the covert nature of the air war. For many,
the pain of not knowing left them trapped in the no-man's land of grief and
facilitated their later belief in the existence of secret camps.

Casualty information from these air campaigns was frequently classified,
and after Richard Nixon became president in 1968, it was often entirely falsified to conceal his illegal broadening of the conflict. Frustrated by the lack
of information about their husbands, wives of the missing banded together
to try to remedy that situation—and by so doing, formed the first American
POW/MIA advocacy group. At the same time, many wives of MIAs found

themselves trapped between mourning loss and hoping for survival, that toxic psychic environment so vital for the birth of the secret camp myth. Their efforts to learn their husbands' fates, particularly via engagement with the Nixon White House, laid the foundation for larger activism after the war and, eventually, the birth of the American secret camp myth.

Vietnam was hardly the first major war in which American servicemen became prisoners or went missing. Indeed, compared with the two wars closest to it in time, World War II and the Korean War, Vietnam's harvest of POWs and MIAs seems almost inconsequential. Well over 70,000 Americans are still listed as not recovered from World War II. Shorter in duration and smaller in scale, the Korean War left just under 8,000 Americans unaccounted for. Compared with these numbers, even the most generous counting of men unaccounted for in Vietnam seems almost incidental, yet neither World War II nor the Korean War spawned such a peculiar form of advocacy of their own. What was it about Vietnam that made it so singular in American imaginations as to facilitate the creation of the long-lasting secret camp myth? In large part, the secretive nature of the air war from which most of those men went missing contributed to the later conspiratorial mindset endemic to POW and MIA activism, particularly the usually covert and occasionally illegal aerial interdiction campaigns.

The Trail: US Interdiction Efforts as a Source of POWs and MIAs

A covert supply route, the Ho Chi Minh Trail was a network of paths and roadways, winding through regions sparsely populated even by the standards of Southeast Asia. The remote, inaccessible nature of the trail made rescue and recovery of those Americans lost during various aerial campaigns problematic, and often left information on their statuses incomplete. The North Vietnamese began infiltrating men and supplies in 1959 to supplement stay-behind cadres and formations already present in the South. The trail itself was built upon the centuries-old network of small footpaths that connected the villages of the interior, which the North Vietnamese expanded and rationalized to the point where by the early 1960s foot, bicycle, and pack animal traffic had given way in many areas to motorized transport, chiefly using Soviet-bloc and Chinese trucks. US efforts to cut the trail concentrated largely on aerial interdiction since it ran through thick jungle terrain barely accessible otherwise, though there were supporting ground operations as well. The remoteness and difficulty of access to targeted areas all but guaranteed that rescue and recovery of airmen shot down during interdiction actions would be a difficult matter, even for a military superpower with first-class air assets. What is more, many of these campaigns fell into legal gray areas, or were explicitly illegal, which helped to restrict already incomplete information about the missing. The inability to determine just what had happened to these men fueled early rumors and suspicions that grew into the American secret camp myth.

As early as 1956 the United States had established and manned facilities in South Vietnam under the auspices of the Military Assistance Advisory Group (MAAG) for the purposes of training the nascent Army of the Republic of Vietnam (ARVN).[1] Over 16,000 of these advisors and other US personnel were in the country by 1963, and some of them ended up missing in action.[2] As an example, on 22 April 1961, enemy guerrillas ambushed and killed a four-man team of advisors operating in Laos. Though the US military initially classified all four casualties as KIA-BNR—"Killed in Action: Body not Recovered"—that classification later changed to "Unaccounted-For," which all four officially remain as of this writing.[3] These early losses were exceptions, however. The United States lost the bulk of its POWs and MIAs following President Lyndon Johnson's escalation, often referred to as the "Americanization" of the war. In addition to the increased use of US ground troops, this escalation caused a dramatic upsurge in attempts to disrupt cross-border enclaves and traffic on the Ho Chi Minh Trail, and as a result contributed to the creation of the secret camp myth via the increased casualty rates.

Who were these men who remain officially unaccounted for? Initially, each service arm was responsible for accounting for its missing men, as was the Department of Defense. At the signing of the Paris Peace Accords in January 1973, the representatives of these separate entities listed a total of 1,986 POWs and MIAs, which dropped to 1,290 after the Operation Homecoming repatriation of known prisoners later that year.[4] By way of comparison, a little over 58,000 American service personnel died in Southeast Asia between 1 November 1955 and 15 May 1975, out of a total 3.4 million who served in some capacity in Southeast Asia during the war.[5]

Following the 1992 Senate hearings on POW/MIA matters, the Department of Defense's POW/Missing Personnel Office centralized all the Vietnam-era casualty records.[6] That office now maintains the official list of the missing and provides valuable insight into exactly who was lost, where they were lost, and in what manner. This last point is an important one: while the list, broadly, is of those "unaccounted for," it is not strictly a list of those

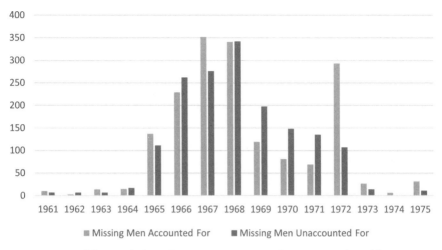

400
350
300
250
200
150
100
50
0

1961 1962 1963 1964 1965 1966 1967 1968 1969 1970 1971 1972 1973 1974 1975

■ Missing Men Accounted For   ■ Missing Men Unaccounted For

"Accounted for" includes POWs, remains returned or recovered, and known deserters. "Unaccounted for" includes MIAs, KIA-BNRs, POWs confirmed dead but not returned, and those presumed dead. Source: Defense Prisoner of War/Missing Personnel Office U.S. Unaccounted-For from the Vietnam War, 26 February 2014, http://www.dtic.mil/dpmo/vietnam/reports/documents /pmsea_una_p_name.pdf.

missing in action. As with the example of the four advisors lost in Laos in 1961, a significant proportion of "unaccounted for" are men whose fates are indeed known. Initial casualty reports did not include these men as POWs or MIAs, but subsequent revisions added them to those categories.[7] The mathematics of the missing is itself an important part of the story. Both pragmatic discovery and political intervention caused men to be added to the rolls of the unaccounted for during the war years and subsequently. Similarly, the delay between discovery and identification of remains confounds the larger question of just how many Americans truly remain missing in action, and has led to an inflation of the potential population in the alleged secret camps.

Indeed, to this day men known to have been killed in action, but whose bodies were not recovered, outnumber those whose deaths are still only presumed, 852 to 749. The small remainder is composed of a handful of missing civilians and POWs known to have died in captivity but whose remains were not returned.[8] In total, Defense Department statistics record 1,649 men still unaccounted for in one of these ways, several of which transparently fail to meet any realistic definition of being truly "unaccounted for." Of these men, over half were air force and navy aviators, numbering 883. Similarly, POWs and remains recovered after the war also come more frequently from aviators than from ground troops. The US Air Force reports 332 POW returnees at war's end, 481 men whose remains were eventually found and returned, and 16 POWs known to have died in captivity, as well as one man (Jasper Page) who managed to escape from captivity on his own.[9]

Breaking these statistics down even further, we see that of those 883 aviators still unaccounted for, the majority went down over Laos, North Vietnam, or Cambodia. The US Air Force lists 197 lost over Laos, 181 over North Vietnam, and 27 over Cambodia, while for the US Navy the numbers are 17 for Laos and 255 for North Vietnam. Conversely, the unaccounted for from the US Army and Marine Corps were overwhelmingly lost within South Vietnam, with only 167 men from both service arms going missing in Laos, North Vietnam, and Cambodia taken together.[10] This is not, of course, to say that adherents of the secret camp myth focused exclusively on missing aviators, or that lost ground troops were entirely absent from those adherents' attention, but pilots and aircrews who went missing over hostile territory were necessarily of greater interest after the war since they had been lost in significantly larger numbers.

The broader background of these men is also telling: 1,151 of those eventually accounted for and 879 of those considered still unaccounted for were officers, opposed to only 442 and 670 enlisted men, respectively.[11] This too sets the majority of the missing apart from the bulk of men who served in Vietnam, for because they were officers they were much more likely to be career men rather than draftees. Additionally, as officers, most of these men were from at least the middle class, as the commissioned ranks required a college degree, the exceptionally rare battlefield promotion notwithstanding.[12] This is not to say that all pilots and aircrew held full commissions; indeed, many army warrant officers in particular flew many of the Bell UH-1 "Huey" helicopters, but as a rule military flyers did not come from the ranks, and generally also not from the working class.

Education contributed as well to racial disproportionality between the missing and the larger armed services more generally during Vietnam. By far the majority of POWs and MIAs were white, and race played a part in the secret camp myth. Upon entering the military, all recruits took the Armed Forces Qualification Test (AFQT). Along with other service-specific exams, this test largely determined what each man's military occupational track would be. High-scoring recruits ended up in categories I and II, which qualified them for technical and intelligence work, including most air service positions, whereas those in categories III and IV were almost always destined either for basic support jobs or the combat infantry.[13] Minority recruits usually ended up in either III or IV due to earlier educational disadvantages, particularly those African Americans who had grown up prior to desegregation.[14] The tests themselves were culturally biased to favor white people and included material with which minorities were considerably less likely to be familiar.[15] Once assigned to categories III and IV, it was exceptionally difficult to gain transfer to more technically sophisticated work; in combination with the college requirement, this contributed further to making the pool of men most likely to end up POW or MIA overwhelmingly white.[16] The air force in particular further compounded this racial disparity by blanket-banning any carrier of sickle cell anemia traits from flying and aircrew positions—traits that are genetically much more common in African Americans.[17] Taken together, we have a clear picture of those men who ended up either missing or in captivity, and it is one that is important to why activism on their behalf persisted for so long. These men came from the established classes within larger American society. To be sure, not every man was a John McCain or James Stockdale, but collectively they were prominent enough to ensure that any group that advocated on their behalf could not be simply written off as a fringe element, or politically unimportant.

Back to the Stone Age: Aerial Campaigns and Their Missing Men

Because airmen form the bulk of the populations of the alleged secret camps, it is important to examine more closely the specifics of those campaigns during which they were lost. In addition to direct support of ground units, American flyers conducted numerous interdiction campaigns against traffic on the Ho Chi Minh Trail, and to break up known or suspected Viet Cong staging areas in Laos and, later in the war, Cambodia. Finally, the United States used strategic bombing against North Vietnam to bring Hanoi to the bargaining table. Of these air campaigns, three concentrated on Laos: Operations Barrel Roll, Steel Tiger, and Commando Hunt. Operation MENU, a conglomeration of six subordinate operations named BREAKFAST, LUNCH, DINNER, SNACK, SUPPER, and DESSERT, targeted suspected National Liberation Front (NLF—also known as the Viet Cong) supply and concentration areas in Cambodia. Finally, Operations Rolling Thunder and Linebacker I and II brought airpower to bear against North Vietnam directly. Taken together, these operations serve as useful examples of the nature of the war in the air, and its casualties.

Barrel Roll and Steel Tiger were the first major attempts to use airpower for interdiction, as well as the first significant incursions into ostensibly neutral Laos.[18] The mutual violation of that state's neutrality by both the United States and North Vietnam predisposed each party to keep the other's secret throughout the conflict, despite temptations to exploit the situation for propaganda purposes. This secrecy also had the unintended consequence of reinforcing the secret camp myth when it later emerged. After all, if both the United States and North Vietnamese governments had been lying about their activities in Laos during the war, why should anyone trust their casualty reports from those campaigns? POW/MIA activists could well be forgiven some skepticism of official accounts of these illegal operations, as they could quite rightly protest that both governments had every reason to minimize and downplay those actions, perhaps even to the point of writing off live MIAs for the sake of mutual convenience.

US efforts in Laos were concentrated mainly against the trail, as well as its North Vietnamese and Pathet Lao defenders. In 1964 the CIA attempted to build up the Royal Laotian Air Force for interdiction purposes via a scheme code-named Project Water Pump. This action served as precursor to both Barrel Roll and Steel Tiger. Those two campaigns ran concurrently and were mutually supporting. Steel Tiger consisted of operations flown over southern Laos and targeted the Ho Chi Minh Trail and border sanctuaries primarily, while Barrel Roll took place over the northern parts of the country and was used more to directly assist the Laotian government in its struggle against the Pathet Lao. Of the two, Barrel Roll began in December 1964 and originally covered all air operations over Laos; in 1965 its purpose was modified into direct support of Royal Laotian forces in the north of the country, when US commanders created Steel Tiger to replace its southern interdiction aspects. In total, the United States lost 131 aircraft during Barrel Roll raids between 1964 and 1973.[19] As with other US-led air campaigns, the number of losses in Operation Barrel Roll were neither particularly heavy nor came at a very high rate. The operation lost 131 aircraft over the course of nine weeks, and during the first week of the operation only two missions of four aircraft each flew over Laos, which the North Vietnamese may not have even noticed as a new US effort.[20]

Operation Steel Tiger split from Barrel Roll in April 1965 to cover interdiction duties over southern Laos. Like Barrel Roll itself, Steel Tiger was a motley affair conducted with many different aircraft and was remarkably reflexive. Unlike Barrel Roll, however, Steel Tiger did not continue right up to the last days of direct American involvement in Southeast Asia. The Tet Offensive in 1968 cast aerial interdiction efforts into harsh light, as Tet should not have been possible if Steel Tiger had been as successful as its proponents claimed. The subsequent pause in interdiction flights elsewhere had the secondary effect of freeing air force resources for use against the trail in southern Laos and South Vietnam itself, as did President Johnson's decision to halt Operation Rolling Thunder raids against North Vietnam. Air Force commanders incorporated the existing Steel Tiger apparatus into these new efforts, called Operation Commando Hunt, which became the largest aerial interdiction campaign of the entire war.[21]

Commando Hunt benefited doubly from inherited institutional experience gained from Steel Tiger and resources from Rolling Thunder, and it massively increased the number and weight of missions against the Ho Chi Minh Trail compared to Steel Tiger. Like Barrel Roll and Steel Tiger, Commando Hunt was not without its share of casualties, the POWs and MIAs from which helped to foster the secret camp myth by the ambiguous nature of their casualty status. In total, just under 500 aircraft of all types were lost over Laos in these three operations. Approximately 400 US airmen died, while a little more than 500 ended up listed as MIA or KIA-BNR.[22] The covert nature of Commando Hunt raids, and the attendant difficulty in rescue and recovery in a country whose neutrality the United States claimed to be respecting, was of equal importance to the creation of the secret camp myth. These men had gone missing in a region where no Americans other than a small number of advisors officially operated. During the war this was concealed by falsified loss reports, which claimed the men had gone missing somewhere on the South Vietnamese side of the border. Such deceptions inevitably angered the families of these men when they eventually discovered the government had been lying concerning the location and manner of their loved ones' disappearance. They also were a significant contributing factor to MIA advocacy groups' refusal after the war to accept any accounting by that government as full and complete.[23] After all, the government had been lying about where and how the men had gone MIA in the first place; who was to say it was now telling the truth when it claimed they could not still be alive in secret captivity?

Laos was not the only geographic point of contention with regard to the missing, and it was not the only "secret war" that contributed to the body of missing men lost under ambiguous circumstances. Less known than the Ho Chi Minh Trail was the Cambodian port of Sihanoukville, from which the NLF smuggled substantial amounts of supplies into South Vietnam. The Cambodian government of Prince Norodom Sihanouk quietly turned a blind eye to such activities and the establishment of sanctuaries and camps on their side of the admittedly poorly defined border. Sihanouk was not a supporter of the Hanoi regime and in particular resented the way it treated his country as a handmaiden, but he was nevertheless a pragmatist and hoped a degree of passive accommodation would keep Cambodia from being further embroiled in the expanding war next door.[24] President Nixon's decision in 1969 to covertly and illegally strike these sanctuary and supply areas not only expanded the war itself but also resulted in another harvest of American servicemen missing in another remote, inhospitable part of Southeast Asia. More important to the secret camp myth, like their missing comrades from Laotian operations they went missing in places where supposedly American troops did not operate.

The first of these Operation MENU raids was BREAKFAST, the brainchild of General Creighton Abrams, who in February 1969 was certain that US intelligence had at long last located the elusive "Central Office for South Vietnam" (COSVN) from which the North Vietnamese and NLF were coordinating the southern insurgency. Abrams believed he had found the enemy's headquarters in a sanctuary area located just across the Cambodian border, in the "fish hook" region.[25] BREAKFAST was conducted by B-52s flying from Guam on the morning of 17 March 1969 that, under guidance from ground controllers who alone knew exactly where the bombers actually were, successfully converted several square miles of Cambodian jungle into flaming ruin, then turned for home without suffering a single loss.[26]

Regardless of whether COSVN was in that area or indeed even existed as a discrete entity, the Nixon administration considered the attacks to be both successful on their own terms and more broadly a validation of covert raids across the Cambodian border. In reality the B-52s did little damage to enemy forces, as a Special Forces Daniel Boone team sent to recon Area 353 later that day found out to its dismay. Sent in to collect the few presumably "dazed" communist survivors, two Special Forces men (Bill Orthman and Barry Murphy) and their eleven accompanying ARVN soldiers found themselves in desperate need of rescue as their helicopters went down under heavy fire. Another helicopter made its way through the hail of bullets to rescue Orthman and three of the South Vietnamese soldiers, but Murphy died on the spot and was not recovered.[27] Like all other MENU casualties, his death was reported as having happened on the South Vietnamese side of the border via a sophisticated system of double-reporting and falsification designed to conceal the raids from the public and, more important to Nixon, the prying eyes of Congress.[28]

Additional missions, code-named LUNCH, DINNER, SNACK, SUPPER, and DESSERT, followed over the next fourteen months with a total of 3,650 more secret B-52 raids on supposed Viet Cong base areas and resupply cadres inside Cambodia.[29] Despite this number of raids, MENU and its attendant "secret" ground incursions resulted in far fewer casualties than the Laotian or Vietnamese aerial campaigns, with only ninety men unaccounted for.[30] Despite this quantitative difference, the men lost over Cambodia had a disproportionate impact on the creation of the secret camp myth. Specifically, the covert and indeed illegal ways the US government had used and then lost these men contributed greatly to their families' distrust of the government's postwar accounting efforts. Because efforts to conceal the violation of Cambodian neutrality were that much more elaborate—and came to light alongside the Watergate scandal via the congressional testimony of US Air Force major Hal Knight—these MIAs may have even weighed more heavily than their Laotian counterparts on those who already distrusted official government POW/MIA accounting efforts.[31]

This is not to say that the secret camp myth was built entirely upon cases of men lost in covert actions at the periphery of the fighting in Vietnam itself. The major air campaigns in both Vietnams brought their own grim harvests of missing men whose ambiguous status contributed to the myth's creation. Though these men were lost during operations that were at least nominally legal, they were lost in larger numbers than the Laotian and Cambodian campaigns. As a result, they contributed to the growing number of casualties whose final fate remained ambiguous and who could conceivably still be alive in secret captivity.

Operation Rolling Thunder was the first major air campaign over Vietnam proper. Casualties were correspondingly higher than in earlier raids due to the much larger scale of Rolling Thunder and to the Soviet and Chinese advisors who had helped the enemy develop increasingly effective air defenses. Hanoi in particular was protected by a sophisticated air defense network consisting of both modern surface-to-air missiles and antiaircraft artillery. In 1965 and 1966 alone the US Air Force lost a total of 489 aircraft over North Vietnam.[32] By the close of Rolling Thunder that number had risen to just under a thousand, with over 800 of their aircrew killed, captured, or otherwise lost. US records report 922 aircraft lost during Rolling Thunder, the majority brought down by Hanoi's air defense network. By contrast, the records kept by Chinese advisors in North Vietnam claim 1,707 shot down and over 1,500 others damaged throughout the campaign.[33]

The final US operations against North Vietnam were called Linebacker I and II. Linebacker I was essentially Rolling Thunder revamped and relaunched in 1972 in response to North Vietnam's Easter Offensive of that year. Linebacker I began on 10 May 1972 and aimed to fatally damage the North Vietnamese attack by cutting off the supplies on which it fed. US aviators concentrated attacks both on the infiltration routes and on the major points of entry into North Vietnam itself, such as the ports and rail crossings through which the Chinese and Soviets provided aid. All told, the United States lost a total of 134 aircraft during Linebacker I and other air operations flown during the Easter Offensive.[34]

Informally known as the "Christmas Bombings," Linebacker II took place 18–29 December 1972 to compel North Vietnam to return to the peace negotiations from which it had withdrawn in November. Unlike Linebacker I, which focused on precise strikes against enemy supplies and supply routes, Linebacker II intended to force the North Vietnamese to come back to the peace table via sheer, brutal, and at times seemingly indiscriminate destruction.[35] In total, Linebacker II resulted in fifteen B-52 losses, with a total of ninety-two crewmen on board. Of those men, eighteen died, fifty-seven were either rescued or captured, and the remaining fifteen were listed as missing in action.[36]

A Full Accounting: POW/MIA Activism
and Wartime Diplomacy

It did not take US leadership long to find ways to make domestic concern over the missing a part of its negotiating strategy and to serve its larger war ends. Well before the conclusion of hostilities, the Nixon administration had raised concerns over POW/MIA issues in ways its predecessors had not. Point 2 of the Joint Peace Proposal written by the United States and South Vietnam, made public 25 January 1973, stated:

> The release of all military men and innocent civilians captured throughout Indochina will be carried out in parallel with the troop withdrawals mentioned in point 1. Both sides will present a complete list of military men and innocent civilians held throughout Indochina on the day the agreement is signed. The release will begin on the same day as the troop withdrawals and will be completed when they are completed.[37]

This proposal carried within it an important seed of the secret camp myth to come. Specifically, the second sentence stipulates that both sides would present complete lists of exactly whom they held throughout not just North and South Vietnam but all of Indochina. In other words, the United States expected North Vietnam to account not just for the POWs its forces had taken but rather for all known prisoners and missing men throughout the war zone, including Laos and Cambodia. The actual number of men unaccounted for was and is disputable, since estimates varied considerably depending on who was counting and which men they chose to consider "missing in action." Officially at least, the United States claimed 1,335 of its men were in captivity at the time of the Paris Peace Accords in January 1973.[38] American POW/MIA activists repeatedly called for more information from the Vietnamese government concerning those men who remained unaccounted for after the 1973 repatriation of known POWs. They almost always invoked some variation on a "full accounting" of the missing when they did so. No group has ever satisfactorily defined exactly what constituted a "full accounting." The vague definition of this demand made it impossible to meet and, coupled with the ambiguous definitions of just who exactly was "unaccounted for," laid the groundwork for belief in MIA survival in secret camps for decades after the end of hostilities.

While the presence of captive and missing Americans in Southeast Asia is necessary for the secret camp myth to exist, it is not sufficient to explain that myth on its own. Since that myth grew from within Vietnam POW/MIA activism, it is important to understand how that activism came to exist, and what motivated the people within the movement. As the war in Vietnam ground seemingly endlessly onward, concerned individuals coalesced around the issue of determining status of POWs and accounting for the missing. The League of Wives of American Prisoners in Vietnam, which later changed its name to the National League of Families of American Prisoners and Missing in Southeast Asia, was the first coherent group that formed from this mass. The league grew to be a driving force in POW/MIA activism during the war and in its aftermath, and though it has never directly advocated for the existence of secret camps, it has played a crucial role in fostering that myth and encouraging believers in it.

Equally important to the rise of recognizable POW/MIA advocates was how the Nixon administration wove the issue into its larger political agenda. By lending official support and breaking from the Johnson-era policy of keeping POW/MIA relatives at arm's length, Nixon sought to use POW/MIA activism as part of his efforts to recast himself as leader of a "respectable" peace movement, separate from the odious street-level rabble-rousing of the peaceniks. Specifically, by making accounting for the missing his own issue, Nixon sought to redirect its constituency into support for ending the war on his own terms and at a time of his own choosing. The way in which Nixon engaged with the league and other POW/MIA activists is important to the rise of secret camp mythology because he overemphasized the number of POWs who could still be alive, then failed to bring home nearly that many in 1973. By setting expectations as high as he did, and then failing to satisfy them, Nixon encouraged the belief that the remainder were still alive, but secretly held elsewhere. More fundamentally, Nixon is personally responsible for the very existence of the term POW/MIA, which had not been used before as a joined descriptor in American wars or indeed anywhere else. In all previous American conflicts, prisoners and the missing were held to be distinct casualties, with the heavy presumption that MIAs were likely to be in fact KIAs. Nixon's deliberate conflation of the two terms into the compound POW/MIA demonstrates his decision for his administration to speak and write of them as if they were interchangeable, which appealed greatly to those who were desperate to believe men in the latter category were, perhaps, in the former.[39]

The rise of POW/MIA activist groups and their complicated relationship with official government accounting efforts helped shaped the emergence of the secret camp myth following the war. Who were these activists, and how did they become engaged in POW/MIA issues? The nucleus of postwar POW/MIA advocacy began long before America managed to disengage from direct involvement in Vietnam. The first real moment of activist organization came in 1967, when a group of San Diego POW/MIA wives coalesced around the remarkable person of Sybil Stockdale, wife of then squadron commander James Stockdale, who had been shot down and taken prisoner two years earlier.[40] POW/MIA wives occupied an odd non-place in the social hierarchy of officer's wives and professional base life. That culture defined a wife's status largely by that of her husband, and the ambiguous state of a captured or missing man thus translated into social distancing for wives and families left behind. Not yet widows, they were viewed by other military wives as something closer to that than not. Isolated and initially lacking any official support mechanism, these women had organically drifted toward one another and become a de facto support group.[41]

Though the military established housing for the immediate families of career men serving in Vietnam on the old Schilling Air Base in Salina, Kansas, no service arm initially notified POW/MIA wives of its existence. Indeed, the administration of Schilling Manor, as the base had been renamed in January 1966, did not want to allow POW/MIA wives to live there at all, fearing the impact their presence might have on the morale of the other wives. This changed in 1967 when POW wife Kathleen Bonnie Johnson found out about Schilling from an *Army Times* article and successfully applied for housing; but even then, POW/MIA wives remained an outgroup among military dependents, albeit one to be pitied more than scorned.[42]

Neither Wives nor Widows: The League and Early POW/MIA Activism

It is important to understand the initial makeup of this group of POW/MIA wives, since the early league grew from a small support group to a bona fide special interest on par with any other in American politics. By their own account, these women initially found out about one another through the unofficial grapevine that lies just beneath the surface of career military life. The women who formed the league first met on 7 October 1966, when Sybil Stockdale and twelve other POW/MIA wives got together for lunch at her home in Coronado, California. By her own account, Stockdale was surprised to learn that some of these women did not know the options available to them for seeking information about their missing husbands. The meeting lasted all afternoon, as the women talked about what they did know, rumors they had heard, and potential points of contact within the military and government of which others might avail themselves.[43] Stockdale and the others met again the next month, and they soon made such meetings a regular event that grew in size as additional wives heard about the group through word of mouth. The group formalized its name—the League of Wives of American Vietnam Prisoners of War—and organizational structure the following year, in 1967. It then prepared itself to contact the government formally in an effort to gain more information about its members' missing husbands, though it did not yet see the need to lobby directly for their release.[44]

The women of the league, and wives of POWs/MIAs more generally, cut very sympathetic figures in the emerging national narrative. Class played a part in this, since they tended to be middle- or upper-class, white, and married to men who were more often than not career officers. While most Americans fighting in Vietnam were working-class draftees, those men only made up a small minority of POWs/MIAs.[45] Given this distinction, the women who initially made up the majority of the league and of early POW/MIA activism generally were predisposed to stand apart from other wartime activist groups, particularly those of the antiwar left, as a "respectable" constituency. That many were also young and photogenic surely did not hurt, either. The initial motivation of the league was primarily informational in nature, a desire to discover just what had happened to its members' husbands. The idea of POW/MIA accounting—of determining what, exactly, had happened to the missing—has been its core mission ever since. Indeed, to this very day the league lists obtaining "the fullest possible accounting for the missing" as its second most important aim, just behind obtaining the release of any remaining POWs.[46]

This quest for information about the missing was crucially important on an individual level to the wives of the league. Many of these women found themselves in a psychological no-man's land, young, often recently married and with small children, separated from their husbands and with no certainty of ever being reunited. "We're not divorced, not widowed, and we're not really married either," was the sentiment of POW wife Eileen Cormier.[47] She was far from the only league woman to experience this sense of ambiguity, of being trapped between hope and mourning. Evelyn Grubb, wife of POW Captain Wilmer "Newk" Grubb, who was shot down in 1966 and subsequently died in captivity, described the situation as "my prison of being legally a wife but actually a widow."[48] Patty Zuhoski, married just over a month before her husband was shot down, had similar sentiments: "It's a very lonely existence. You're married but you're not married. You're not single. You're not divorced or widowed. Where does that put you in society? That puts you in your own world."[49]

This ambiguous sentiment was neither a new phenomenon nor unique to Vietnam itself. Historian Jean-Yves Le Naour examined an example during World War I where the wives of French MIAs found themselves similarly trapped and expressed themselves in language similar to the women of the league:

> It's strange—I always hold out hope. It seems as if an extraordinary thing had happened and the word *missing* doesn't mean *death*. . . . Why shouldn't we be among the many families who have had no news for two or three years because the missing were kept from writing? It's a mad hope, maybe, but it has never left me.[50]

MIA wives in particular experienced this sensation of increasingly unrealistic hope, which persisted in the absence of concrete proof of death, to a greater degree than their POW counterparts who, often, had at least some information pointing to their husbands' survival. That need to know, and hope, made it much easier to believe any new rumor or scrap of information that suggested potential survival. Caught in such an unenviable emotional position, such women found subsequent talk of secret camps containing live MIAs particularly appealing.

The league's initial efforts to clarify husbands' statuses also led to its involvement in the politics of the war. By serving as a resource for wives of captured or missing men, the league also served to focus the dissatisfaction of those women with what they perceived as inattentiveness on the part of the Johnson administration. They believed that the government was not doing nearly enough to ensure humane treatment of their husbands, as well as regular mail communication. Specifically, the league membership was very much disturbed by the government's official position that keeping quiet about POWs/MIAs was the best way to guarantee Hanoi's humane treatment of those men, as well as its adherence more generally to Geneva Convention standards of behavior—standards that both sides frankly honored more in the breach than observance. Some of the wives believed this hands-off position indicated that the government was blandly indifferent toward American POWs generally, including Stockdale herself, who had direct evidence of her husband's mistreatment. Though mail delivery was irregular, some contact was possible between families and POWs, and James Stockdale managed to get word to his wife via clever use of invisible ink about various tortures he had endured.[51]

Though often very frustrated with the US government for failing to keep them properly informed about their missing husbands, the women who made up most of the league's early membership were not yet all that politically active, particularly by the standard of activists of the period. As "members of the last generation of hat-and-glove military wives called upon by their country to pack without question, to follow without comment, and to wait quietly with a smile," they did not initially concern themselves with the larger issues surrounding the war, save in those instances where such issues directly touched upon the fate of captured and missing men.[52] The manner in which these women, and other POW/MIA activists, became enmeshed in the toxic politics of the Vietnam War and its aftermath helped fertilize the ground from which the secret camp myth grew.

Politicization of POW/MIA Activism

POW/MIA activism's engagement with the Nixon administration is crucial to understanding how the American secret camp myth grew and the specific form it took. Indeed, Nixon's impact is difficult to overstate, as his efforts unintentionally fed both key aspects of secret camp advocacy. First, his efforts to co-opt POW/MIA relatives away from the antiwar movement supported and reinforced the idea within the league that many, perhaps most, of their missing husbands were still alive in enemy captivity, chiefly through the "Go Public" publicity campaign. Those league members and others who were trapped in the no-man's land of grief found reasons to keep hoping for reunion with their missing men. When they did not get that expected reunion, many among them had been hoping too much, and for too long, to give up, and they instead embraced the idea of secret camps to avoid facing the unendurable reality that their men were dead and had been all along.

Second, the Operation Homecoming repatriation heavily and explicitly emphasized the heroic, redemptive qualities of the POWs. Nixon intended that these men should serve as unimpeachable counter-examples to the various elements of the popular left whom he so loathed. However, by expending so much effort in building them up, and simultaneously only returning a fraction of those his efforts had led POW/MIA activists to believe survived, Homecoming fed the myth that the remaining missing, now fully realized as hero-victims, must still be alive in secret captivity. As a result, the league continued to agitate for further accounting, and other fringe elements of POW/MIA activism began to articulate for the first time the idea of secret camps in which the remaining MIAs *must* still survive. When these groups discovered Nixon's duplicity regarding their cause, they became even more distrustful of official practices, especially those that presumed the death of the MIAs in the absence of evidence to the contrary.

Peace with Honor: POW/MIA Activism's Initial Embrace of Richard Nixon

To be sure, the women of the league never were mere puppets of the White House, nor did they uniformly support Nixon's policies. Frustrated by irregular communication with their captive husbands and incomplete information on whether they were even still alive, the women of the league grew increasingly active through the last years of the Johnson presidency. The league especially resented the effectiveness of North Vietnam's propaganda use of prisoners, and what it saw as a reluctance or refusal of its own government to attempt any countermeasure or refutation. Combined with the late-term disasters that drove Johnson not to seek reelection, these two elements naturally inclined the league to favor Nixon's candidacy in 1968. In particular, Nixon's promise of an about-face on the war and "peace with honor" led the league to believe that here at last was a president whom they could trust to do right by them and their missing husbands.[53]

For his part, Nixon needed little persuasion to make the POW/MIA issue much more public than had Johnson, though not solely out of any great empathy for those men or their families. Nixon had campaigned on what appeared to be a peace platform, albeit one very different from and hostile to that of the antiwar movement. Specifically, he had promised that he would bring "an honorable end" to the war in Vietnam.[54] His definition of that honorable end presumed, however, the long- or at least medium-term survival of South Vietnam. Additionally, Nixon quite correctly gauged that to accomplish this goal he would need to reverse, or at least halt, the increasing popularity of the larger antiwar movement, which called for a rapid withdrawal from the conflict. Having campaigned loudly, though nonspecifically, on ending the war Nixon was determined to recast himself as the leader of a peace movement distinct from the squalid baying of the street demonstrators.[55]

One method he seized on to accomplish his rebranding scheme was key to the popularization of the secret camp myth: co-opting the POW/MIA issue, both as an excuse to remain engaged in Southeast Asia and to steal so potentially potent a weapon from the hands of the peaceniks Nixon so despised.[56] This is not to say that members of the league were dupes, but it is undeniable that at least initially the league had high hopes for this new president. However, by accepting his assistance, POW/MIA activists unintentionally joined their cause to Nixon's covert plans to continue and extend the war.

The POW/MIA issue gave Nixon an excuse to revitalize public support for the war and also to justify continued involvement despite public troop withdrawals. By embracing that issue, he argued that staying militarily engaged in Southeast Asia was necessary lest America abandon its brave boys behind the wire. The circularity of this argument, that America must continue to fight to bring back the POWs it had lost in earlier fighting, was muted by the argument's emotional weight, which helped with "winning the hearts, if not the minds" of a public rapidly wearying of the seemingly endless quagmire.[57] Nixon also aimed to make the POWs and MIAs into figures worthy of proper celebration at war's end, a status that other Vietnam veterans were much more rarely afforded, and never automatically.[58] The Go Public campaign combined these elements into a cross-media publicity blitz, which included both official government messaging and also efforts by the league and other POW/MIA activists.

The official kickoff to the campaign came at a press conference given by Secretary of Defense Melvin Laird on 19 May 1969. Laird appealed on humanitarian grounds for the immediate release of all American prisoners in Southeast Asia, whom he numbered between 500 and 1,300.[59] Laird also accused the North Vietnamese of failing to live up to their Geneva Convention responsibilities regarding prisoner notification and contact via neutral third parties. Similarly, he called on North Vietnam to allow international inspection of its holding facilities to ensure the "proper treatment" Hanoi insisted it was delivering.[60] He argued, "The North Vietnamese have claimed that they are treating our men humanely, I am distressed by the fact that there is clear evidence this is not the case."[61] This sentiment became a common one among POW/MIA activists, who elevated Hanoi's supposed duplicity to an article of faith. It also reinforced a key aspect of secret camp mythology, for if the enemy was treating known POWs abominably, how much worse must be the suffering of the MIAs in the secret camps?

Another idea contained within Laird's statements is equally important to the emergence of the secret camp myth: casting doubt on exactly how many prisoners the North Vietnamese claimed to hold. Laird's wide numerical range of suspected American prisoners gave family members a reason to hope their missing man might in fact be a prisoner who just had not yet been identified. So too, by prominently calling out North Vietnam's refusal to allow international inspection of its prison facilities, outside of a handful of heavily managed, Soviet-directed incidents, Laird added more sinister implications to how North Vietnam handled its prisoners. After all, if they had not treated known prisoners humanely and were not forthcoming about even those they held, who was to say that the villainous Vietnamese communists might not have kept some secretly after the war, for whatever depraved reason?

Laird quickly followed up his statement with another two days later after Xuan Thury, head of the North Vietnamese delegation to the peace talks, had turned down his appeal for full prisoner disclosure. Playing to the moment, Laird said he was "deeply shocked and disappointed by this cruel response of Hanoi's representative to such a basic request for humanitarian action."[62] Laird here framed the refusal of North Vietnam to account for its prisoners as a cruel and intentional act, thus reinforcing how Hanoi could not be trusted on matters relating to POWs and MIAs. Laird was personally an enthusiastic supporter of Go Public within the Nixon administration, so such statements are hardly surprising. He had gone out of his way to make POW/MIA affairs a priority within the Defense Department upon taking office, and he lent considerable support from on high to POW/MIA accounting efforts within that department and elsewhere.[63]

Laird also won support for Go Public from the service arms themselves through such media grandstanding. They needed little encouragement in any case, as the leadership of each had felt stifled by the Johnson administration's reluctance to act more directly on POW/MIA issues. The air force in particular had proposed its own public relations initiative in 1967 only to see it shelved, and it felt that public pressure was the only way to force Hanoi to treat captured Americans appropriately. Somewhat more cynically, the navy felt that officially publicizing the plight of POWs and MIAs would at least reassure the American public that the government really was doing all it could on behalf of those missing men.[64]

The military was not alone in reacting positively to this new publicity campaign. In November, Congress unanimously passed a bill designating the ninth of that month to be National Day of Prayer for POWs. Simultaneously, United We Stand (UWS), a front group founded by Texas billionaire and longtime POW/MIA activist H. Ross Perot, launched an ad blitz demanding immediate release of all Americans held in Southeast Asia.[65]

In addition to these and other media events, the Nixon administration embraced those activists whom the Johnson administration had kept at arm's length. The first direct area of cooperation between activists and the Nixon administration occurred against this backdrop of increased government activity, when Sybil Stockdale wrote to Nixon in her capacity as national coordinator of the now-renamed National League of Families. The president had given a prime-time press conference on 3 November 1969 in which he failed to mention POWs and MIAs at all, which Stockdale and others within the league feared signified the White House was backing off from Go Public:[66]

Many of the families were deeply disturbed that you did not mention the plight of the prisoners in your message to the nation on November 3, 1969. We are at a point where we feel we must meet with you personally so that we may be reassured about your own personal interest and thoughts pertaining to the most desperate straits in which our husbands and sons find themselves. If you can find time to see a representative group from our number, we would be deeply grateful. We have been and remain your loyal supporters.[67]

Stockdale need not have worried. Nixon was from the very start of his administration attempting to seize the mantle of peacemaker away from the antiwar movement. In the first dozen drafts of his 3 November speech, he included the following: "For as long as the desire for peace occupies the nation, no other goal occupies my thoughts and energy. My every day as President has been a day of dedication to ending the war."[68] He followed this up with the idea that while Americans might be united behind wanting the war to end, the real issue was whether to continue to search for what he termed a "just settlement," or rather just accept defeat and cravenly pull out.[69] While staff revisions did result in less specific language, the overall rhetorical emphasis on peace remained.[70] This emphasis on charting a new course toward peace on his own terms served Nixon's ambitions well in the main. Gallup polling following the 3 November speech indicates that the overwhelming majority of those polled both had heard the speech (72 percent) and agreed with his plan to end the war (80 percent). Furthermore, in light of his speech, most (72 percent) agreed that public demonstrations were detrimental toward the achievement of that peace.[71]

Even before Stockdale wrote to Nixon, his staff was planning on incorporating POW wives into their larger plan to sell Nixon's "secret plan" for peace. Among other elements, one of the proposed actions on this front was assigned to his deputy assistant Alexander Butterfield; it read, "Push passage of Congressional Resolution to pray for POW's November 9th and *tie-in POW wives—unanimous support for the President*"[72] (emphasis mine). This was hardly the only directive to push for greater incorporation of POW/MIA advocacy into Nixon's agenda. In the more substantive "November 15th Gameplan" talking paper, Nixon's staff cited how important it would be to "arrange for the POW wives to unanimously endorse on that day [9 November] the President's plan for peace."[73]

Nixon's staff had already by autumn 1969 explored the potentialities of using the POW wives for their own propaganda purposes. Ken Cole, in a memo to H. R. Haldeman on 22 September 1969, commented that "the President noted the report regarding the wives of the captive pilots and the POW's" and agreed with meeting a delegation from their group.[74] Haldeman for his part was not slow to forward this on to National Security Advisor Henry Kissinger, repeating how Nixon had personally found the stories of POWs and their wives to be useful countermeasures to North Vietnamese propaganda efforts.[75]

Stockdale and a handful of other POW/MIA wives accepted the proposed invitation and visited the White House on 12 December 1969 to discuss the issue in person, which marked a significant change from how the previous administration had kept several layers of bureaucracy between them and the president.[76] Nixon viewed this meeting explicitly as a way to assuage league fears that his "Pursuit of Peace" speech signaled a turn away from POW/

MIA activism, and also to further bind the league to the service of his own Vietnam policy.[77]

The meeting itself was almost more than anything for which Stockdale and the other relatives could have hoped. Nixon appeared to say all the things they had so long wanted to hear, that North Vietnam was subjecting American prisoners to "unconscionable" behavior and that the president was personally willing to go on record publicly demanding that their rights under the Geneva Convention be guaranteed. At last, the league members and others present felt that progress was being made on the behalf of their missing men. Stockdale herself claimed that the evening following her White House visit was the first time she slept soundly since her husband's capture four years prior.[78] She was not alone in seeing Nixon as an inspiring new hope for POW/MIA families, at least initially. The wife of missing pilot John J. Hardy Jr. later commented that "President Nixon can do something about this, he's the only one that can."[79]

The league was not the sole nongovernmental actor to involve itself in Go Public. Established veterans and activist organizations responded to the Go Public appeals, particularly a UWS-backed ad campaign of November 1969. The UWS received a staggering volume of responses to its 10 million newspaper ads and postcards targeting groups like the Veterans of Foreign Wars and American Legion.[80] Of greater significance, an initially obscure group called the Victory in Vietnam Association (VIVA) also involved itself in Go Public. As the name suggests, VIVA's primary concern was achieving some manner of victory in Vietnam for the United States, but with the advent of Go Public it shifted efforts to the POW/MIA issue. How it did so led to the creation of the first major physical symbols of POW/MIA activism, and eventual secret camp advocacy: the POW/MIA bracelets. Spiritual ancestors of the yellow ribbon magnets still common across bumpers and tailgates of any current mall parking lot, these bracelets were each engraved with the name of a missing man and proved wildly popular with those looking for a convenient way to show solidarity at a bargain price.[81] Indeed, the very convenience of the VIVA bracelets brought staggering numbers of Americans into at least superficial contact with POW/MIA activism during and after the war, with over 4 million sold by 1973. This included A-list celebrities and prominent politicians, H. Ross Perot and Ronald Reagan among them.[82]

Perhaps still worried that he had not fully secured the POW/MIA constituency, Nixon made his point more clearly with a policy statement on 15 December, three days after meeting with representatives of the league.

Again, he emphasized that North Vietnam was responsible for accounting for America's missing men and simultaneously castigated them for not having done so satisfactorily already. Similarly, he used that failure as an example of Hanoi's overall unreasonableness, thus blaming the North Vietnamese for the continuation of the conflict he supposedly had a "secret plan" to end, calling such alleged failures "cruel, indefensible action[s]" and "a shocking demonstration of the inflexible attitude they have taken on all issues at the negotiating table in Paris."[83]

Talk *Only* about Prisoners: The Political and Propaganda Value of the Missing

Paris itself would serve as an important touchstone of the evolving nature of POW/MIA activism during the war years. Encouraged by the statements and actions of the Nixon administration, several family members of missing men traveled to Paris at year's end 1969 in a much-publicized attempt to pressure North Vietnamese negotiators, though ultimately without much success. While this trip was not Nixonian in origin, the White House was interested in how it could use the visit for both diplomatic and propaganda purposes. Discussing the possibility earlier in September 1969, Kissinger mentioned to Nixon that the head of the American delegation, Henry Cabot Lodge, considered the trip by a select group of wives to be a potentially useful if unorthodox way to make North Vietnam look bad.[84] These wives were themselves potent symbolic proxies for the suffering of their missing husbands, and the North Vietnamese had already made efforts to spin POWs and their families to their own ends. Hanoi previously had announced that those wives would be more likely to get information about their missing husbands via involvement with the peace movement.[85] Additionally, during an earlier informal visit, the North Vietnamese embassy had told two wives that if they had any hope of seeing their husbands again, they should demonstrate against the war as soon as possible.[86] Neither those individual wives nor the league generally responded positively to such heavy-handed approaches, but the possibility that it might shift in that direction was more than a little concerning to the Nixon administration.

As it happened, the North Vietnamese had little time for league representatives when they reached Paris in December, meeting with just three of them on Christmas Eve 1969, and then only briefly. During the meeting, which lasted a little over an hour, the North Vietnamese representatives refused to answer any substantive questions about the fate of missing and captured Americans and insisted that the only thing that might benefit them would be to pressure the US government to end the war as quickly as possible.[87] Clearly, both Nixon and the North Vietnamese were willing to at least try to use the POW/MIA wives as bludgeons against one another. More important to the creation of the secret camp myth, such a direct refusal by the North Vietnamese to offer any information about the missing even during a face-to-face meeting helped reinforce the idea that they had something to hide on the subject.

Symbolic exploitation of POWs and MIAs was not limited to the international stage. Nixon was more than willing to use POW/MIA family members as campaign props during his 1972 reelection bid. He feared his enemies at home would find a way to turn the sympathetic women of the league against the war, or him, despite his years of engagement with that constituency. During the last months before the general election, National Security Council Staff member James Fazio warned Kissinger that Radio Hanoi had broadcast several interviews purportedly with captive US pilots, all of whom pledged their support for George McGovern in the upcoming election, and requested their wives to make contributions to McGovern's campaign.[88] More conspiratorially, Kissinger advised Nixon not long thereafter that news of a possible small-scale POW release might well be a scheme on the part of the North Vietnamese to embarrass the administration and throw the election to McGovern via the high-profile participation of antiwar activists in those prisoners' release.[89]

It should surprise no one that Nixon was more than willing to use as potent a symbol as America's missing men in his unique style of campaigning. In his "Assault Book" plan for the 1972 campaign, Haldeman summarized McGovern's position on POWs as one of abandonment, that the United States should "a) pull our [*sic*] all our troops and forces, and all our leverage over Hanoi; b) abandon our ally to the enemy, —and c) then hope 'on faith' that Hanoi will give us back our prisoners and d) rely on world opinion to get our prisoners back."[90] Predictably enough, he then went on to propose Nixon could find ample room to attack McGovern over this position.[91] Drawing such a contrast inadvertently helped to nurture secret camp paranoia. By popularizing the idea that all of America's missing would only come home if Hanoi was made to release them, Nixon fostered the belief that Hanoi would *not* release all its prisoners if not forced so to do. Such sentiments helped create a default mindset whereby the North Vietnamese were presumed to always prefer retaining American prisoners and would only ever give them back when induced or compelled to do so.

The idea that McGovern planned to abandon America's POWs and MIAs found a very receptive audience, further demonstrating how effective Nixon's engagement with POW/MIA activism had been in recasting that aspect of the war in his own favor. So too, it served to reinforce the larger narrative that Nixon, and only Nixon, could bring all the boys home. The plan was to hammer how wrong McGovern had been about everything related to Vietnam and if he did get elected, "the SOB would leave our prisoners in Hanoi—and count on the good will of that barbarous regime to get them back."[92]

Nixon employed the power of the bully pulpit to sell his framing of POWs/MIAs as a prominent war issue outside of election season as well. One of his administration's very first foreign policy reports to Congress made it abundantly clear just what the official line was going to be regarding missing Americans in Southeast Asia, lest anyone mistake his earlier statements and actions for mere grandstanding:

> In human terms no other aspect of conflict in Vietnam more deeply troubles thousands of American families than the refusal of North Vietnam to agree to humane treatment of prisoners of war or to provide information about men missing in action. Over fourteen hundred Americans are now listed as missing or captured, some as long as five years, most with no word ever to their families. In the Paris meetings we have sought repeatedly to raise this subject—to no avail. Far from agreeing to arrangements for the release of prisoners, the other side has failed to even live up to the humane standards of the 1949 Geneva Convention on prisoners of war: the provision of information about all prisoners, the right of all prisoners to correspond with their families and to receive packages, inspection of POW camps by an impartial organization such as the International Red Cross, and the early release of sick and wounded prisoners.
>
> This is not a political or military issue, but a matter of basic humanity, There may be disagreement about other aspects of this conflict, but there can be no disagreement on humane treatment for prisoners of war. I state again our readiness to proceed at once to arrangements for the release of prisoners of war on both sides.[93]

Nixon's rhetorical linking of POWs to the Paris talks was intentional. POWs played a prominent role in Nixon's overall negotiating strategy—or, rather, his strategy to stall negotiations long enough to secure some sort of quasi-victory that his "peace with honor" required. Specifically, by putting

POWs at the forefront of his negotiators' priorities, he could then insist on dealing with nothing else until all sides had agreed a solution to that issue. Indeed, one does not need to look far to see this specific impetus in play. Nixon wrote a note to Kissinger on the back of a copy of his 27 February 1970 daily briefing on the Paris talks, saying, "I have changed my mind— From now on until further direction from me—[Ambassador] Habib is to talk only about prisoners."[94]

Such an emphasis, in both public relations and closed-door diplomacy, on accounting for the missing and bringing the boys home, contained potential pitfalls. Publicity on the POW/MIA issue necessarily created public expectation for more than just speeches and media events. If the government cared so greatly about obtaining the release of American prisoners, what exactly was it waiting for? After all, repatriation of POWs traditionally came after the cessation of hostilities, so the longer the Nixon administration continued to prosecute the war in any fashion, the hollower rang its supposed concern for those prisoners. The North Vietnamese themselves played to this usual aspect of prisoner repatriation by insisting that POW/MIA families would be best served by urging an immediate end to the war. They also periodically released small numbers of prisoners while making complete release contingent on a full American withdrawal and end of support for the southern regime, thus making the POW/MIA issue serve their own ends.[95]

Indeed, some POW/MIA advocates even took the North Vietnamese at their word. Since these advocates' primary concern was obtaining prisoner release and MIA accounting, they began to demand an immediate and complete withdrawal of US troops.[96] By awakening this constituency, Nixon had inadvertently set a clock ticking on how long they would wait for him to make good. Once the heady excitement of the December 1969 meeting wore off, the league in particular developed a complicated relationship with the government's efforts on POW release and MIA accounting. Its members were initially grateful to apparently have an ally in the president, but elements within the league's ranks quickly grew suspicious of both his sincerity and the government's actual capacity to do anything substantial to force POW/MIA concessions from the enemy during wartime. It did not take long for many in the league to start running out of patience for an administration that talked a big game but never quite managed to accomplish anything concrete. The family of Army Warrant Officer Quentin Beecher, a helicopter pilot lost in bad weather 11 June 1967, took exception to the refusal of the military to change his status to KIA, as they were convinced he could not have survived the crash. Additionally, his widow could not remarry due to his persistent MIA status. Beecher's family ascribed this refusal not merely to bureaucratic inertia or incompetence but rather to specific government policy aimed at using POWs and MIAs in Vietnam to justify the continuing US military presence in Southeast Asia. Beecher's mother stated, "I think they're misleading us for their own purposes."[97]

Others were willing to go even further in their criticisms of Nixon's motives in publicizing POW/MIA issues. Several wives of missing men gave interviews to the *Wall Street Journal* in 1971 and explicitly stated their belief that the Nixon administration was using POWs/MIAs as an excuse to continue the war:

> [The government] sees the POW issue as an excuse to keep a "residual force" in Vietnam.[98]
>
> It shook me when the administration made it appear we were there (in Vietnam) because of the POWs. This is a bunch of bull. I resent using the POWs as an excuse to stay in Vietnam. Washington is just trying to save face.[99]
>
> We've been used to drum up support for the war.[100]

These women were admittedly a minority within the league's constituency, but they were nevertheless correct that prisoners and the missing made for exceptional propaganda tools. Even prior to Go Public, North Vietnam had already made a concerted effort to parlay American concerns about their missing and captured men into pressure to end the war. In 1967 two East German reporters, Walter Heynowski and Gerhard Scheumann, visited and extensively photographed those Americans being held at Hỏa Lò Prison, the notorious "Hanoi Hilton." *Life* magazine republished their article in October of that year, albeit with extensive annotation concerning those areas that the editors of *Life* considered questionable or entirely manufactured. Among the key points that article made, which *Life* disputed, were that prisoners were well treated, had access to regular mail service, and were not brainwashed or abused, and that the benign Vietnamese guards philosophically considered the prison a "hotel for unasked guests."[101] Even less believably, Heynowski and Scheumann reported that each prisoner they spoke with praised the level of medical care they had received and, crucially, that each man invariably spoke of a longing for home and family.[102] *Life* editors took exception with much of the article, going so far as to compare it to a Potemkin village, and the prisoners in question later confirmed the entire visit was heavily orchestrated and largely at odds with standard brutality of life in the Hilton.[103] Nevertheless, that the Vietnamese went out of their way to orchestrate elements so certain to play upon the heartstrings of those back in America demonstrated how well they understood the propaganda power of the POW and missing man.

The Vietnamese were hardly the only ones to use those men as propaganda tools. Recasting POWs and MIAs into heroic, sympathetic figures lay at the heart of Go Public and other elements of US POW/MIA activism, transforming them into hero-victims of a war not of their own making. A series of league newspaper advertisements demonstrated this clear transformative intention by stressing Vietnamese inhumanity toward prisoners and how that affected the families back home. Each one of these ads heavily accused Hanoi of refusing to accommodate reasonable requests for information on which prisoners it held and other violations of mandated Geneva Convention behavior toward POWs.[104] Photos of worried wives appear prominently in these ads, next to such pleas as "My husband, Alexander, is a Lt. Commander in the Navy. Four years ago he was reported missing in action. There's a chance he was taken prisoner and is still alive. But I don't know. And I can't find out. Hanoi won't tell our government. Hanoi won't tell me."[105]

Every one of these appeals invariably ends with the statement "We ask no more than we give. All American and South Vietnamese prison camps are inspected regularly by official neutral observers—The International Red Cross."[106] Such statements helped to frame the larger narrative that this series of ads and much POW/MIA activism generally sought to establish as canon: we Americans are fighting this war cleanly and fairly, and the evil Vietnamese communists are not. Our poor boys are being victimized, as are their families by extension, while we are the only ones to scrupulously observe international conventions on fair treatment. The language used in these league ads was remarkably similar to that used in the official statements being used by US negotiators in Paris, and that similarity was hardly an accident.

To be sure, the crafters of Go Public and league members were not at this stage secret camp advocates, and none of these messages mentions or implies the existence of secret camps, but their efforts at elevating the missing to such heights served secret camp advocacy well after the war. After all, if the returning POWs were heroes for having endured victimization at enemy hands, how much more heroic must be the men who continued to suffer in the alleged secret camps? Furthermore, that very suffering, which these advertisements claimed the North Vietnamese uniquely were inflicting on their captives, played to another core aspect of the secret camp myth: the appropriation of suffering. Such coordinated messages resonated emotionally with the American populace, but in casting Americans and South Vietnamese so simplistically as good guys who played by the rules, they were hugely at odds with the ugly realities of the war. While some American facilities were indeed inspected by international third parties, many were not—especially not those run by the South Vietnamese. Additionally, US authorities usually transferred their prisoners to South Vietnamese facilities in a deliberate evasion of the Geneva Convention. South Vietnam was not a signatory to the 1949 convention, and the United States, which was, violated Article 12 of that treaty each time it transferred captured insurgents and North Vietnamese fighters to South Vietnamese facilities, which it regularly did.[107] Conditions in these prisons often were as bad, if not worse, than the hardships and tortures endured by American POWs in the Hilton. North Vietnamese officials were quick to point out this hypocrisy, including national premier Pham Van Dong:

For their part, the US troops and their agents in South Viet Nam [use] the most barbarous tortures [on] the Vietnamese patriotic fighters and ordinary citizens captured by them and they have instituted a horrible penitentiary regime as evidenced by the "tiger cages" in the Pulo Condore prison. . . .

For their part, the US Government has carried out very perfidious and wicked maneuvers. It has made every effort to distort the above-mentioned humane policy of the Democratic Republic of Viet Nam Government. It has put forth hypocritical contentions about "humanitarianism" in the so-called "prisoner of war issue," etc. The US Government is using the "prisoner of war issue" to cover for its odious crimes against the Vietnamese people, its war acts against the Democratic Republic of Viet Nam, and its schemes to prolong and extend the war of aggression.[108]

Admittedly, this was a diplomatic exchange between two high-level public officials and should be treated as such, but neither was it the first public airing of US failures to live up to its own lofty rhetoric on prisoner treatment. In 1969 *Christian Century* reporter Don Luce toured several South Vietnamese facilities and found them squalid, brutal places rife with prisoner abuse. Con Son Prison in particular was notorious, both for its miserable conditions and also for how it was historically a dumping ground for those political prisoners considered dangerous by the Saigon regime. Among others, Luce interviewed an NLF cadre there who described how guards would routinely beat prisoners for minor infractions, in her case failure to salute the South Vietnamese flag and sing the national anthem.[109]

A visit by an American congressional delegation to Con Son and other facilities that same year had even greater public impact. The South Vietnamese made some efforts to cover up the worst aspects of these prisons by hiding the most abused prisoners and concealing the basest conditions from visiting American eyes. However, congressional staffer Tom Harkin bluffed his way into a restricted area and discovered the brutal everyday conditions of the prison. What is more, he documented what he saw with a personal camera, despite insistence by dismayed South Vietnamese guards that such behavior was prohibited. Even more impressively, he managed to hang onto the film all the way back to the United States, despite several attempts by both the South Vietnamese and American officials to deprive him of such damning evidence.[110] The photos shocked the public when *Life* magazine published them several months later, with their graphic depiction of just how America's ally was treating the prisoners consigned to its care. The prisoners depicted showed unmistakable signs of abuse, neglect, and malnutrition.[111]

The *Life* story also revealed that US officials were fully aware of how the South Vietnamese were mistreating their prisoners, contrary to Go Public statements about how the nation and its allies always treated captives humanely. Frank Walton, a former Los Angeles Police Department commander and American advisor to the South Vietnamese administrators of Con Son, was on-site at the time of Harkin's visit and had initially described the facility as a "place more like a Boy Scout recreational camp."[112] Walton's pleasant accommodation of the delegation quickly turned hostile when he learned Harkin had told the horrified congressmen exactly what he had seen in the restricted areas. Attempting to get Harkin to turn over the damning film, Walton angrily insisted that "You aren't supposed to go poking your nose into doors that aren't your business."[113]

POW/MIA activists were no more affected by Harkin's photos than they were by any other of the ugly revelations concerning the war, and they generally held the *Life* story to be an isolated occurrence, or possibly even a fabrication. This is understandable, as part of the plausibility of the American secret camp myth depended on the North Vietnamese enemy alone not behaving honorably toward their prisoners. After all, the rationale went, since the North Vietnamese had refused to allow inspectors into their prisons during the war, who is to say that they had even been honest about how many American prisoners they actually held? North Vietnam's supposedly unique inhumanity was therefore a necessary precursor for the existence of the secret camps and the survival of MIAs hoped to be in them.

There is another important element of the larger secret camp phenomenon present here as well: without denying the barbaric conditions American POWs endured in North Vietnamese captivity, Harkin's photos and other accounts demonstrate how such suffering was not unique to them, and that the United States and South Vietnam rarely treated their prisoners with much greater solicitude. After the war, for secret camp advocates the story of suffering was a strictly one-sided affair, thus making it a tale of American victimization, appropriating the pain of their own victims and making it their own via POW proxy.

Complete and Official Identification:
The Impossible Standard

The Go Public campaign not only promoted the idea that North Vietnam was brutalizing American POWs but also, via the constant repetition of "Hanoi won't tell our government, Hanoi won't tell me" and similar statements, reinforced the idea that there could be a far greater number of POWs present than was in fact the case.[114] Nixon's diplomatic strategy also reinforced this idea by using the supposed refusal of North Vietnam's government to disclose how many prisoners it really held as a reason to stall more substantial peace negotiations. During his remarks at the opening of the 1970 session of the Paris peace talks, US Ambassador Philip Habib claimed that North Vietnam's refusal to make a "complete and official identification" of its prisoners was an intolerable roadblock to any further talks, and "This is a matter that cannot be held in abeyance. It cannot wait until the end of the war."[115]

Though Nixon's diplomats were not secret camp advocates and made no explicit mention of secret camps, such an emphasis contributed to that myth by making the North Vietnamese appear that much more dishonest and also by playing up POW victimization. Ambassador Habib's use of the phrase "complete and official identification" in his 1970 statement, without defining what would constitute "complete and official," demonstrates the former point. Such slipperiness made such charges virtually impossible for North Vietnam to refute, regardless of how much information Hanoi disclosed on the subject. The existence of MIAs and KIA-BNRs all but guaranteed Hanoi could know little or nothing about some missing Americans, which effectively prevented any genuinely "complete and official" accounting. This infinitely moveable goalpost became a useful tool to justify continued American troop presence in Vietnam, for as Habib concluded, "This is a matter that cannot be held in abeyance. It cannot wait until the end of the war."[116]

Two years later, Habib's colleague Heyward Isham, head of the American delegation, had very similar things to say. Hanoi had by that point provided a POW/MIA list, and so Isham now argued that that list was intentionally incomplete and that men known to have made it to the ground alive failed to appear on the "so-called 'complete' list."[117] Though Isham had changed the rhetoric slightly, Nixon's larger tactic remained clear: so long as one man remained unaccounted for, North Vietnam had not lived up to its obligations and so the peace talks could not proceed. Isham's focus on airmen known to have safely ejected is also important to the creation of the secret camp myth, for it constructed the expectation that therefore such men must be in enemy captivity, despite Hanoi not mentioning them in its prisoner lists. Though neither Isham nor anyone else at the time took this idea to its logical conclusion, secret camp advocates after the war certainly did.

Importantly, Isham's assumption that aircrew who made it to the ground should be on such lists was fundamentally flawed, despite being a convenient excuse to keep the war going. Outside of urban areas, Southeast Asia was not particularly densely populated, and relatively few people lived in the dense, vast jungles of the interior. It was a very easy part of the world for people to disappear in without a trace. Even during the war, the American military acknowledged this reality with regard to its downed pilots. When interviewed by the *Wall Street Journal* in 1967 on the subject of jungle survival, US Marine Corps lieutenant colonel Pat Caruthers was bleakly realistic on a pilot's chances. After speaking on how common it was for airmen to suffer serious or debilitating injuries following even textbook ejections, he commented on just how hostile was the environment in which those men usually found themselves, concluding with the dry understatement that "If a man's not found within 10 days, he's got a real personal problem."[118]

Caruthers was not alone in understanding how making it to the ground was no guarantee of survival. Testifying before Congress in the 1990s, former air force intelligence officer William Gadoury similarly explained how aircrew faced formidable challenges when parachuting into the jungles of Southeast Asia. Gadoury had served three years in Vietnam during the war and had worked at the Joint Casualty Resolution Center in the 1980s where by his own admission his highest priority was "to find hard, credible evidence that Americans were still alive in Indochina, evidence which I dearly hoped would lead to the return of some of my former comrades in arms."[119] Gadoury admitted he had never found any such evidence, though he continued to hope that some men might somehow still survive. More to the point, he argued that even those men who made it to the ground uninjured would have found survival exceptionally difficult. He described his own experiences in the jungles during recovery operations, that even with the benefit of proper survival equipment, supplies, and medical aid as needed, "Sometimes, laying in my cot I wonder[ed], if I didn't have the cot, if I didn't have the mosquito net, the military rations and all the things we have out there, how long could I last?"[120]

Men Redeemed: Operation Homecoming and POWs as War Heroes

The Nixon administration was remarkably successful in engaging with POW/MIA activism and folding it into the administration's own plans for the war via Go Public and Nixon's diplomatic emphasis on POW/MIA accounting. In particular, the government believed it had succeeded in recasting the POWs and the missing as war heroes of the new type, whom it could now use to manufacture a triumphant exit from the war. Having achieved at last "peace with honor," Nixon was determined to use POW repatriation to publicly validate his efforts in Southeast Asia, completing their transformation into long sought-after heroes of a war that had produced precious few others. Unlike the largely anonymous return of most troops who had completed their tours of duty throughout the war, Nixon had in mind for the POWs something that recalled the celebrations that marked the end of World War II. In practice, this all coalesced into Operation Homecoming, and the manner in which Operation Homecoming ultimately failed to satisfy POW/MIA activists accelerated the growth of the secret camp myth—both by failing to bring home as many POWs as activists believed still alive and also by treating those men who did return as hero-victims to be celebrated.

The Pentagon had done exploratory work for Operation Homecoming as early as 1967 when it established a POW working group to write policy on how to handle returning prisoners. This group initially concerned itself with avoiding some of the stumbles of the Korean War repatriation, where returning POWs suffered the stigma of cowardice or even of sinister North Korean brainwashing. In 1971 Defense Secretary Melvin Laird established a larger POW/MIA Task Group to coordinate repatriation and related matters.[121]

Assistant Secretary of Defense for International Security Affairs Roger

Shields headed the new task group, with Rear Admiral Horace Epes Jr. heading the subordinate task force that was to act as staff for the group.[122] That task group's preparations show clearly that the Nixon administration believed the image of the POW as a beaten but unbroken hero was important. They created instructions for returning POWs: how to properly address the press, specifically by limiting their answers to patriotic love of country and how they looked forward to family reunions, and to avoid any political commentary on the war or captivity.

Such spin was likely unnecessary. Many prisoners had already internalized an idea of themselves during their captivity that meshed well with the hero narrative Nixon and others were so eager to create. The origins of this attitude lay in the Code of the US Fighting Force, which was adopted after the Korean War, in 1955, in part to address the communist taint with which some of that war's prisoners had supposedly returned.[123] North Korea's frequent propaganda use of coerced POW confessions and statements led the American public to suspect all POWs had been ideologically contaminated during their imprisonment. The Department of Defense commissioned a special advisory committee following widespread media reports of alleged misbehavior among returnees, to both determine the degree of truth to those stories and ascertain what could be done to repair the damage. That committee discovered that reports of collaboration were highly exaggerated, but it nevertheless recommended that a new code of conduct be written to make explicit that such behavior was unacceptable and must not be repeated, despite how rarely it actually occurred.[124]

The code dictates expected behavior for all service members, should they wind up prisoners of war. Among other things, it requires that those taken prisoner have a duty to continue to resist and attempt escape whenever possible, as well as keeping faith with fellow prisoners and making no statements of disloyalty to the United States and its allies. It also insists that every serviceman "never forget that I am an American, fighting for freedom, responsible for my actions, and dedicated to the principles which made my country free. I will trust in my God and in the United States of America."[125] The inherent message is clear: all members of the armed forces are expected to continue their struggle even in captivity, albeit in a less direct manner. American POWs in Vietnam internalized this expectation to such a degree that predisposed them to the passively heroic image Nixon wanted them to be, and that later secret camp advocates needed them to be.

Prisoners like James Stockdale knew full well that the resistance required by the code of conduct would anger his North Vietnamese captors and result in violent retaliation, but he was determined to hold to it regardless. He was hardly alone in such sentiments.[126] Fearing that cooperation with the North Vietnamese would aid their propaganda efforts, Stockdale and other prisoners employed various forms of passive resistance, such as playing dumb and, when brought to breaking point, doing their best to limit their utility to their captives. These men also actively worked to keep others from taking the easy route of cooperation, or at least to make sure there would be a postwar accounting for those determined to have violated the code of conduct.[127]

Other prisoners were quick to attest to holding the same mindset of patriotic resistance during captivity after repatriation, and to having rejected all communist cajoling to support the antiwar movement:

I would like to say that so far as I know every man who has been a prisoner supports and has supported our President and his policies. At no time during my imprisonment have I failed to support my President, my country, and my President's policies.[128]

For years and years we've dreamed of this day, and we've kept faith—faith in God, in our President and in our country. It was this faith that maintained our hope that someday our dreams would come true and today they have.[129]

The official agreement for prisoner repatriation on which Operation Homecoming was based includes another seed of the secret camp myth. The 1972 negotiations that led to the Paris Peace Accords one year later included substantial discussions on POWs. Both sides agreed to simultaneous repatriations of those prisoners, and, crucially, Hanoi agreed to arrange the release of all prisoners held throughout all of Indochina, not just those in North Vietnam itself.[130] That element of the larger peace agreement reinforced the already strong presumption among POW/MIA activists that Hanoi knew the status of all Americans captive or missing elsewhere in Southeast Asia and also was able to make its various allies and clients comply with those terms.

The Nixon administration ensured that Operation Homecoming was heavily televised, and that it was at times scripted to manufacture the appearance of a victory America had manifestly failed to win outright militarily. In total, 591 prisoners came home to much pomp and fanfare, and the government lavished them with attention and material comfort, including but not limited to back pay for their time in captivity, lifetime passes to major league baseball games, use of new cars, and trips to Disneyland.[131] Nixon personally wanted to make sure the returning prisoners felt appreciated, going so far as to direct his staff to put together souvenir baskets for POWs and their families when a group came for a high-profile dinner at the White House in May 1973.[132]

The attention paid to these men at times bordered on the obsessive, and it is hard not to see in such activity a willing turn away from the reality of Vietnam to a reimagined version of the war. Indeed, at times the rejection of that reality was almost physical, demonstrated by no less drastic an action than an executive order that the flags that had been lowered to mark the death of LBJ be returned to full height.[133] Johnson's failure to win in Vietnam was thus symbolically eclipsed by Nixon's "victory," as demonstrated not so much by the end of direct American involvement but by the return of the prisoners he had for so long claimed were the existential reason America had persisted in its long struggle in that country. Those who accepted this rewriting of the Vietnam War narrative thus preconditioned themselves to accept the later secret camp myth, which took the idea of "POW return as victory" one step further and applied it to those men still unaccounted for from the conflict.

Nixon hoped to build upon the success of Operation Homecoming to transform celebration of the POWs' return into a larger recontextualization of the whole conflict. He had already made his position on this matter clear in February 1973 when he told the Joint Chiefs of Staff that while he did not want to exploit the POWs, nevertheless, "we now have an invaluable opportunity to revise the history of this war. For eight years the press has called the Vietnam war immoral and those that went to Canada moral."[134]

This was not the only time Nixon had expressed such sentiments concerning the usefulness of returning POWs. After Operation Homecoming's completion, he confirmed such intentions with Roger Shields: "They [the POWs] should be recruiters, speaking on college campuses, and writing. They have thought deeply about themselves and their country and we should benefit from it. They must be used in an effective way." Shields affirmed that that should be entirely possible, since "they see changes in the United States that they don't like and want to change these." Clearly pleased, Nixon replied, "These men can inspire and we shouldn't lose this opportunity."[135] Importantly, Nixon considered these men to be so potentially useful because of their status as hero-victims. They had kept the faith throughout their imprisonment and torture at communist hands, only to come home to find long-haired peaceniks running amok. As a result, Nixon believed them perfect instruments for reinserting a moral tone he believed the country had lost due to the social upheaval of the war years. Secret camp advocates later seized upon this same sentiment and applied its hopes for moral renewal to the MIAs they claimed survived in the secret camps.

It is possible to find a few dissenting voices among all the celebrations surrounding the POWs' return. In an issue that also featured three major stories on the returnees, *Newsweek* included a story about the much larger population of ordinary Vietnam veterans who had received no such fanfare upon their return, often faced serious obstacles reintegrating into the civilian world, and found precious little official assistance in overcoming such problems. These men were essentially left to their own efforts once out of uniform, and they suffered disproportionate unemployment as a result. Unlike their POW counterparts, the public at large far more frequently viewed these veterans negatively, as uncomfortable reminders of the war's turmoil, or even as drug-addled, potentially violent lunatics. *Newsweek*'s story also highlighted the irony of the disproportionate attention the nation paid to POWs versus other veterans by pointing out how there was one government that made reintegration, training, and employment assistance a high priority for all veterans, regardless of their status: North Vietnam.[136]

Of course, not all Americans agreed with the narrative of POWs as hero-victims. Commentators disagreed about how to label these men, as well as whether they were ready or fit for the hero role in which so many Americans seemed determined to place them. While many lauded these men unconditionally, others were more apprehensive that the public at large was assigning an identity regardless of whether those men all wanted it. A *Time* magazine article tellingly entitled "A Celebration of Men Redeemed" expressed such skepticism with its opening lines: "If it was a war without heroes, many Americans were intent on making the prisoners fit that role."[137]

Nixon certainly fit this particular model of behavior, both politically and on a personal level. For him, the prisoner release not only gave America some heroes at last but also served to validate those military actions he had ordered supposedly on their behalf. Speaking at length with UN ambassador John Scali in early February 1973, he commented:

President: Did you see the POW release? Wasn't it great?
Scali: Yes.
President: Like Armstrong on the move [*sic*]—God bless America. It's good for the American people to see some brave men. The POWs felt the bombing got them out.[138]

Nixon was not alone in his satisfaction with having at last filled the long-empty role of Vietnam war hero, regardless of what the men themselves might have to say on the matter. *Newsweek* commentator Shana Alexander noted how eagerly other Americans accepted the idea of POWs as war heroes:

> World War I had the Rainbow Division. World War II had Iwo Jima and the Bulge. Even Korea had the men at Changin Reservoir. But until last week the longest and most dismal of all America's wars had victims, casualties and the faceless brutalities and braveries common to all wars, but no heroes at all. Well, we have them now.[139]

Alexander's purpose was to highlight how selection of this heroic role for returning prisoners was in a way artificial and dissimilar from previous wars, where the heroes usually emerged from battlefield actions of one sort or another. At the same time, she noted how imposing that role upon men who often came back from captivity with any number of problems and traumas might well do them more harm than good. "The final irony," she concluded, "may be that after eight cruel years as prisoners of war, they have now become hostages of propaganda, prisoners of peace with honor."[140]

Ultimately, Operation Homecoming did succeed in its short-term goal of manufacturing at least an ersatz triumph out of POW repatriation and thus generated something to which the Nixon administration could point to justify its policies in Southeast Asia. Indeed, Nixon's staff estimated they had gained considerable political capital from the "euphoria" of the prisoner return, which hopefully could be turned to the service of other items on the Nixon agenda.[141] Homecoming, and Nixon's engagement with POW/MIA activism more generally, had unintended consequences, however, that fueled growing discontent within that activism, and that ultimately laid the foundation for the American secret camp myth. Nixon's decision to work with the League of Wives of American Vietnam Prisoners of War raised hopes that POW/MIA relatives at last had a champion, and the Go Public campaign gave them reason to hope that far more POWs survived in enemy captivity than was indeed the case. Go Public and Homecoming both also contributed to the concept of the POW/MIA as hero-victim, whose repatriation signaled a triumphant end of American involvement in the Vietnam War. However, far too few men actually came home, with Operation Homecoming only resulting in the return of fewer than 600 of the roughly 1,300 men activists hoped were still alive. This was not nearly enough to satisfy

POW/MIA activism, particularly after Go Public had gone to such lengths to convince them that North Vietnam had not been honest about how many POWs it held. Where were the rest? As one MIA mother said shortly after Homecoming's conclusion, "When the prisoners of war came home, everyone said the war was over. Everyone was talking about peace with honor. But when you abandon 1,300 men there is no peace with honor."[142] Subsequent attempts and failures to satisfy these families and their allies were the final contributing factors to the birth of the secret camp myth—and they were crucial to its longevity in American politics.

❧

FOUR

Radicalization of POW/MIA Advocacy and the Emergence of the Secret Camp Myth

Operation Homecoming had raised hopes for MIA survival too high for its comparatively small number of actual returnees to satisfy. Individuals within POW/MIA activism had believed in that survival for too long, and too fervently, to accept that their loved ones were dead—and likely had been the whole time. At the same time, POW/MIA activism as a whole was becoming more militant, for two key reasons. First, many early members of the National League of Families of American Prisoners and Missing in Southeast Asia (as it was then known) disengaged from public activism, either because their missing man had come home or because they were able to find a way out of the no-man's land of grief. Second, new activists joined the league and otherwise became active, and they demanded not just the truth about whom among the missing might still be alive, but in a very real way, also the resurrection of the dead. The Go Public campaign had convinced these activists that the MIAs must still be alive, and so they rejected the finality of Operation Homecoming when those men did not reappear. In the absence of strong evidence to support such a belief, they seized upon conspiratorial concepts to justify belief in MIA survival, prime among them the secret camps. When a congressional investigation in the 1970s failed to reveal any surviving MIAs, these individuals saw such a failure not as debunking the idea of MIA survival but rather as a cover-up. Having progressively made space for themselves within POW/MIA activism, secret camp advocates redefined that activism through the 1970s in such terms as to prefigure its revival on more hysterical, even less believable terms in the 1980s. More important, they helped to popularize and normalize the idea that the US government had knowingly abandoned live POWs in Vietnam, who now survived in secret captivity.

"Have You Forgotten Him?": Why They Continued to Believe in MIA Survival

For all its fanfare, Operation Homecoming had failed to address the concerns of many within the POW/MIA community, and the discrepancy in men returned versus men expected was fertile ground for the growth of the secret camp myth. For many individuals within POW/MIA activism, the only alternative to believing in something like secret captivity was to accept that the missing were actually dead, which they were unable or unwilling to do. What was it that fostered such a belief? Beyond the basic emotional need for it to be true, there are several specific reasons that encouraged POW/MIA activists to believe that secret camps had to exist.

Most immediately, a few supposedly dead men did resurface during Operation Homecoming. Most notable among this handful of individuals was Marine Private Ronald Ridgeway. The Marines had reported Ridgeway killed in action near Khe Sahn in 1968, and his family received a set of remains purported to be his for burial. However, in 1973 Marine Corps officials informed Ridgeway's mother that they had located her son alive in North Vietnamese captivity, validating his mother's refusal to accept the finality of his alleged death. Admittedly, the body had only conditionally been identified as Ridgeway's and had not been found with his dog tags, but nevertheless this startling tale of death and resurrection helped fuel belief that other Americans could still be alive in Southeast Asia.[1] Ridgeway's family was not the only one to experience this sort of reversal of expectations. The air force believed that Captain James Wilder had likely died in captivity but abruptly informed his wife of his survival shortly before he too reappeared during Homecoming.[2] Such remarkable reappearances of supposedly dead men encouraged other hopeful relatives of the missing to believe their man might reappear as well.

The failure of supposedly living POWs to appear similarly encouraged belief in MIA survival, interestingly. The parents of MIA James Ray believed that their son was a live POW on the strength of reports from earlier returnees, but despite this, the army subsequently informed the Rays that their son had died in captivity. For their part, neither the NLF nor North Vietnam officially acknowledged they had captured Ray or that they knew anything about him. Believing the first reports of his survival, his parents rejected subsequent claims of his death and suspected instead that the US Army or the Vietnamese must have been lying for reasons unknown.[3] Similarly, Hanoi radio announced the capture of navy pilot Lieutenant James Teague in 1967, but did not include him on the Homecoming lists of expected returnees. When Teague did not reappear, his suspicious father claimed, "The North Vietnamese are holding out on us. We know this."[4] Thus, while "dead" men reappearing fostered hopes for MIA survival, "live" prisoners failing so to do did not always discourage family members from believing they were still alive. Belief in secret prison camps where these missing men might survive built upon such hopes.

In addition to misclassifications like these, there were cases of deliberate status falsification. This generally stemmed less from any sinister motive on the part of North Vietnam, however, than from well-intentioned but short-sighted actions of the friends of this or that man. Witnesses from time to time spun their loss reports in such a way as to foster illusions of survival that they knew to be impossible:

> A guy is flying, he does see his wingman shot down. Two guys go in, and they're deader than a doornail. He's thinking to himself, "If I report that they're dead, the wife's going to be brokenhearted, she'll get death gratuities, and that's it." If I report him MIA, his pay keeps going, and it will cushion the blow for a little while.
>
> Now put me in that position, and I come back and tell you I just saw your son flew into the ground. Do you think I'm going to tell you that? Hell no, because the way I think, if I tell you your son got target fixation and flew into the ground, to my way of thinking, what I would be telling you is, "You know, what you had for a son is a real idiot." That's not true, so what am I going to say?
>
> So what are we going to do? We twist the report. But now I've given you a shred of hope. It's not an out-and-out false report. I told you he flew into the ground, but I just twisted "why." So now he has the option of ejecting.[5]

Men employed this sort of spin out of a sense of compassion for their dead comrade's family, but doing so often had unintended consequences.

Family members who thus received such a "shred of hope" became remarkably resistant to later reports of their man's death. They did not take well to learning that he had been dead the whole time after believing he was alive for so long. Additionally, learning that they had been lied to actually could lead to a retrenchment of original survival belief:

Now, I come back 6 years later. You know all the stories, the different reports, the conflicting stories: this guy tells you that; that guy tells you something else; you talk to the other people here, they've got conflicting stories, and now I come back and tell you, "Your husband flew right into the ground, I saw him." What are you going to believe? You're faced with, "Well, yes, here's one more guy. He really knows. Oh, yeah? Well, get lost, buddy."[6]

What is more, family members often grew paranoid after such revelations and sometimes came to doubt *all* wartime information about their missing man, while at the same time holding fast to the core belief in that man's potential survival:

Where are you left? Exactly as you were before I showed up. It's very simple if I just give you one story and then seven years later we forget everything that happened and I give you a second story and explain it to you. Now, after all you have heard and all the frustration and all the pain that you've been through for seven years, if I come back and give you that story you probably will not believe it. You are faced with a situation of "what the hell can I believe?"[7]

The US government's position before and during Operation Homecoming also reinforced belief in MIA survival. Throughout Go Public and well afterward, the official line was that Hanoi knew far more about America's missing than it had disclosed, with the heavy implication that its leaders were purposefully holding back information about live POWs. This included the Homecoming returnee list, which the Defense Department considered provisional at best. In its press releases on the subject, that department repeatedly amended the estimated POWs and MIAs and moved men back and forth from one column to the other, which created the impression that any number of unlisted men might still be alive. More specifically, the Defense Department believed that 54 of the men Hanoi claimed had died in captivity were more likely still alive. As a result, official US POW lists contained those men despite their names being on Hanoi's dead list, regardless of Hanoi's repeated insistence that all 54 were dead.[8]

The controversy surrounding those men casts into sharp relief the shifting nature of POW/MIA activism after 1973. Indeed, the 54 men were one of three major concerns the league communicated in early 1973 to President Nixon's military assistant, Brigadier General Brent Scowcroft. On the basis of their own "good evidence," the league found it suspicious that the men did not appear on Hanoi's list of confirmed prisoners.[9] More generally, the league was dismayed that so few MIAs had resurfaced among the POW population contrary to its optimistic expectations. Only 51 out of the estimated 1,334 MIAs came home during Homecoming, and only 7 had reappeared from the 317 missing in Laos.[10]

This is not to say that league membership uniformly believed the MIAs all survived in secret captivity. Some league members, and others, already suspected the belief in MIA survival owed less to factual inconsistencies in Hanoi's accounting and more to the psychological inability of the families of the missing to give up in the absence of firm evidence of their loved one's death. In other words, they recognized firsthand that many of their compatriots were trapped in the no-man's land of grief. Reporting on the subject, Steven Roberts of the *New York Times* commented, "More significantly, many simply cannot believe that their men are dead."[11]

Some MIA activists recognized this behavior in themselves—that their refusal to accept the likely death of the MIAs was a factor in their continued involvement in league affairs, and that such sentiments stemmed more from personal need than any reasonable expectation or observable evidence. League national board member and MIA father Colonel John Scott Albright admitted that psychological need played a part in his belief in secret camp survival: "Each of us who has an MIA is personally convinced he's all right. That's what drives us. Some believe in the face of insurmountable odds, but what is the alternative?"[12] That alternative was, of course, to accept the unacceptable, and so many MIA family members instead looked for some specific excuse to keep hope alive.

Regardless of personal motivation, the members of the league continued their publicity campaign after Operation Homecoming with a modified message tailored toward MIA survival. In February 1973 the league and other advocacy groups ran a full-page advertisement in the *Washington Post* and other major newspapers. "Have You Forgotten Him?" appeared in large block text across the top of the ad, over a grainy photograph of North Vietnamese army (NVA) troops herding navy lieutenant Ronald

Dodge into captivity in 1967. In accusatory tones, the ad spoke of how the North Vietnamese had shot Dodge down but had not disclosed his status.[13] The league's advertisement argued Dodge was just one example of how Hanoi's POW/MIA accounting was "inaccurate and incomplete."[14] Though this advertisement does not explicitly mention secret prison camps, "Have You Forgotten Him?" heavily implies their existence. After all, by February 1973 the North Vietnamese had returned all the POWs they had admitted holding and emptied out their known POW camps, so where exactly were they keeping Lieutenant Dodge?

On the surface, "Have You Forgotten Him?" stands as an example of a continuation of the same message from Go Public: Hanoi is being dishonest and we must continue to agitate as long as even a single man remains unaccounted for. Its subtext, and that of similar advertisements, heavily suggested that these missing men could still be alive, in enemy custody. The White House reinforced this mindset as well when administration officials met with league representatives on 29 January 1973. Nixon made a brief appearance, and Henry Kissinger told them that the government believed Hanoi's POW/MIA lists were incomplete and as such unacceptable. He went on to outline how the government planned to force a full accounting from North Vietnam. Interestingly, while he stated that "we also did not believe they [North Vietnam] will hide any POWs," and that "in North Vietnam it is almost inconceivable that they will hide any POWs," nevertheless, "they have tended to collect their prisoners together. They can't use the men for blackmail if they don't know they hold them."[15] Via such shifting rhetoric, Kissinger was able to reassure the league of the government's due diligence on their behalf, maintain their hopes that the missing would soon be accounted for, and also manipulate their fears that even with the coming of peace the dastardly communists might be acting duplicitously with regard to some minority of live prisoners held outside North Vietnam.

Despite such reassurance, the league had other reasons to fear the completion of the Homecoming repatriations. League members knew how the US government had dealt with MIAs following previous conflicts. If precedent held, many of those men would be automatically reclassified from missing in action to presumed dead after a relatively short period of time. As some of the older league members were well aware, after the Korean War the Defense Department had wasted little time before doing just that. Barely a month after the end of official prisoner exchanges in September 1953, the Defense Department announced:

In light of casualty reporting experience in Korea, it is now the considered opinion of the Department of Defense that most of these men must eventually be presumed dead. They have not been reported so before because of strict requirements that there be reasonably conclusive evidence of the fact before a man is reported as having died.[16]

That final line is crucial to understanding one of the fears of Vietnam POW/MIA activists following Homecoming: if men were only declared dead following "reasonably conclusive evidence of the fact," as the Defense Department had done just one month after the Korean War prisoner repatriation, how much time remained before their missing men were written off as well? As league national coordinator Helen Knapp commented within months of Homecoming's completion, "It's becoming much more desperate. . . . Too many of our officials and news media are saying all the men are home now."[17] Such desperation led many to seize upon any seemingly plausible excuse to believe in MIA survival, including the existence of secret camps.

Fundamental Uncertainty: Changes in POW/MIA Activism after Homecoming

At the same time, POW/MIA activism generally was experiencing a demographic shift, which signaled a move toward secret camp advocacy. Relatives of POW returnees, as well as others who accepted the verdict of Operation Homecoming, often departed from activism. In particular, the wives who made up the original league constituency became a much smaller percentage of overall membership, and they no longer controlled the direction of the movement as they had during the war. The public face of POW/MIA activism generally shifted from being primarily the photogenic "hat and gloves" wives of career men who made up the bulk of league membership during the war to the parents, siblings, offspring, and other relatives of the remaining MIAs. Total league membership also shrank noticeably as most POW family members withdrew from active participation.[18] Indeed, for many of the founding members of the league it appeared that their mission was essentially over and there was little or no further reason for the league as an organization to exist. Even those old hands who did believe in further accounting activism often found themselves shouldered aside during the reordering that followed Operation Homecoming. These new activists, both in the league and elsewhere, carried into POW/MIA activism a new strain of militancy and an even more potent refusal to accept the likelihood of MIA death. More important, they also were the first to explicitly articulate the idea of secret prison camps in Southeast Asia.

Other advocacy groups similarly experienced a shift in emphasis on POW/MIA issues after Homecoming. MIAs played a much more prominent role at the 74th National Convention of the Veterans of Foreign Wars than they had previously. During that convention, the membership of the VFW agreed that the return of POWs and accounting for MIAs were unsatisfactory and resolved "that the President and the Congress of the United States be petitioned to increase action in obtaining information on the fate of the MIAs."[19] To be sure, the VFW was talking about locating MIA remains and determining how and when they had died, not locating live men in secret camps, but nevertheless such a change of focus from POWs to MIAs speaks to the larger move away from men known to be alive and toward ambiguously missing men.

The shift of emphasis from POWs to MIAs also signaled a change in the emotional landscape of POW/MIA activism. The missing were a much more ambiguous subject than known POWs had been. John Sarr of the *Washington Post* reported that, at a post-Homecoming league rally, "This fundamental uncertainty underlaid [*sic*] the rally—it was neither a wake for men known to be dead nor angry protest on behalf of the living."[20]

Beyond this "fundamental uncertainty," additional external factors raised hopes for the possibility for the survival of the missing in covert captivity. A cottage industry of POW/MIA information vendors had arisen among the refugee communities clustered around the periphery of the war zone, Thailand in particular. Those who had fled often carried with them rumors they had picked up along the way about missing Americans. The most common type of evidence turned in to American authorities was missing dog tags. Well over ten thousand sets of tags as well as supposed copies of tags surfaced in the years following the war. Often, individuals approaching US officials with such tags claimed to have further information or a set of American remains to sell.[21] Though there was no official reward policy for returning artifacts or remains of missing Americans, many in Southeast Asia nevertheless believed that handing them in would result in either money or immigration assistance.[22]

Even setting aside possible ulterior motives of those who turned in dog tags or copies thereof, their existence was not a good indicator of MIA survival—as the sheer volume of lost tags alone should have indicated. American servicemen routinely lost their tags throughout the long period of US involvement in Southeast Asia. Knowing this, investigators with the Defense Intelligence Agency (DIA, the intelligence arm of the Defense Department under which official accounting work began) placed very little weight on dog tag reports. Later analysis determined that close to 90 percent of all tags turned in belonged to Americans who had returned from the war in one way or another.[23]

Investigators and POW/MIA activists took other sources of evidence more seriously. Chief among these were the "live sightings" reports of alleged MIAs following the American withdrawal. Much like the dog tags reports, live sightings came chiefly, though not exclusively, from refugees. The Defense Department's POW/Missing Personnel Office reported in 2010 that since the collapse of South Vietnam in 1975, there had been 7,576 live sightings, though fewer than 2,000 of those are purportedly firsthand accounts.[24] Such volume alone implied that there might be some Americans left behind in Southeast Asia—an attractive possibility for those predisposed to believe precisely that.

As with the dog tag reports, this source of evidence is misleading, however. As Joint Casualty Resolution Center investigators noted, the majority of these accounts were secondhand at best, which made verification extremely difficult. Speaking later in the 1980s, air force lieutenant colonel Paul Mathers, who worked on MIA accounting through the 1970s, commented, "There's so much mythology about this, but we have no proof that would stand up in court. We hear hundreds of secondhand accounts. We're always traveling up to the refugee camps to check the stories out. But we never seem to be able to find the guy who'll say, 'I'm the one who saw them.'"[25]

In addition, the rationale behind most "live sightings" presumed that any Caucasian seen in Southeast Asia was likely an American prisoner. This is faulty for two reasons. First, Vietnam was closely allied with the Soviet Union, a relationship that only grew closer as Sino-Vietnamese relations soured. Visitors from the USSR and Warsaw Pact states could be and often were mistaken for Americans. More conspiratorially, secret camp advocates claimed that these visitors were, in fact, the missing men from the secret camps who had been transferred from Vietnamese to Soviet custody, interrogated and brainwashed, and later sent back to Vietnam with new Russian identities.[26] Second, there were some nonprisoner Americans known to have stayed behind after the war, including a handful of deserters and collaborators. These men were from time to time mistaken for live MIAs.[27] Even if these two points had not been the case, live sightings suffer from another problem in common with the dog tag reports: witness unreliability. While it is of course wrong to cast blanket aspersions upon every person who came forward with an account, dog tag, or live sighting report, it is also undeniable that a shadier element within the refugee communities in Southeast Asia very much desired to make money off MIA hunters and desperate family members of the missing. [28] Regardless of motivation, almost all live sighting reports were vague, lacked details, and failed to identify the alleged POW in question, beyond being supposedly an American. That POW/MIA activists considered such reports believable in the face of such limitations again points to how much personal need played into belief in MIA survival and the existence of secret camps.

Neither the league nor other activist groups had concerned themselves with these sorts of evidence during the war, preferring instead to seek information from official sources. Such a shift in focus signaled two things. First, it was another indication of the new demographic gaining prominence within POW/MIA activism after 1973. These new activists were frequently at odds with the old guard. To this point, POW wives had been the face of such activism, but now other types of relatives challenged their leadership. Wives were, after all, often less willing to wait endlessly for final determination of their husbands' status compared to other family members. These women needed some form of closure to escape the netherworld between wifedom and widowhood, even if their husband never came home. Along the same lines, MIA wives needed a presumptive declaration of death for their lost husbands if they wished to legally remarry, as many did. As Knapp herself acknowledged during the league's contentious 1973 national convention in Washington, DC, "A father or mother or sister or brother can wait forever for a finding, but wives and children cannot."[29]

Second, the turn toward dog tags and live sighting reports marked a growing distrust within POW/MIA activism for official sources of information. The new entrants into POW/MIA activism were much less likely to trust government sources due to Watergate revelations of how dishonest the Nixon administration had been and also because of the looming threat of what league members termed "arbitrary" status changes for MIAs. The potential mass-shifting of missing men's status from "unaccounted for" to "presumed dead" aggravated the growing friction between wives and other relatives of the missing. This practice had been rationalized and codified during World War II via the Missing Persons Act, which mandated that "a lapse of time without information" was enough for the death of any given missing man to be presumed.[30] Influential figures within the league decided to take preemptive action. Specifically, Albright hired New York attorney Dermot Foley to file a class-action suit to block any such status changes.[31] On 20 July 1973 the US District Court for Southern New York granted a temporary injunction against any further status changes, which in practice put an end to unrequested status changes.[32]

Though league attitudes were indeed shifting and hardening, league members remained uncertain as to how to proceed after Operation Home-coming ended. Donald Barker acknowledged how the role of wives within the league was changing, in his reporting on the league's 1973 national convention. Without discounting the real emotional pain felt by other relatives, he identified how the conflicting desires of the remaining wives were causing disunity within the league itself over the subject of status determinations. Barker is perhaps most telling in his depiction of Knapp herself, whom he describes as the "wife (or is she a widow?) of a missing pilot."[33]

The growing conflict between family members of the missing was not confined solely to the 1973 league convention. Those relations whom the league had previously restricted to secondary roles now lobbied vigorously for greater roles within the league in the 1970s. Among other changes that accompanied this power shift, the league altered its membership rules, enabling entry for all relatives of the missing. This included the so-called adoptive relatives, people who were not actually related to any of the missing but who could "adopt" this or that MIA, for the bargain price of $5 a month.[34] The adoptive members were admittedly not full participants, but their inclusion marked a move away from the more pragmatic attitudes of the wartime POW wives, concerned first and foremost with the fate of their missing husbands, to a broader political—and at times frankly paranoid—position. Many of these new members were much more concerned with validating the war and redeeming America's war efforts, a desire that predisposed them toward redemptive reconstruction of the missing into hero-victims.

It is important to discriminate between POW/MIA activists generally and secret camp advocates in particular. Admittedly there was no hard and fast line between the two, and the degree to which any given activist believed in the existence of secret camps varied by person and over time. Nevertheless, some distinctions exist. First, older league members tended to be more skeptical of secret camps and of POW/MIA conspiracy theories generally. Those who became active during and after the mid-1970s tended to be less personally invested in discovering the fate of a specific missing man than the wives who had started the league, and more broadly invested in conspiratorial ideas concerning men left unaccounted for. What is more, this new activist demographic was politicized to a much greater degree. Specifically, they tended to be exceptionally distrustful of official government accounting, especially when it told them things they did not want to hear.[35]

The league's annual meeting in June 1974 was a telling example of the power shift within POW/MIA activism and the rise of secret camp advocacy. Radical elements of the newer membership mocked and catcalled league executive director Albright so much that he left the stage without even completing his opening statement.[36] He resigned soon afterward, signaling a radicalization of the league as militant newcomers then took over leadership positions. Compounding this change was an increase in cross-pollination between newer league members and Voices in Vital America (VIVA), an energetic lobbying group previously allied with the league but with disparate goals of its own. This is the same VIVA that originally went by the name Victory in Vietnam Association and that had been active in wartime POW/MIA activism; the change of name came about once its original namesake goal became patently impossible. Unlike the league, VIVA was concerned not solely with accounting for the missing but more broadly in justifying and validating US actions in Southeast Asia.[37] Similarly, many of the newer, more extremist members of the league and POW/MIA activism generally were less concerned with discovering the fate of the missing and more focused on redeeming the legitimacy of the war itself. Even for those who were direct relatives of missing men, those men seemed to have served better as symbols of a noble effort cravenly abandoned than as actual human beings with undetermined fates.

Many of the older members felt alienated by these newcomers, whom they often regarded as zealots lacking any real personal stake in the larger POW/MIA question. League founding member and MIA mother Iris Powers testified:

> I've been condemned and vilified for seeming to care more about the families of our missing men than of the men themselves; but I believe that's the way our men would have wanted it, if there had to be a choice. I bitterly resent having "concerned citizens" hysterically tell me that they care more about my son than I do—and this has happened. I wonder what motivates people who have made our problem their crusade![38]

Most prominent among those who rose within the league during this shift was Ann Mills Griffiths, sister of missing navy lieutenant commander James Mills. Griffiths had been an early member of the league but, unlike many among the old guard, had always been unusually militant in her desire to discover the fate of her missing brother; she sided with the new element coming into the league.[39] She had connections to VIVA as well via their own "Support our POW/MIAs" suborganization that she headed, and into which VIVA dumped its assets when the larger association shut down in 1976.[40]

In addition to the power shift among league members, the 1974 meeting marked a change in overall attitude throughout the POW/MIA community generally. This new demographic now assuming leadership roles within the league employed symbols and images already in use in POW/MIA activism and attempted to associate more broadly with the overall war itself. This was a deliberate effort to recast Vietnam as a story of the missing, with other aspects of that larger conflict subordinated to that narrative of missing, victimized men. The metal bracelets first promoted and sold by VIVA in 1970 prefigured this shift by asserting the vital importance of the missing while at the same time subtly downplaying the visibility of the much-larger body of conventional war veterans. Those bracelets continued to symbolize the missing even after 1973, as the league and VIVA both continued to refer to them in their post-Homecoming campaigns. "Don't take your bracelets off!" thundered a full-page advertisement in the Washington Post, "there is more you must do!"[41]

When it comes to long-lived POW/MIA symbols, however, one cannot find a more persistent or pervasive piece of iconography than the black POW/MIA flag itself. The league commissioned World War II veteran and commercial artist Newt Heisley to design the flag in 1971. The image centers on a male POW in silhouette, head bowed, with barbed wire and a menacing guard tower in the background. The words "POW/MIA" above this tableau and "You Are Not Forgotten" beneath it complete the overall design. Heisley used his Marine son, recently returned from training, as the model for the flag's iconic central figure. The flag quickly surpassed even VIVA's bracelets in terms of popularity and became the premier symbol of POW/MIA activism, as indeed it remains to this day.[42] More than that, the flag has become a de facto icon for the war itself, helping to refine that war in terms of POW/MIA victimization and abandonment.

The Hostage Hypothesis: Initial Rationale behind the Secret Camps

Secret camp advocates also faced a significant challenge in explaining why North Vietnam had built the alleged secret camps to begin with. What possible reason could they have for such camps, and for retaining the prisoners within them? Though answers to that question varied depending on which secret camp advocate one asked, the earliest and most common one given was that North Vietnam retained POWs for ransom against secretly promised reconstruction aid. Since the United States had never delivered that aid, North Vietnam had never returned the last of the prisoners.

North Vietnam had made reconstruction aid a sticking point during the Paris talks, but one of the apparent triumphs of Henry Kissinger's negotiating team had been to get them to drop the issue as a precondition to prisoner repatriation.[43] Domestically there was considerable pressure on this front. In February 1973, Republican congressman Jack Kemp had written to Kissinger that the United States should not even consider reconstruction aid until all POWs had been returned and Hanoi accelerated its MIA accounting programs.[44]

Article 21 of the Paris Peace Accords complicated matters by stipulating that the United States would "contribute to healing the wounds of war and to postwar reconstruction of the Democratic Republic of Viet-Nam and throughout Indochina."[45] However, POW return and MIA accounting were explicitly not provisional upon the fulfillment of Article 21, and the agreement covered their particulars in Article 8. Even in early drafts of what eventually became Article 21, the North Vietnamese acknowledged that reconstruction aid and POW repatriation were separate issues.[46] They also were well aware that any such aid would have to come from separate congressional action. However, among the many bits of dirty laundry to eventually surface following Watergate was a secret letter from Nixon to Premier Pham Van Dong written 1 February 1973.[47] In that letter, Nixon informed Pham that "Preliminary United States Studies indicate that the appropriate programs for the United States contribution to postwar reconstruction will fall in the range of $3.25 billion in grant aid over five years."[48]

This too was admittedly well short of any definitive agreement for specific amounts of aid, and viewed on its own merits it appears just to have been an estimate on what could be worked out in the future. However, secret camp advocates read into it the implication that American POWs were collateral to an eventual aid deal. Since Nixon had reneged on that promised deal, surely that was why the Vietnamese never released those prisoners. While plausible within the mindset of the secret camp advocate, in reality there was a fatal flaw in such reasoning: the Vietnamese government has always maintained that it held no remaining prisoners after 1973, nor has it ever offered to return missing Americans in exchange for cash.[49] If the missing were actually hostages, it is strikingly odd that Hanoi never bothered to send a ransom note.

Regardless of why they chose to believe in MIA survival, secret camp advocates were united with most in larger POW/MIA activism in fearing their hard-won national prominence was endangered. More than just general worries of the nation giving up on the missing after Operation Homecoming, they had reason to believe the federal government, so long an ally, was turning against them. Specifically, they felt threatened by William Clements's appointment as deputy secretary of defense in 1973. Not only was he no ally of the league or any other group, Clements believed the time had more than come to start presuming the deaths of the remaining MIAs. Such a process had been the practice in prior American wars, and given how few men were still to be accounted for, Clements might well have been forgiven for at least initially imagining that this move would be mostly uncontroversial. It is doubtful he would have changed his mind even if he had fully appreciated how such action would incite the worst fears of POW/MIA activism: Clements did not think much of the league, VIVA, or any other advocacy group to speak of, finding their activism to smell not a little of a con game. In August 1973 he went so far at one point as to state,

> There is not a shred of evidence, not one hard piece of evidence, that would give us hope that there are survivors among the MIAs. The crudest thing going on is the profit-making on bracelets and bumper stickers and fund raising that uses the sadness of the families of these men and the sympathies of their countrymen for profit. The rumor-mongering by charlatans makes my blood boil.[50]

Clements rejected the idea that there needed to be some sort of forever search for the missing or that the United States should deviate from how it had handled such matters in earlier wars. Writing to Nixon in July 1973, Clements had already raised the concern that outside influences might well disrupt the accounting process and divert that process from properly authorized government bodies into the hands of those with personal axes to grind:

> I am concerned that the process for equitably determining status of the missing in Southeast Asia may be unduly influenced by emotional factors rather than the law governing such determinations and the facts bearing on each individual case. For example, some family members are seeking an immediate change from missing to deceased, regardless of whether

available information justifies such a declaration. Conversely, others are demanding a complete moratorium on status changes until Southeast Asia can be swept for grave sites and combat locations where men were lost.

In my view the status determination process, as established by law and experience, should be allowed to function as prescribed if we are to maintain fairness, credibility, and consistency. It is not our intent to write off our missing men prematurely, but at the same time we cannot condone building undue hope for the family members without justification.[51]

Going further, Clements noted just how unlikely survival was for virtually any of those still listed as missing, citing both statistical evidence and also the testimony of returned POWs.[52] Finally, he concluded with the recommendation that the United States follow standard postwar operating procedure with regard to the missing:

In the past, many were continued in a missing status because of lack of information from the other side. Now that the men have returned, the positive information that they have given us has been added to the data already available. The fact that reports from our returned prisoners of war indicate that many others apparently did not enter the captivity environment is also a significant factor that must be considered.[53]

Clements did not foresee that this would be seen as an attack by POW/MIA activists and probably would not have cared if he had. More important, whereas POW/MIA activists saw his actions as abandonment, secret camp advocates perceived his supposed haste to close the book on the missing as intentionally covering up MIA survival. Testifying later, Roger Shields claimed that in 1973, Clements had all but ordered him to give up on finding any more live prisoners. After Shields argued that he could not say that there were no more live Americans, he claimed that Clements angrily replied, "You didn't hear me. I said they're all dead."[54] For the league and other groups, revelations of Nixonian dishonesty and the appointment of Clements seemed to confirm two dreaded fears: the government had been stringing them along as convenient war boosters, and it now planned on sweeping any remaining hope for MIA survival under a rug of political expediency.

The league did not speak with one voice on this issue. Some members held faith that the Joint Casualty Resolution Center would eventually determine the fate of the MIAs. Others even went so far as to publicly call out their radicalized compatriots, arguing those members were "simply refusing to accept reality."[55] Such reasonable objections were, however, increasingly in the minority as POW/MIA activism narrowed what were and were not acceptable realities with regard to the remaining MIAs.

The Montgomery Committee: POW/MIA Activism's First Congressional Inquiry

Disillusionment with the Nixon administration did not, yet, mean an overarching rejection of all official accounting efforts. In 1974 the league and other groups lobbied for congressional hearings on the missing, which eventually led to the September 1975 formation of the House Select Committee on Missing Persons in Southeast Asia.[56] That committee's stated purpose

> is to conduct a full and complete investigation and study of (1) the problem of United States servicemen still identified as missing in action, as well as those known dead whose bodies have not been recovered, as a result of military operations in North Vietnam, South Vietnam, Laos and Cambodia and the problem of United States civilians identified as missing or unaccounted for, as well as those known dead whose bodies have not been recovered in North Vietnam, South Vietnam, Laos and Cambodia; (2) the need for additional international inspection teams to determine whether there are servicemen still held as prisoners of war or civilians held captive or unwillingly detained in the aforementioned areas.[57]

The press generally referred to this committee as the Montgomery Committee after its chairman, G. V. "Sonny" Montgomery (R-Mississippi), and POW/MIA activists had reason to be optimistic at that choice. Montgomery had a history of being sympathetic to veterans' issues, and of opposition to the antiwar movement generally.[58] More to the point, Montgomery had not been silent in his belief that men had been left behind in Southeast Asia and that the government was not doing enough to locate them and hold the Vietnamese accountable. Though he never articulated a belief in secret camps as such, Montgomery claimed to be the loudest voice speaking for the missing in Congress.[59]

Despite such promise, the Montgomery Committee proved a massive disappointment to the league and other activists. Chairman Montgomery notwithstanding, others on the committee were less than enthusiastic about the prospects of finding any more live prisoners. Furthermore, some even rejected the idea that Vietnam should shoulder any further responsibility for America's missing men. Representative Richard Ottinger noted during the opening comments of that committee's deliberation, "I think the attitude of the North Vietnamese is that we made a moonscape out of their country, we killed thousands and thousands of their people, and disrupted their economy completely, and the notion that they should have to come forward first in these circumstances seems incongruous."[60]

It is unlikely Vietnam could have provided better information about the missing even had it been so inclined. Ottinger correctly observed that the recently reunited country was still dealing with the physical devastation of the war, particularly the ravaging of its communications and logistical networks. The North Vietnamese had acknowledged how this had limited their capacities to keep track of prisoners during the war, with Pham Van Dong privately acknowledging how hard it was to keep track of prisoners held outside the capital, the numbers of whom changed daily as new reports came in.[61] Prior to 1970 the North Vietnamese had an even harder time tracking their prisoners due to the decentralized ad hoc system of their camps and holding facilities. After the US Special Forces raid on the Son Tay prison facility that year, the North Vietnamese consolidated virtually all of their POW camps into three main facilities in and around Hanoi (the "Hilton" and the smaller and less well-known "Plantation" and "Zoo").[62] They still did not keep records of prisoners in transit prior to their arrival in Hanoi, however.

Further dampening league hopes, witnesses testifying before the House Select Committee did not support the idea that live MIAs remained in captivity in Southeast Asia. On the contrary, many spoke of how difficult POW/MIA survival was and how unlikely it was that missing men could have survived the destruction of their aircraft. Dr. Roger Shields, head of the Defense Department's POW/MIA task force, testified before the committee on 30 September 1975 that aircrews, comprising the majority of the missing, were often lost under such circumstances that even identifying the wreck of a given aircraft was quite difficult, to say nothing of the crew it carried:

Now, to implement the accounting procedures, which we felt was going to be very difficult, we know that many of our men—most, in fact—were lost in aircraft accidents, incidents, shoot downs, and so forth. We know that in the case of high-speed aircraft carrying ordinance and other explosive munitions, that oftentimes it's very difficult even to find enough of the airplane to identify.[63]

Striking more directly at the foundation of the secret camp myth, he testified that while the Vietnamese probably did have some American remains left to return, there was nothing to indicate they retained any live prisoners. Further, Shields testified that it was unreasonable to expect the Vietnamese or anyone else in Southeast Asia to have perfect knowledge of what happened to every American who had disappeared during the war:

> We know, on the other side of the coin, that there are a substantial number of men who were lost, about whom North Vietnam and its allies have very little information, men who were lost in isolated areas, analogous to airplane crashes in this country in which wreckage and remains are not located for many years.[64]

For their part, league representatives offered testimony on the feasibility of continued MIA survival, attempted to frame the overall debate in terms that presumed survival as the starting point, and especially argued against any policies that could lead to presumptive status changes. League executive director Earl Hopper maintained that not only was the league fundamentally opposed to the idea of presumptive findings of death for MIAs but also it opposed the idea that the relatives of a missing man could request a status review by the military if it could potentially lead to a status change. Hopper argued that even when instigated by next of kin, such reviews violated the civil rights of the missing since they could hardly represent themselves, and that such processes were just an excuse to conveniently move MIAs into the KIA category. He contended that only "factual proof" or an "extensive documented search effort" could justify such a change, though he failed to define exactly what he considered acceptable levels of either.[65]

E. C. "Bus" Mills, the chair of the league's board of directors, made points similar to Hopper's, adding specifically that the traditional status change process abnegated the government's "legal and moral obligations" to the missing and "declaring them dead without substantial proof is not justified and is a violation of the individual rights of that prisoner or missing man."[66] The league position here was clear: these men should be presumed alive unless shown to be otherwise, regardless of how unreasonable that might be for any specific missing man. Since all not proven dead should be presumed alive, the government therefore should continue to search for them and press Vietnam for further accounting. Being even more specific, Mills used the example of a POW by the name of Sparks who supposedly had written his parents about how well he was managing in captivity. Though Sparks did not return during Homecoming, and the Vietnamese claimed to never have held him prisoner, Mills argued his letters demonstrated that "the burden of proof should not be with those parents to prove that he is still alive."[67] To be clear, Mills did not claim that this example demonstrated the existence of secret prison camps, but his argument was premised on Sparks, and others like him, surviving in enemy captivity.

Such presumptions of survival were deeply unrealistic, as the league's board well knew but apparently chose to ignore. Navy lieutenant commander and former POW George Thomas Coker had testified before that body in 1973 about various aspects of the POW/MIA experience. Among other things, he explicitly told the board just how heavily the odds were stacked against anyone whose aircraft went down over the jungle. Presuming the airman's parachute opened correctly, which was not a given, he still risked getting killed by whatever had disabled his aircraft in the first place. If he then made it to the ground in one piece, there were numerous instances of NVA forces, NLF guerrillas, or even enraged locals killing pilots while they attempted to evade capture, or following surrender.[68]

Coker went on to testify that as dangerous as capture was, it was also often the only way a man had even a chance at survival. Men who suffered injuries during ejection or on the ground found the Southeast Asian bush and jungle exceptionally inhospitable, as indeed did even healthy men. Deadly infections set in very easily even for minor wounds, and life-saving treatment could only come from the enemy under such conditions. Even then, death was as real a possibility as survival, as Coker personally attested:

> To give you a very real example of this, is my own case. My leg was injured. It became infected. If I had been 1 week later getting to Hanoi, I don't think I would have lived. When they finally got me there, I had to go to the hospital for an operation—this was 3 weeks later. When they took me in there I thought they were going to cut my leg off. But they cut it all open and drained all the junk out, and they gave me enough medication to overcome it. And I consider myself one of the luckiest medical cases up there. It was a very small injury, really superficial, nothing major—but it became infected. One more week and I would have been dead.[69]

If a man with such minor injuries could barely survive, clearly anyone with more substantial wounds would have far slimmer chances. That the league's board heard this testimony only to ignore it points to how much hope overrode the reality that MIA survival was not likely, or in some instances even possible.

Committee hearings continued through late 1975 and into 1976, with the committee publishing its final report on 13 December 1976. That report did not speak favorably toward there being any real possibility of live American prisoners remaining in Southeast Asia. It recognized that the unaccounted for of all classifications were a very small percentage of those Americans who had served in Southeast Asia throughout the war, and that evidence for their continued survival was cursory and circumstantial at best.[70] The report cited extensive witness and expert testimony when it stated that "the experiences of rescued airmen and returned POWs does little to contribute to the belief that many airmen now missing in Southeast Asia could have survived. Indeed, the record indicates that possibility as very slight."[71]

That report struck even more directly at the hopes of POW/MIA activists and especially secret camp advocates when it pointed out that to date all MIA survival investigations had turned out to be based on evidence that ranged from scanty to entirely fabricated. The committee acknowledged that despite this, family members of the missing might well continue to hold out some hope. Nevertheless, "The committee, therefore, reluctantly concludes that no Americans are still held as POWs and the focus must be on gaining an accounting for men who lost their lives in battle or after capture."[72]

This would have been bad enough in activist eyes had the committee not then gone a step further. The committee recognized not only that there were no more living American prisoners in Southeast Asia but that there likely would not ever be a full accounting for every single man still missing. Having examined how Americans had gone missing, and where, the committee concluded, "A total accounting for all 2,546 Americans who did not return from Southeast Asia is not now, and never will be, possible."[73]

Above all, the conclusions of the Montgomery Committee existed within a narrative of the missing that had functioned well enough in previous wars but was so unsatisfactory to Vietnam's MIA families: the missing belong among the heroic dead, not the victimized living, and it was time to move on. They should be commemorated, mourned, and have their remains recovered if possible, but be no longer frantically searched for:

It would seem correct, then, to pay tribute to all those Americans who served their country in Indochina but failed to return and whose fate is unknown. Theirs was not the task to determine the political and military conditions under which the struggle in Southeast Asia would be waged; rather it was their often thankless task to give of their youth in sweat and blood. They answered the call to fight a difficult and unpopular war in a distant land. They fought with honor and with pride, hoping that through it all they might make possible for others the way of life with which they were familiar and which they loved. In so doing, this report concludes, they paid the ultimate price in service of their country. . . .

It is the final recommendation of this report that a memorial be erected on the grounds of Arlington National Cemetery, and that, after an accounting has been achieved, the name of each man who never returned from that war in Southeast Asia be inscribed thereon, and that appearing above the names be written:

IN GRATEFUL REMEMBRANCE OF THOSE WHO GAVE THEIR LIVES IN SERVICE OF THEIR COUNTRY, AND WHO SLEEP IN UNKNOWN GRAVES. THIS IS THEIR MEMORIAL—THE WHOLE EARTH IS THEIR SEPULCHER.[74]

For all the apparent compassion of its conclusion, the Montgomery Committee findings did little to assuage POW/MIA activists and nothing at all to dissuade true believers in the secret camps. This failure derives more than anything else from a fundamental misunderstanding by that committee as to why the older MIA narrative failed to satisfy families of Vietnam's missing men. As Earl Hopper's testimony shows, the presumption of POW/MIA activism was that the missing were alive until proven otherwise, rather than vice versa. Those activists who were trapped in the no-man's land of grief *needed* the MIAs to be alive, so they necessarily rejected any conclusion that did not support and reinforce that need. What the Montgomery Committee intended to be tribute and memorialization the league and its allies saw instead as dismissal and cover-up, the latter being a particularly strong suspicion in the wake of Watergate. Montgomery himself personifies the older mindset, for though he opened the hearings inclined to believe in MIA survival, he did not presume it or continue to hope for it in the absence of positive evidence.[75] What is more, the Montgomery Committee had failed entirely to grasp the second key feature of the secret camp myth: the heroic recasting of the missing as redemptive victims. The men its report spoke of were definitively dead. Heroic perhaps in their sacrifice, but not sufficiently so to redeem the otherwise compromised national enterprise that was war in Vietnam.

For this failure, many within POW/MIA activism symbolically cast Montgomery aside and vilified him for coming to the wrong conclusions. Some even went so far as to brand him a traitor on par with Jane Fonda and refer to him as "V. C. MontGOMERy," thus to childishly imply that the true sympathies of a man known for physically assaulting antiwar demonstrators actually lay with the communist enemy.[76] League director Ann Mills Griffith avowed that "the conclusion that all P.O.W.'s and M.I.A.'s should be declared dead is ludicrous, particularly in light of recently initiated negotiations between the United States and Vietnam."[77] Another league member, Carol Bates, angrily proclaimed the committee's hearings "inept," and "incompetent," alleging that Montgomery himself spent his time "sitting in his office in Washington, and playing golf in Meridian, Miss[issippi]," rather than actually getting to the truth about live MIAs.[78] Though both stopped short of openly declaring their belief in the existence of secret camps, these two long-time league members clearly felt the Montgomery Committee had abandoned live MIAs to their fate.

Going further than Griffiths and Bates, Bruce W. Most, who had reported on POW/MIA issues through the early 1970s, wrote an editorial for the *Los Angeles Times* in which he argued that the committee's report was "presumptuous at best" and "ignored such blatant cases as that of Navy Lt. Ron Dodge." Though he too did not use the term "secret camps" explicitly, Most did mention "numerous reports" of live Americans being held by the enemy, and he cited a Vietnamese defector who Most claimed said it was "common knowledge" that there were live POWs in Haiphong.[79]

The league's 1976 meeting coincided with the end of the Montgomery Committee hearings and shows how clearly the league had turned against that committee's chairman, even before they had seen the final report. Montgomery attended in person and reviewed the findings of his committee before the league membership present. While he did promise to do everything in his power to ascertain the fate of the MIAs, nevertheless he made the mistake of presuming their death was more likely than survival. Montgomery remarked that "our MIAs lost their lives in service of their nation" and that future accounting efforts must be based on "reason, not emotion, and facts, not rumors."[80] A "concerned citizen" in attendance, Jo Ann Waller, thought Montgomery's speech was merely an attempt to mollify the angry league membership and that "It stinks what's going on here. Only 4 of the 10 members of the committee are here today. Our men didn't ask to go over there to fight, and they didn't ask to be abandoned by the government, either."[81] Other league members reacted even more harshly to Montgomery, with a mother of two MIAs screaming in response to his speech, "You are not God! You are a servant of the people!"[82] Clearly, for some within the league, keeping faith in MIA survival had come to mean literally just that. So too, they expected the "servants of the people" to keep looking for MIAs until the people were satisfied, regardless of how unrealistic it was to expect further live Americans to be found.

This should not be surprising, given those factors that contributed to the birth of the American secret camp myth. Years of well-meaning falsities spoken by comrades of dead men, of government reporting errors and discrepancies, and indeed active deception and manipulation by the Nixon administration, had engendered hopes too great to be denied. Families of the missing could not accept that such hopes had been misguided and their men had almost certainly been dead all along, and so they latched on to the most appealing remaining explanation: the missing must be in secret captivity somewhere in Southeast Asia. Their own government had abandoned them there and could not be trusted to ever bring them home, as demonstrated by the craven betrayal of the Montgomery Committee report. More than anything else save Watergate, that report poisoned any remaining POW/MIA activist trust in official MIA accounting. From this point on, the "cowardly government bureaucrat" stereotype, more concerned with covering up embarrassing realities than getting to the truth, would dominate POW/MIA activist narratives, rising eventually to be as much a villain of the piece as the Vietnamese communists themselves.

However, this is not to say that the rest of the 1970s was a time of renewed vigor for POW/MIA activism generally, or for the league in particular. On the contrary, while opinions did harden and radicalize within that community, external interest diminished as Vietnam fatigue gripped the nation. League involvement in national political contests did not help matters. Particularly damaging for the league was the bitter Republican primary of 1976, in which longtime league ally and original VIVA sponsor Ronald Reagan challenged President Gerald Ford for the nomination. Reagan made MIA accounting a subordinate element of his foreign policy platform, seamlessly if not entirely coherently combining Ford's failure to force an accounting from the Vietnamese with the impending return of the Panama Canal Zone, détente with the Soviets, and normalization of relations with China as all collective signs of weakening American power on the world stage, remediable only via a Reagan presidency.[83] More specifically, he appealed directly to the league for support during the primary season, promising if elected he would appoint a secretary of state to take "every reasonable and proper step" to get the league what it wanted.[84]

Reagan failed in his primary challenge, but that he had included MIA accounting in his platform pulled the league further into his orbit and thus left that group in the unenviable position of having bet on a losing horse.[85] Though temporarily embarrassed by this, the league had by that point a long history with Reagan, who had been part of POW/MIA activism since the war years. That relationship only grew more pronounced as Reagan's political star rose.

For his part, Ford made the mistake of admitting that what the league wanted might just be impossible to deliver. Addressing the league convention himself, he promised that while his administration would continue to "employ every effective means to account for your loved ones," nevertheless, "information for every missing man may never be available."[86] League membership strongly applauded other points in his speech, particularly when he asserted that no normalization of relations with Vietnam was possible without first resolving the MIA issue, but they did not receive him with unqualified zeal.[87] League coordinator for Oregon Barbara Parker, meeting with the president briefly after his speech, informed him that she "didn't think he was doing everything he could" and, after he replied to the contrary, added, "do more."[88]

Beyond national politics, however, America was tired of Vietnam and all the problems associated with it. The POW/MIA movement in general reacted to all these various setbacks by digging in its heels and continuing to insist that Vietnam would never be truly over until the missing had been fully accounted for. Surviving the wilderness years of the 1970s, POW/MIA activism experienced a dramatic revival of fortune and also public visibility in the 1980s. That revival moved belief in the secret camps from being a fringe one within the POW/MIA community to a much more mainstream, popular opinion. Frustrated by the failure of officialdom to resurrect the missing, secret camp advocates discovered new justification for why the black POW/MIA flag should continue to fly high. They were aided in this pursuit by political opportunists who saw in POW/MIA activism a way to rewrite the history of the Vietnam war, as well as charlatans who used the desperate hopes of MIA families to line their own pockets and, somewhat surprisingly, Hollywood's.

◦◦

FIVE

High-Water Mark of
the Secret Camp Myth

The 1980s heralded a revival in national interest in Vietnam POW/MIA affairs and subsequently the secret camp myth as well. Such was the reversal of fortune that those activists who had felt themselves betrayed by the Montgomery Committee in the mid-1970s would regain not only national attention, but also a second congressional inquiry on the matter. Three issues led to this resurgence of interest. First, the Iranian hostage crisis at the end of the 1970s reawakened the image of the prisoner and hostage in the American consciousness. Second was the appearance of lurid allegations that the Vietnamese had secretly warehoused hundreds of sets of American remains. Third, POW/MIA activists embraced a new cinematic subgenre, the POW/MIA rescue film, which gained popularity among the gloriously pulpy action movies of that decade. These three factors combined with a concerted push by right-wing politicians and others to recast POWs and MIAs as American heroes cravenly abandoned by their government, and so attempted to make their heroic suffering the face of the larger Vietnam experience. Such was the revival of interest in the missing from Vietnam that Congress once more launched hearings into the possibility of live POWs and secret camps, only to once more conclude that none of the former still survived and the latter likely had never existed at all.

Prisoners Again: The Iranian Hostage Crisis

In November 1979 radical Iranian students stormed the US embassy in Tehran and seized the staff they found there. This was a moment of particular importance for the revival of both POW/MIA activism and secret camp advocacy as graphic images of subdued Americans being paraded through the streets of Tehran, surrounded by angry crowds, evoked similar images of downed pilots being led through Hanoi. The national media soon noted the thematic similarities between the Iranian hostage crisis and the missing men from Vietnam. As one example, *New York Times* reporter Steven Roberts describes how the entire situation resonated with the American public: "It was as if the whole nation had been blindfolded and hogtied, hauled through the streets of a strange city with people taunting them in a foreign tongue. Americans' sense of futile rage grew even sharper last April after they tried and failed to rescue the hostages."[1]

Roberts here uses language that was already a staple of the POW/MIA community and had been used during the Go Public campaign, such as the pictures of Ron Dodge's capture and humiliation in the "Have You Forgotten Him?" advertisement after Operation Homecoming in 1973.[2] Though not blindfolded in those photos, Dodge is being led through the streets under North Vietnamese guard in a very close match for the American prisoner experience in Iran. So too, the helpless frustration of those earlier league pronouncements ring through in what Roberts calls America's "futile rage."

Roberts goes further to symbolically link the hostage crisis and Vietnam prisoner-rescue failures:

No myth goes deeper in the American character than the belief that good will triumphs in the end, that the cavalry will ride over the hill at the last minute and save the day. Accordingly, the spectacle of American troops, trapped by swirling sand and faulty helicopters in a remote desert, then crashing into one another in their haste to escape, could hardly have been more humiliating . . . *the good guys had lost—again.*[3] (emphasis mine)

Roberts is alluding to a direct antecedent of the failed Iranian hostage rescue. On 21 November 1970, US Special Forces staged a rescue attempt on the North Vietnamese prison at Son Tay, then thought to be the main concentration point of American POWs. While technically spectacular, featuring among other things the deliberate crash-landing of the main assault helicopter within the prison walls to effect the fastest and most violent possible entry, that raid was unsuccessful because the North Vietnamese had evacuated their prisoners days before.[4] Despite their best efforts, the "good guys" had lost, as had their counterparts almost ten years later over the Iranian deserts.

Roberts was not alone in seeing the ghosts of Vietnam interwoven with that more recent crisis. Many Americans saw the failed rescue not just as an international embarrassment but also as a symptom of a more troubling disease that stretched back to Vietnam itself. In this understanding, America's humiliation at Iranian hands was just the latest evidence of a larger national decline that began with the failure to win in Southeast Asia. Kathleen Kennedy, wife of a retired air force officer, told Roberts, "We should have gone in a long time ago, a strong President and a strong Government wouldn't let Iran get away with that."[5] Her husband, Frank Kennedy, voiced similar, bitter sentiments:

> I've lived all over the world, and years ago when I went into the service, the United States had respect in foreign countries. *Then along came Vietnam, and we fought a pitiful war—we wouldn't really let the military fight—and we ended up losing.* I agree with Teddy Roosevelt. Walk softly but carry a big stick. And club the hell out of them if you need to. Our stick is down to a toothpick.[6] (emphasis mine)

Though the Kennedys were not part of the POW/MIA community, their words mirrored those used by others for years. In that viewpoint, Iran's seizure of the US embassy staff would not have been possible if America had not been so humiliated and diminished by the Vietnam War. Indeed, their language was part of a growing chorus that reimagined the United States not so much defeated by Vietnam as defeated by cowards and traitors within the nation.

Some voices went even further than simply seeing POW parallels, linking the Iranian crisis specifically with the secret camp myth. In February 1980 the *Los Angeles Times* published an op-ed from MIA father Wallace S. Wiggins, who argued that the two crises were entirely connected and that he could not understand why everyone was so keen on the fifty Iranian hostages while at the same time they ignored the much-larger number of missing Americans in Vietnam. Wiggins claimed that those men, including his son, were being held in secret captivity by Hanoi, and that the National League of Families of American Prisoners and Missing in Southeast Asia "has obtained sufficient evidence to prove that American prisoners (alive) are being held in Southeast Asia."[7]

The league in particular saw in this shift a clear opportunity to bring its cause back to the forefront of the American consciousness. New York State league coordinator Gladys Brooks noted that publicity on the Iranian crisis resulted in "a great surge of interest in our POW/MIA issue."[8] What is more, family members of the Iranian hostages quickly organized their own advocacy group, the Family Liaison Action Group (FLAG). Commentators at the time noted that group's close resemblance to the early league in both form and function.[9] Among others, President Ronald Reagan referred to the just-returned hostages as "prisoners of war" in his first cabinet meeting in 1981.[10] To be sure, the Iranian hostage crisis existed on its own terms in American politics and popular culture and was not just an extension of half-buried Vietnam neuroses. Nevertheless, those who wished to force POW/MIA issues from that war back to the forefront of the national conversation found it a useful tool.

Them Bones: Remains of the Fallen, Rumors of the Missing

The Iranian hostage crisis reawakened American interest in matters of captive Americans abroad generally, but other specific events appeared to cast new light on the idea of Americans being held in Southeast Asia more explicitly. Refugees had reported any number of supposed live prisoner sightings, but by 1979 there was still no credible evidence confirming their existence. However, late that year one particular refugee came forward with seemingly explosive news of Vietnamese duplicity in the accounting process. Tran Vien Loc, a refugee from Hanoi, testified at the league's annual conference that he had been a mortician in North Vietnam during the war. He claimed to have processed the remains of American personnel through 1975 and to have seen POW/MIA corpses as late as 1977. Only 26 of these latter sets of remains were ever reported to US officials, though Tran claimed more had subsequently been put into long-term storage as future diplomatic bargaining chips.[11] Tran had more sensational news than this, however. While taking questions at that same meeting, he affirmed that he had seen live POWs in his Hanoi office as late as 1974, one year after the supposed return of all live prisoners.[12]

What made Tran's account more believable than prior live sightings, from which nothing useful had been gleaned so far? Unlike those reports here at last was a firsthand account, not some half-remembered viewing-at-a-distance refugee tale told at one or more removes. Tran himself was more compelling a witness as well—not just some penniless refugee but an actual former functionary of the enemy government, albeit one who had operated at a very low level. Whereas Joint Casualty Resolution Center officials like Paul Mathers had despaired in the 1970s of ever getting closer than two or three steps from a live-sighting claim, here was the man himself, in the flesh and ready to testify.

This is not to say that everyone within the league believed what Tran had to say, of course. Most prominently, Dermot Foley, outgoing legal counsel of the league, alleged that the mortician was, in fact, a member of the Vietnamese secret police purposefully spreading disinformation. Foley based this claim on information he had from his client Robert Garwood, the notorious wartime deserter who had only recently returned to the United States and was then standing trial for desertion and collaboration.[13]

Most of the league was nevertheless far more receptive than Foley. Carol Bates, who had expressed belief in MIA survival following the Montgomery Committee report, took such a belief to its logical conclusion and claimed that Tran's evidence finally proved the existence of secret prison camps: "Over the last 18 months, the abundance of reports of live Americans have been enough to convince us that there is substance to our longstanding beliefs there are men held against their will."[14] Going further, Bates argued that there were over "300 first-hand sightings of Americans in captivity," which she considered "overwhelming" evidence of the existence of secret prison camps.[15]

Unfortunately for POW/MIA activists and secret camp advocates, Tran's story broke at the height of the Iranian hostage crisis, in particular just as the daring escape of six American diplomats via a joint US-Canadian operation made headlines. The *Washington Post* spent many pages discussing the hostage rescue but limited its coverage of Tran's supposed revelations to a very modest story occupying a corner of page A13. Even in that small space, the *Post* made no mention of his claim of having seen living prisoners postwar but rather focused on charges leveled by New York congressman Lester Wolff that Hanoi had been warehousing US POW remains.[16] The article also contained a statement from California congressman George Danielson, who, with Wolff, had recently returned from an official trip to Vietnam and was less than convinced of the reliability of Tran's testimony. Danielson believed Tran had "a variety of motives in presenting his account."[17]

Tran's story did eventually gain some momentum. In June 1980 the *San*

Francisco Chronicle ran a story about his appearance before a House sub-committee chaired by Wolff. Tran wore a helmet with an opaque face-shield throughout his testimony, which added more than a touch of spy-thriller sensationalism to the proceedings. This was supposedly a defensive measure to prevent sinister Vietnamese agents from being able to identify him.[18] His actual testimony was less exciting, as Tran merely repeated his earlier claims to have processed as many as 400 sets of US remains by 1977, and identified the facility where this supposedly took place as "the citadel" or "the plantation." Representative Wolff added that his delegation had been barred from visiting a particular former POW complex when it had visited Hanoi in January, heavily implying that that location could also be used to warehouse unreturned remains.[19]

More important for secret camp advocates, Tran crucially reaffirmed that he had seen live Americans in Vietnam after the end of direct US involvement. "I saw three Americans who came into the military law division jurisdiction area," he claimed, as well as giving brief, fairly generic descriptions of the men in question.[20] Though he had not met these alleged prisoners face to face, he claimed they were given "special care" by the Vietnamese administrators and that he had personally seen them "many times" in the body processing area, most recently in 1974.[21] Tran did not explain how he knew these men were actually American prisoners, and no one on the committee ask him to clarify that assumption.

Tran's testimony reinforced a core element of the secret camp myth: the fundamental dishonesty and inherent cruelty of the Vietnamese regime. Pentagon director of East Asia and Pacific affairs brigadier general T. C. Pinckney said that Tran's testimony was further evidence of how the Vietnamese "have stonewalled any meaningful resolution of the [MIA] question."[22] MIA father Charles Walker went further and argued Tran's testimony helped re-awaken the POW/MIA issue in the American public consciousness as it "exposes that claims by the Vietnamese have been absolutely unreliable."[23]

Nevertheless, both sides were seeing in Tran's testimony what they wanted to see and were giving it much greater weight than it deserved. The majority of what Tran had to say was focused on POW remains rather than live prisoners. He was right that Vietnam did use the return of remains as diplomatic leverage from time to time, and so that might seem to lend credence to his live POW claims. The Vietnamese have never denied holding or delaying the return of some American remains, though they have on occasion obfuscated just how long they have had this or that set on hand. However, they have never once acknowledged, and have repeatedly denied, having live prisoners and never made any offer to return live POWs in exchange for anything.

Tran was not that dissimilar from the standard model of "live sighting" witnesses, despite his uniqueness as an alleged firsthand witness of live POWs. He had emerged from within the Southeast Asian refugee community and had parlayed his supposed knowledge of missing Americans for his own ends. His claims were more plausible than the usual live-sighting report but ultimately just as unconfirmable, and he never did substantiate his live prisoner claims.

Regardless of whether Tran had fabricated his story about seeing live POWs, one cannot avoid the fact that others who made similar claims had done so. As was the case in the 1970s, live-sighting witnesses in the 1980s usually came from refugees from the former war zone, and more often than not their motivation was primarily or exclusively financial. Former Royal Laotian Army officer Khambang Sibounheuang was a prime example of this more self-interested type of live-sighting witness. Khambang settled in the United States after the war and made repeated attempts to capitalize on continuing POW/MIA investigations. He approached the Defense Intelligence Agency (DIA) in 1985, offering to assist in POW/MIA accounting in exchange for $4,000, which he claimed would be used to fund the neutralist faction within the Laotian anticommunist resistance.[24] The DIA considered his usefulness suspect and did not take him up on this offer upon learning he had been expelled from the neutralists for malfeasance. Undaunted by this rejection, Khambang resurfaced periodically throughout the late 1980s and into the 1990s, usually in connection with various sensational MIA survival claims. He provided supposed photographic evidence of a survivor to secret camp advocate Senator Robert Smith (R-New Hampshire), which turned out to be an aged Laotian highlander, and subsequently provided a wealth of alleged live POW evidence, all of which the DIA debunked after cursory examination.[25] Not everyone who reported a live sighting was as unreliable as Khambang, but even sincere witnesses failed to provide anything more substantial.

A War Someone Else Lost: Hollywood Refights Vietnam

Though the Iranian hostage crisis may well have reawakened the American consciousness to Vietnam-era POW/MIA issues, and the mortician's report excited and reinvigorated those within the movement, Hollywood provided the final element necessary for the popular articulation of the secret camp myth. No one who paid the slightest attention to the movies of the 1980s can be unaware of the "Vietnam POW Rescue" subgenre of action films. Most big-name action heroes of the period starred in one at some point, from less-likely castings such as Gene Hackman in *Uncommon Valor* to Chuck Norris in *Missing in Action* and its two sequels, to probably the most well-known of them all, Sylvester Stallone in *Rambo: First Blood, Part II.*

As archetypes of the subgenre, these movies all share plot elements seemingly taken directly from POW/MIA activism, with the existence of putative secret camps being only the most prominent example. Their heroes are invariably veterans and usually from Special Forces or some other sort of elite unit. These gritty protagonists are invariably disillusioned with the bureaucratic foot-dragging and cover-up that typifies US officialdom in such films, particularly with regard to live POW allegations. In *Uncommon Valor* this contrast manifests when CIA agents intercept and disarm Colonel Rhodes (Hackman) and his team just as their mission begins. The agency is concerned chiefly with preventing Rhodes from causing an international incident and is not interested in whether there are any POWs to rescue. Undaunted by the loss of his team's state-of-the-art gear, Rhodes rearms his men at bargain-basement rates with World War II cast-offs and goes on to liberate a secret camp. The better-armed, villainous but incompetent Vietnamese guards fall by the dozen before the swaggering heroics of Rhodes's team, which suffers some casualties but wins the day regardless. Not only is Rhodes able to liberate the secret camp and thus prove that the United States abandoned living prisoners in its rush to cut and run, the manner in which he does so demonstrates another key genre element: even at a disadvantage, big strong Americans can always beat the evil Vietnamese communists, if they are only allowed to do so.[26]

Released in 1984, *Missing in Action* portrays this concept even more blatantly, though somehow more clumsily, than *Uncommon Valor*. During the final scene, weak-willed and conciliatory State Department civilians prepare to sign off on an agreement with the oily, villainous Vietnamese communists that the POW/MIA question has been satisfactorily resolved. At the last second, headbanded Colonel James Braddock (Chuck Norris) bursts into the negotiating room with just-rescued POWs beside him, sweeping aside the armed-but-ineffective Vietnamese door guards in a triumphant and redeeming display of unfettered American might.[27] The viewing public was not slow to recognize, and sympathize with, this cinematic reimagining of the reality of the war. William Broyles, who served with the Marines in Vietnam, mentioned this redemptive theme in a 1985 article about his postwar return visit to that country:

> The thought preys on the mind: there may still be some Americans there. Did we commit the soldier's cardinal sin—did we leave comrades on the battlefield? Two recent movies, *Uncommon Valor* and *Missing in Action*, have played upon that nagging doubt and, in bursts of satisfying action, *sent their heroes in to save American POWs and, belatedly, our honor.*[28] (emphasis mine)

In *Rambo* all of these elements reach their apex. The "sinister yet cowardly bureaucrat" archetype inhabits a larger and more directly antagonistic role in the character of Marshal Murdock (Charles Napier), a slimy congressman who radiates insincerity and duplicity. Murdock sends Vietnam veteran Rambo (Stallone) back to Vietnam to get evidence of any living POWs, expecting he will find none. Murdock secretly knows the camps he is sending Rambo to photograph are empty, and he has no intention of really learning the truth about the MIAs. His plan is to "prove" no Americans were left behind and thus provide cover for the government to ignore calls for future searches and rescue attempts. Despite being thus set up for failure, Rambo finds living prisoners and in defiance of orders attempts to extract one against all odds. However, Murdock cravenly aborts a helicopter rescue just when it has come within feet of reaching the imperiled hero. Importantly, Murdock betrays Rambo not out of some villainous conviction but rather from the fear that rescuing American POWs will have political consequences when America learns those men had been abandoned in 1973.[29]

Each of these movies contains the subordinate theme of rescue as validation of American martial prowess and as symbolic victories denied by bureaucratic interference during the actual war itself, as do all other movies within the subgenre. Upon being recruited for the mission by his wartime superior and holdover character from the original *First Blood*, Colonel Sam Trautman (Richard Crenna), Rambo initially responds sarcastically with "do we get to win this time?"[30] This sentiment, coupled with Rambo's unstoppable fury even when underarmed/unarmed and outnumbered, served to further reinforce the same "stab-in-the-back" trope present in *Uncommon Valor* that had long been popular within POW/MIA activist circles, and which was gaining broader acceptance by the 1980s. The POW rescues that occur at the climax of these movies symbolically demonstrate how brave American soldiers could have won the actual war itself, if Washington had not tied their hands. It is no accident that POW rescue movies treat the rescue of MIAs as the symbolic refighting of the war, with America emerging victorious this time around.

There are uglier sides both to these movies and to the new Vietnam narrative they represent. Race plays an uncomfortable role throughout them, with even the "good" Asian characters being subordinate if not downright submissive to the American hero, who towers over them both narratively and often literally.[31] The Vietnamese enemies are invariably vicious, cruel to the fettered POWs, yet militarily incompetent and unable to stand up to unrestrained American valor and firepower. They lack any real martial prowess when it comes to actual combat, despite being brutal sadists in the seemingly mandatory torture scenes. This disparity reinforces the trope that America's real-world defeat came primarily from traitors and weaklings at home rather than from the enemy in the field. Vietnamese camps and hamlets are almost uniformly squalid and backward, and their cities are seedy and run-down in the films' rare urban scenes, such as in *Missing in Action*.[32] Taken together, this heavy-handed subtext exists to suggest to the audience that it should have been easy to defeat such an enemy, so why exactly did America lose? The POW/MIA rescue movies thus demonstrate a unique feature of the American secret camp myth: not only are American POWs the heroic victims of the war but also those heroes could have easily won the war had someone not tied their hands and subsequently abandoned them. The racialized reimagining done in these movies dovetailed with secret camp paranoia of imagined US government complicity in covering up the existence of the secret camps. Though duplicitous and sneaky, the Vietnamese communists surely could never have kept such a matter secret had not cowardly American bureaucrats done much of the obfuscation for them.

Hollywood helped to popularize POW/MIA activism and the secret camps myth in other ways as well. Prominent figures in Hollywood were involved in a series of bizarre private rescue efforts that took place in 1982. Retired Special Forces officer and Vietnam veteran James "Bo" Gritz, a larger-than-life figure who had devoted himself to rescuing any live POWs that might exist, led these two missions, which he rather melodramatically named Operation Lazarus. Gritz argued that he alone could lead any rescue attempts since "both Teddy Roosevelt and John Wayne are dead."[33]

One can only describe his efforts as almost comedically botched. Gritz's team was disorganized and poorly equipped to begin with, and they had barely made it across the border from Thailand to Laos when they blundered into rival Laotian anticommunist guerrillas, whom Gritz mistook for Pathet Lao troops. The guerrillas quickly sent Gritz's team running for their lives under a hail of gunfire.[34] More embarrassingly, Gritz may have had to pay a ransom of $17,500 for one of his own men captured by those guerrillas, though Gritz himself denied that any such ignominy befell the team.[35] It should come as no surprise that no live POWs were encountered during this brief affair, as none were either in a second, equally ineffective attempt Gritz made several months afterward. He delivered none of the photographic evidence he had previously, and loudly, promised to Congress, but he did produce a small collection of remains he claimed were from a dead American POW. Laboratory analysis later determined those bones were actually a mismatched collection from two different Asians and several animals.[36]

There is a deeper connection between Gritz's rescue attempts and the POW rescue movies. Almost as if reading from an early draft of *Rambo,* for which Gritz later claimed to have been the direct inspiration, Gritz himself characterized his actions not just as rescuing prisoners but ultimately redeeming American martial pride.[37] In his own words, Gritz answered criticism of his private rescue missions by arguing, "We are the gladiators—not the arm-chair critics, bureaucrats, politicians and pot-bellied has-beens. . . . There may be [someone] better than us—but where are they? Let them either lead, follow, or get out of the way."[38] Gritz spoke not just along similar lines as the movies but also in the language of the secret camp advocates who argued that cowardly politicians had abandoned live prisoners in the first place.

As tempting as it is to dismiss Gritz's efforts as fantastical and marginal to the larger POW/MIA story, his story has larger connections to the popularization of the secret camp myth, and like the movies that connection runs through Hollywood. According to Gritz, William Shatner paid $10,000 for the film rights to the mission and Clint Eastwood contributed $30,000. Though both men prudently made themselves unavailable for comment during the immediate aftermath of the Lazarus fiasco, their involvement has since been confirmed.[39] More significant, Gritz subsequently claimed to have been in indirect communication with President Reagan, with Eastwood acting as intermediary. In Gritz's version of events, the president spent the raid waiting breathlessly for any evidence of live POWs so he could then inaugurate some nonspecific but presumably overwhelming official military response. Furthermore, Reagan supposedly had assured Eastwood, who had subsequently passed word along to Gritz, that "if you bring out one US POW, I will start World War III to get the rest out."[40]

Whether Reagan ever made so grandiose a promise is unclear, but he did meet with Eastwood prior to the Lazarus raid. According to subsequent White House statements, Eastwood made the president aware of Gritz and his plans. Administration officials advised Reagan not to get involved with anything as flaky as what Gritz had proposed, and the president agreed that the official position on the matter should remain that "These cross-border forays and other independent efforts were discouraged."[41]

Though Reagan may not have endorsed the actions of an unbalanced character like Gritz, he had been connected with POW/MIA activism for years before reaching the White House. As a whole-hearted supporter of the war itself, Reagan was one of the key architects among those seeking to recast the quagmire of Vietnam as a noble cause betrayed by liberal peace-niks. Speaking at the Veterans of Foreign Wars' national conference on 18 August 1980, he expressed ideas very similar to those on display in *Rambo: First Blood, Part II*. Candidate Reagan claimed that the Vietnamese enemy

> *had a battle plan, it was to win on the city streets of America and in our news media what they could not win on the field of battle.* . . . There is a lesson for all of us in Vietnam; if war does come, we must have the means and determination to prevail or we will not have what it takes to preserve the peace. *And while we are at it, let us tell those who fought in that war that we will never again ask young men to fight and possibly die in a war our government is afraid to let them win.*[42] (emphasis mine)

Reagan had long been a devoted believer in MIA survival, and he spoke frequently while in office of his belief that live Americans were still being held in Southeast Asia, according to his national security advisor, Richard Allen.[43] Reagan did not limit such expressions to private conversation. During the official unveiling of the Vietnam Veterans Memorial on Veterans Day, 1984, he spoke of the remaining unaccounted-for men from the Vietnam War, saying, "some [of them] may still be saved."[44] He repeated such sentiments in his 1988 Veterans Day remarks, following his comments about ongoing MIA accounting with "And we have told Hanoi that it must prove to the American people through its cooperation whether men are still being held against their will in Indochina. Otherwise we will assume some are, and we will do everything we can to find them."[45] Reagan's default state here is clear: live prisoners presumably existed in Southeast Asia until Hanoi proved otherwise to his satisfaction.

One can trace the genesis of this belief to Reagan's acting career in the

1950s, specifically when he played the lead in 1954's *Prisoner of War*, a lurid war drama about the experiences of American prisoners during the Korean War. Reagan himself acknowledged the impact that role had and continued to have upon him when addressing a group of former POWs in 1984, saying that the movie was "the only experience I had that was in keeping with what you have gone through."[46] Considering the president by his own admission occasionally confused past movie roles for reality, one wonders how much of an influence that movie had had on his belief in secret camps.

Reagan had been a vocal supporter of the league and a member of VIVA since the war years, and his connection to activism and the secret camp myth is hardly surprising. Moreover, his prominence typifies a trend toward that style of new conservatism that had been growing within POW/MIA activism since the Nixon years. The at-times paranoid rejection of government present within that emerging ideology married well with suspicions within secret camp advocacy that live MIAs had been intentionally abandoned after the war. Similarly, Reagan's oft-expressed sentiments on how government itself was a problem resonated with those within activist groups who suspected previous administrations were intentionally dragging their feet on POW/MIA accounting.[47]

"We Are That Close!": Knaves, Charlatans, and 1980s POW/MIA Hysteria

POW/MIA activism and the league both revived greatly in the 1980s with the help of rousing movies and a sympathetic president, but it must also be said that that activism unintentionally encouraged less savory elements with distinctly less admirable reasons to keep the secret camp myth alive and well. Specifically, individuals and shady organizations preyed upon the more desperate among the families of the missing through the 1980s by claiming to provide services locating and rescuing MIAs. A prime example is Operation Rescue, one of many smaller groups that were less concerned with ascertaining the final fate of the missing and more with cashing in on the distress of MIA families and their supporters. The following mailer sent out by Operation Rescue founder Jack Bailey is typical of this sort of group and how they operated:

Right now an American serviceman is caged like an animal in Southeast Asia. . . . I have spent all of my time and all of my own finances trying to find our POWs. Because time is running out for these men. They suffer from malnutrition and all kinds of disease. Brave American POWs are mistreated and tortured and worked at hard labor from dawn to dusk. They deserve better! . . . That is why I refuse to give up! . . . But I can't do it alone. And frankly, I can't afford to do it much longer. I'm exhausted. I'm broke. And I'm reaching the end of my rope. But, I believe we are very, very close to getting our first POW out. I can't give you any more details. But you may wake up tomorrow morning and hear that the first American POW has been rescued. We are that close![48]

The emotion-drenched language Bailey employed is common among such groups, who regularly evoked bedraggled American POWs in tiger cages, brutally exploited by their vicious communist captors, as the reason why it was so important that people donate as much as they can, as frequently as they can. This specific letter appears handwritten and hastily jotted down, and Bailey claims he has only just returned from some unspecified but no doubt dramatic mission hunting for living prisoners, which is why he lacked time for a more prepared missive.[49] In reality, the mailer was penned in West Virginia, not the most promising location from which to launch secret missions in Southeast Asia. Similarly, Bailey's "headquarters," the supposed rescue ship *Akuna III*, never left dock in Thailand, and there is little to suggest that he was even on board or in Asia all that frequently. Far from patrolling the coast of the former war zone in search of covert POW camps, Bailey's vessel was sarcastically referred to by local fishermen as "the ship that never sails."[50] Virtually all his efforts, and nearly 90 percent of funds raised, were directed toward further fund-raising.[51]

Such efforts could be quite lucrative. There was a considerable amount of money to be made in fostering hopes for survival of missing men in secret camps. Bailey claimed he needed from $20,000 to $40,000 a month to keep the *Akuna III* afloat, though the specific sums he mentioned seem to shift arbitrarily, and he appears to have had few problems getting it despite supposedly being exhausted, broke, and desperate. Eugene "Red" McDaniel's American Defense Institute was another organization that operated along similar lines; it reportedly collected $1.85 million in donations between 1983 and 1984. Yet another was Operation Skyhook II, founded by former congressman and secret camp advocate John LeBoutillier, which managed half a million dollars a year by the mid-1980s, largely from repeat donors.[52] Despite all that money, none of them ever rescued a single American POW from Southeast Asia or provided credible evidence that any existed to begin with.

To its credit, the league considered Operation Rescue and other secret camp organizations like it to be detrimental to legitimate POW/MIA activism. The league's official position on the subject might well have been a broadside directed squarely at Bailey, but it applied equally well to the others:

> Numerous legitimate POW/MIA organizations are helpful to the process; however, emotionally charged, inaccurate information is distributed by a few to gain public support. Some financial appeals graphically portray the alleged captivity environment and imply that the rescue of a live POW is imminent. Distribution of false or misleading information undermines the credibility of the issue which is compelling on its own, requiring no elaboration or distortion. It is important to note that *no* valid information has ever been provided by these groups. The League urges all concerned Americans to seek the facts and support *responsible* efforts to return our missing relatives.[53]

More than just an example of the exploitative nature of POW/MIA activism's shadier fringe, Bailey's fund-raising letter also serves to illustrate a crucial element of the secret camp myth itself: Vietnam's motive. This lack of plausibility was always a major stumbling block for secret camp myth adherents. Why would the North Vietnamese, or anyone else in Southeast Asia for that matter, want to keep secret prisoners once the war was over? The hostage hypothesis continued to predominate, being pervasive enough an idea to make it into *Rambo: First Blood, Part II* itself, where Colonel Trautman angrily proclaims, "We were supposed to pay the Cong $4.5 billion in war reparations! We reneged! They kept the POWs!"[54] Of course, this argument had seen the light of day in the 1970s when President Nixon had gone back on his secret commitment of reconstruction aid as soon as he could find reason so to do.[55] Many secret camp advocates believed that since the United States had failed in its aid obligation, it made sense to assume the Vietnamese had held back some prisoners against such an eventuality.

While the "hostages" idea dominates secret camp motive discussions, Bailey's letter contains a second motivation attributed to the Vietnamese: POWs as slave laborers. Much like the hostages/reparations idea, this was a common plot element in the POW rescue movies, with both *Uncommon Valor* and *Rambo: First Blood* prominently featuring POW slaves in tiger cages. Though there is little evidence for the concept outside of silver screen creativity and vivid imaginations, it was a popular idea second only to the hostages hypothesis. Hollywood's support for the "slaves" idea came not only from within movies but also from celebrity activism on behalf of secret camp myth advocates. Actor Charlton Heston recorded a telephone message for use in Operation Skyhook II's 1984 donation drive promoting this idea. Heston was by the mid-1980s increasingly involved in conservative political and cultural causes, and he chose to associate with Skyhook II since he thought it "defied logic" not to believe that American prisoners survived in secret camps across Southeast Asia.[56] In this recording, Heston spoke as only he could, arguing that

> Many of our men were held behind, they're still there to this day. Locked in bamboo cages in the jungle or in caves in the mountains. Some of our men are used as slaves, forced to drag plows in rice paddies. . . . America can't forget these men. We have to bring them home, all of them. . . . They're ours and they're heroes, real heroes.[57]

The emotional weight of Heston's recording came from how he seamlessly used the "POWs as slaves" idea to promote the "POWs as hero-victims" narrative that had come to dominate POW/MIA activism generally and secret camp advocacy in particular. So too, Heston held that Skyhook II's sort of private action was necessary as both Democratic and Republican administrations had been far too timid on the live MIA front. Heston argued that those prior administrations feared the potential for embarrassment should live American prisoners surface in Southeast Asia. Such an accusation that the government feared how "destructive to international relations" such a discovery might be could well have come from the rationale for abandonment and cover-up espoused by the oily Murdock in *Rambo: First Blood* itself.[58]

Heston's Skyhook II recording has much else in common with Jack Bailey's written appeal. Lurid imagery and emotive appeals lay at the heart of each message, and each used the weight of urgency to manipulate its intended audience into donating. Over and over, these direct mail and phone solicitations pressed home two points: American POWs are suffering unbelievably, and we are so very close to finally rescuing them, if only your dollars keep coming! So too, these sorts of appeals had much in common with the *Rambo*-esque fantasies and ersatz heroics of Bo Gritz, particularly in how they often described in vivid, unrealistic detail the plan to bring the boys home. Another example, this time from a Skyhook II mailer, is also representative of such militaristic daydreams:

Late one evening, as prison-camp guards kick and flog a group of our boys along the trail back to their cages, the last-few Communists in line might be swiftly and quietly dragged into the jungle. Then, a few seconds later, the bedraggled American POWs they were guarding might also vanish suddenly from the rear of the plodding group. The Americans, of course, would now be in friendly hands. (we won't talk about the guards' fate.) In a matter of just a day or two, the rescued Americans would be smuggled across the border to our SKYHOOK II Project group in Thailand. . . . In just a few weeks—for a relatively few thousands of dollars—six, ten, perhaps dozens of these abused and forgotten American servicemen could be brought back to America *and allowed to tell their story to the world!*[59]

As exciting as this plan sounds, and as compelling as Heston's recording likely was, there was little reason to believe any suffering prisoners actually existed. Retired Marine Corps colonel and former director of field operations in Laos of USAID Loren E. Haffner wrote to Senator Daniel Inouye in 1986, adding his voice to those who expressed skepticism on the possibility of MIA survival. Haffner had spent the war years in Southeast Asia and was intimately familiar with the terrain and climate of that region. Citing the inhospitable environs and sparse population of that country, he argued it was exceptionally unlikely that any American prisoner survived in covert captivity. More to the point, he also stated that in the Laotian case in particular, that nation's very basic economy had no need for slave laborers and thus was even less likely to retain live American prisoners after the war.[60]

While advocates offered the "hostages" and "slaves" hypotheses to justify belief in secret camps most frequently, they had others as well. As with much else concerning secret camp advocacy, one finds more than a few conspiratorial and at times downright crazy ideas. To give only a few examples, there was the racist idea that the Vietnamese had retained POWs with technical knowledge to translate operational manuals for them and repair captured US military equipment for their postwar use, since they were too backward and inferior to manage it on their own.[61] Another rationale, sometimes interwoven with the more popular "hostages" concept, was that the Vietnamese had handed some POWs over to the Soviets for intelligence purposes, who returned them to Vietnam months or years after the end of the war. Moving from the implausible to the downright paranoid, there was a companion theory that the missing men had been transferred to Soviet brainwashing facilities, presumably deep in Siberia, for conversion into "Manchurian Candidate"–style sleeper agents for communism.[62]

Black Flags over Washington: The Political Zenith of the Secret Camp Myth

Regardless of why they believed in the secret camps, adherents of the myth were undeniably very dedicated to the cause. They rode the rising tide of POW/MIA activism and its cinematic popularity to once more put their issue on the forefront of American politics in the late 1980s. President Reagan was already a longtime ally of the league and other groups, but he was not alone among politicians who supported the idea of live Americans in Southeast Asia. Other officials found ways to express their solidarity with activists and secret camp advocates, usually through legislation focusing on displays of the black POW/MIA flag. In 1988 that flag was raised for the first time over the White House on National POW/MIA Recognition Day, and the following year it was displayed in the rotunda of the US Capitol. Congress easily passed legislation authorizing such a display—House Congressional Resolution 28 and its analog Senate Congressional Resolution 9—each with strong bipartisan support.

Solidarity with POW/MIA activism appears to have mostly cut across partisan lines, at least when it came to symbolic expressions of support.[63] However, congressional support for secret camp advocacy tended to come from the political right. Representatives Robert Dornan (R-California) and William Hendon (R-North Carolina) both lobbied Reagan in 1985 on the grounds that he was being fed false information about the existence of live POWs, in whom they both believed.[64] A year later, a POW task force of six members of Congress, headed by Hendon and Dornan, wrote to the president that "Our analysis of data is now complete. Based on the extensive classified briefings we have received and clarity of information we have seen, we write to inform you that American POWS remain captive in communist prisons in Southeast Asia."[65] The task force report used other language also common to secret camp advocacy: "We are firm in this belief and have not been, nor will be, dissuaded by the arguments to the contrary made by bureaucrats who have handled this issue since the end of the Vietnam war."[66] Five of the six members comprising this task force were Republican, with Representative Frank McCloskey of Indiana being the sole Democratic voice.[67]

Indeed, by the 1980s the POW/MIA lobby had grown considerably from the wives' support group it had been during the war years, and it wielded considerable influence on Capitol Hill. Representative Paul McCloskey (R-California), a member of the House Select Committee on Missing Persons in Southeast Asia, predicted this ascension back in 1976 when he commented, "No one's got the guts to tell these people there's no *rational* basis to believe any of these men are still alive."[68] Though McCloskey was a few years early, he was nevertheless entirely correct in describing *why* POW/MIA activism was so powerful in the 1980s: despite lacking any solid basis for their claims, their constituency had grown so large and wielded a message of such emotional weight that opposing it was more trouble than it was worth.

Moreover, their message dovetailed easily with those who wished to redefine the Vietnam experience into something positive and redemptive. During the 1976 congressional session, Representative Leon Panetta sponsored legislation that would require US diplomatic and consular posts to display the POW/MIA flag. Panetta argued that requiring that flag to fly would both act as a symbol of the nation's continuing commitment to the missing and also serve to lessen any feelings of abandonment felt by their families.[69] His bill died in the House Foreign Affairs Committee following unfavorable comments from the State Department, but it was an early example of the growing popularity of the POW/MIA flag, prefiguring its emergence as a dominant symbol of the war itself.[70] To be clear, Panetta was not a secret camp advocate himself, but his championing of the POW/MIA flag demonstrates how the promotion of POW/MIA causes generally unintentionally served secret camp advocacy.

Congressional discussions surrounding POW/MIA activism in the late 1980s illustrate how symbols of POW/MIA affairs and the secret camp myth were making that transformation, while other less comfortable aspects of the war either slid into the national subconscious or were forgotten entirely. The language used in those debates shows how potent secret camp imagery was at the end of that decade:

> I think the placing of a flag in the Capitol rotunda today will be a very fitting and proper Reminder to all Americans that we in Congress and we as a nation have not forgotten the POW's and MIA's and will not forget them as long as they remain missing and unaccounted for.[71]
>
> It is a symbolic reminder that we have not forgotten those men who are still missing in action over a decade after the end of the war in Indochina, and it will enable us to serve notice to the Vietnamese that so long

as we have not received a full accounting of the fate of those men it will be difficult to actually formalize our relationship with them.[72]

To see that black flag with that handsome symbolic face, head bowed because of the tragedy of the issue, not because the spirit of any fighting man that may be alive is broken, the 400 boxes of our heroes [sic] bones in some couple warehouses somewhere in Hanoi or the outskirts thereof, someday those remains of our heroes will come home.[73]

Admittedly, some of this rhetoric surely derives from that instinct to grandstand present within the souls of all legislators, but it would be a mistake to dismiss it wholly as such. Though these pronouncements all speak solely about accounting for the missing and bringing the bodies home, they nevertheless feed into a narrative necessary for the existence of the secret camp myth: Vietnam has not fully accounted for the missing, and the war could never be fully laid to rest without it having done so.

By the early 1990s it was undeniable that the POW/MIA lobby and its secret camp advocates had restored any influence lost during the early to mid-1970s. According to a *Wall Street Journal* poll, 69 percent of Americans then believed that live prisoners were being held in secret camps, and three-fourths of those surveyed thought the government was not doing enough to bring them home.[74] With such popular belief behind them, secret camp advocates were only waiting for an excuse to explode once again onto the national scene. They found their moment in 1991 when President George H. W. Bush announced a "Road Map" for normalization of relations between the United States and Vietnam. This plan consisted of four separate stages, with each stage contingent on Vietnam making "satisfactory" progress on the cases of men still unaccounted for, but even the mere idea of normalization was enough to provoke reaction from the POW/MIA lobby as a whole and from its congressional supporters in particular.[75]

Specifically, a cabal of Republican senators led by Jesse Helms released a document entitled *Examination of US Policy toward POW/MIAs* under the official heading of the Foreign Relations Committee on which Helms sat but for whose permission he somehow forgot to ask.[76] This sensationalist screed had been constructed largely by Helms's staffers and purported to contain reams of apparently overlooked evidence of POW/MIA survival, not merely from Vietnam but also from any number of other conflicts in which the United States had fought during the twentieth century. Going much further than any Defense Department estimates, that report alleged that thousands of American prisoners survived in secret camps. Finally, it fully embraced the conspiratorial mindset pervasive among the fringes of POW/MIA activism by claiming that the government was actively covering up evidence of surviving prisoners, for reasons as provocative as they were vague.[77]

Upon sober reflection, the *Examination* proved to be almost entirely groundless. It contained evidence that was circumstantial at best and was riddled with errors and outright lies at worst.[78] Testifying under oath, Deputy Assistant Secretary of Defense Carl Ford stated of the hundred-plus-page document, "There are numerous other factual inaccuracies throughout the report. To catalog the inaccuracies would require a document of equal length."[79] Helms later attempted to disavow his own involvement in the *Examination* once he could no longer deny the flaws in his staffers' work, going so far as to sack longtime aide James Lucier and POW investigator Tracy Usry.[80]

Such repudiation took time, of course, and the initial sensational impact of the *Examination* was more than enough to provoke a media circus. Allies of POW/MIA activism were quick to capitalize on such publicity. Long-time secret camp advocate Senator Bob Smith sensationally released three photographs of several alleged live US POWs—John Robinson, Albro Lindey, and Larry Stevens—shortly after the publication of the *Examination*. Two more, supposedly of Daniel Borah and Donald Carr, appeared subsequently. Taken together with the *Examination*, these photos created more than enough public pressure to ensure passage of Smith's resolution creating a Senate Select Committee.[81]

That committee's hearings proved to be the high-water mark of POW/MIA activism and the secret camp myth in the United States. Chaired by Vietnam combat veteran Senator John Kerry and including other veterans and POWs such as Senator John McCain, the Senate committee examined material from the earlier Montgomery Committee hearings and also new evidence that had surfaced in the meantime. This included material that the *Examination* purported to have uncovered, as well as other sources. Much of the *Examination* had been debunked in the months between its release and the convening of the Senate Select Committee, and most of what remained withered under close examination.

The sensational photos allegedly of Robinson, Lindsey, Stevens, Borah, and Carr turned out in short order to be completely fraudulent. Notorious POW/MIA con man Jack Bailey, founder of Operation Rescue, was responsible for their creation. Bailey faked the Robinson, Lundy, and Stevens photograph by altering an image he found in a 1989 issue of *Soviet Review*, and the man he claimed to be Donald Carr was in fact an East German rare birds dealer, who was himself serving a prison sentence for fraud at the time of the Senate hearings.[82] In addition, no one ever confirmed any of the new "live sightings," though in those instances the committee did not dismiss them out of hand. The committee found that live sightings were troublesome for the same reason as had earlier investigators. Such reports suffered from the unreliability of refugee memories as well as a new complication: by the early 1990s European and American tourists were much more common in Vietnam and were even more easily mistaken for POWs than had been the Soviet bloc visitors of the 1970s.[83]

It is perhaps less than surprising the Senate Select Committee had to debunk any number of frankly ludicrous ideas and conspiracy theories throughout the hearings, in addition to the more serious work it performed. Committee chair Kerry personally felt the need to refute claims of something called Operation MIA Hatchet Squad. This shadowy organization supposedly operated within the government to prevent the rescue of live POWs, or to brainwash those who did make it back to keep their story under wraps.[84] While such an idea sounds like something taken from a bad spy thriller, such concepts were part and parcel of the POW/MIA activist fringe by the early 1990s. In 1987 self-proclaimed special operations hero Scott Barnes made a very similar claim in his book *BOHICA*, with considerable innuendo but little convincing evidence. Barnes was by all accounts dishonest even by the standards of the grifters who lurked around the edges of POW/MIA activism, and at times he claimed to have been a secret agent variously of the CIA, DIA, DEA, and FBI, among many other things. In *BOHICA* he claims to have personally found live POWs, only to be stopped from rescuing them by sinister agency men out to conceal the truth. Needless to say, this owes less to actual experience in Southeast Asia than to opportunism and a particularly active imagination.[85]

More prominent figures than Barnes made similar arguments, though none managed to substantiate their claims with any greater success. Senator Bob Smith claimed to have accumulated evidence over fifteen years that proved the existence of an undisclosed compound in Hanoi that contained about 200 live American POWs. According to Smith, this prison was dug deep underground, right next to Ho Chi Minh's tomb, which he acknowledged sounded like "something out of a Tom Clancy novel" but nevertheless insisted was true.[86] He ultimately offered little new evidence on the subject, however, and the DIA wrote off such claims in part because the Hanoi water table would not permit the excavation such a structure would require.[87]

More serious testimony significantly damaged both the conspiratorial claims about secret camps and the long-standing league argument that Vietnam was not living up to its obligations in accounting for the missing. Former chair of the Joint Chiefs of Staff and Reagan-era special presidential emissary to Hanoi John W. Vessy Jr. testified that the accounting efforts he had overseen were moving well, and league claims that Vietnam was hoarding vast amounts of POW remains were at best greatly exaggerated.[88] League president Ann Mills Griffiths's attempts to deflect this assertion met with little success, as the committee sided with "the guys in the field, on the team doing the work who do not believe they are holding remains."[89] To Kerry, the league seemed to "not want to see progress."[90]

To their dismay, the league and other groups found that the Senate hearings did not differ substantively from the House hearings of 1975–1976, despite what seemed on first impression to be a mountain of explosive new evidence of MIA survival. Unlike the Montgomery Committee, the Senate Select Committee did admit that "There is evidence, moreover, that indicates the possibility of survival, at least for a small number, after Operation Homecoming."[91] So too, it paid requisite tribute to the sacrifice of the missing and their families and couched its conclusions in less definitive language than had the Montgomery Committee.

On first inspection this would otherwise appear to be a modest win for POW/MIA activists, who had campaigned so long against the idea that the missing ought to be presumed dead in the absence of other evidence. However, those statements were merely prelude to the committee's larger conclusions, which were far less favorable. Even on their own terms, the committee's use of the phrase "indicates the possibility of survival" was conditional in the extreme, particularly as it only even granted that possibility for "a small number" of POWs, not hundreds or thousands. What is more, the committee's report went further in dashing any hopes that might otherwise be raised. Like their House colleagues before them, the senators who sat on the select committee had hoped to discover evidence of surviving American MIAs, but:

Unfortunately, our hopes have not been realized. This disappointment does not reflect a failure of the investigation, but rather a confrontation with reality. While the Committee has some evidence suggesting the possibility a POW may have survived to the present, and while some information remains yet to be investigated, *there is, at this time, no compelling evidence that proves that any American remains alive in captivity in Southeast Asia.*[92] (emphasis mine)

The ubiquity of the black POW/MIA flag demonstrates how fully that image and what it represents continues to dominate the American cultural narrative about the Vietnam War.

Hardcore believers argued that this second official negative result only further confirmed the existence of a government cover-up. Senator Smith, who had reluctantly signed off on the committee's findings, still argued, "I believe that there is evidence that people survived after 1973 and may be alive today. There is evidence, but not enough to prove it."[93] Smith would, later that same year, take to the floor of the Senate to accuse DIA witnesses of perjury, much to the consternation of his former committee colleagues.[94] However, for the most part mainstream America accepted the committee's findings and turned its back on the hysteria that had brought the whole matter into public view in the first place. This is not to say that the league, POW/MIA activism, or even the secret camp myth itself died out following the conclusion of the Senate Select Committee hearings, however. Indeed, all three are still very much alive, but none are as powerful within the American public narrative as they once were. They owe a large part of this decline to those hearings, as well as to the unfortunate involvement of POW/MIA activism in league patron H. Ross Perot's quixotic and at times entirely bizarre 1992 presidential campaign. Proving some things are too crazy to fade away, Scott Barnes resurfaced during that campaign and claimed that members of George H. W. Bush's staff planned to ruin the wedding of Perot's daughter by circulating doctored pornographic photographs of her at the event. Perot was somehow convinced by Barnes's claims and temporarily suspended his campaign as a result.[95] Perot was a long-time supporter of POW/MIA activism, and association with his much-publicized odd behavior on the campaign trail made that activism seem even less serious than had the various conspiratorial claims aired during the Senate hearings.

The 1990s was not, however, a time of collapse for the league or secret camp advocacy, though both never fully recaptured the dynamism or relevancy they had in the 1980s. Though Perot's campaign had made more obvious POW/MIA activism's links with the politics of the weird, it had also served to keep it in the public eye, and by casting himself as the sole champion of America's abandoned men Perot successfully appealed to cultural conservatives who might well have otherwise won George H. W. Bush's reelection.[96] Though no longer able to command congressional or presidential attention, belief in secret camps has proven remarkably persistent across the American political landscape.

You Are Not Forgotten: Persistence of the American Secret Camp Myth

While Vietnam-era POW/MIA activism and the secret camp myth no longer claim nearly the national prominence they once did, both do survive to this day and show little sign of disappearing entirely. Both have achieved this remarkable longevity by becoming virtually synonymous with that war itself, at times even coming close to obliterating all other aspects of Vietnam. There are few better symbols of this transformation than that of the POW/MIA flag, as potent an image today as it was when it first appeared back in 1971. The following advertisement ran in the 20 October 2013 issue of *Parade Magazine*: "Get your FREE Vietnam War 50th Anniversary Coin," reads the ad's headline.

It should be emphasized that this ad ran not in some POW/MIA-specific magazine or newsletter but as a supplement to the Sunday edition of the *Boston Globe*. In that ad's own words, the POW-MIA image now stands without qualification for the war itself and "pays tribute" to all "the men and women who served" during the Vietnam War, not merely that small minority that were captured or lost.[97] Other aspects of the war are subsumed behind the black silhouette of a soldier imprisoned behind the wire, all other experiences of the war overshadowed by that of the forever prisoner and the eternally missing man. While those men "are not forgotten," the larger realities of the Vietnam War disappear in this retelling. By focusing on America's reminted hero victims, such emphasis necessarily diminishes all the others who fought in that conflict. Other American veterans now play a secondary role, and the Vietnamese themselves are almost entirely absent, save as the villains responsible for the suffering of those POWs and MIAs. By inflating the real suffering of POWs and conflating it with the entire war experience, secret camp advocates thus appropriate the actual victimization of the Vietnamese and recast the United States as victim of its own war. At the same time, by connecting the continued existence of the secret camps with refusal by their own government to rescue surviving MIAs, those advocates not only reject American responsibility for the war, they also reject the reality of the defeat itself.

Conclusion

What, ultimately, do these two case studies reveal about the secret camp myth itself? Both are examples of postwar reconceptualization of morally ambiguous defeats. West Germans and Americans found the idea of secret camps useful, for reasons both personal and national. Personally, belief in secret camps constituted an escape hatch for those trapped in the no-man's land of grief. Civilians who could not bring themselves to mourn missing men in the absence of positive proof of death clung to the idea of MIA survival in those secret camps. Nationally, POW/MIA activism transformed prisoners and the missing into nationally redemptive heroic figures by emphasizing their victimization at enemy hands. Secret camp advocates within POW/MIA activism took this trend to its logical conclusion by asserting that the missing still survived, and still suffered, in those secret camps. The process by which these individuals and organizations transformed prisoners and the missing into hero-victims also served to recast the nature of the war and mute—even reject—the verdict of defeat. All the while, they appropriated the suffering of wars they started onto their POWs, and especially onto the men purported to be alive in the secret camps.

For all the commonality between the two examples, it is undeniable that only one of them persisted long beyond the end of its war. More interesting, it was the less plausible example that lasted while the more believable one faded from public consciousness in a relatively short period of time. Here, the differences between the German and American cases best illustrate why the one disappeared and the other survived.

Both the United States and Germany fought their respective wars with draftee armies, and in both cases that practice had been the norm for years. However, despite this similarity each nation's missing came from very different segments of their overall populations. Germany's POWs and MIAs came from a broad spectrum of German society and from the many ranks within the German military, with most of those men coming from the working classes.[1] America's missing from Vietnam came largely from officers in the air services, and as a result tended to be career men from at least the established middle class.[2] As a result, America's missing mostly came from a demographic used to political prominence and to receptiveness from its government.

The two examples diverge as well with regard to casualties, both in absolute number of men lost and the ratio of POWs/MIAs. As of the end of direct American involvement in Vietnam in 1973 there were 1,290 men unaccounted for in one way or another following Operation Homecoming.[3] These men constituted a tiny fraction of overall American casualties, and an even smaller one of the over 3 million Americans who served in one capacity or another in Southeast Asia during the war. Contrarily, somewhere between 540,000 and 1.3 million Germans were either Soviet prisoners or missing on the Eastern Front in May 1945, according to their own estimates—and over double that according to the Soviets.[4]

This difference in numbers of prisoners, both real and imagined, contributes to another distinction between the two examples: plausibility of MIA survival. There was little to suggest American MIAs could survive long in the Southeast Asian jungles even if they escaped their aircraft uninjured, particularly given the hostility of the environment. As US Marine Corps pilot and jungle survival instructor lieutenant colonel Pat Caruthers observed, "If a man's not found within 10 days, he's got a real personal problem."[5] This is not to say that survival for missing men in the vast spaces of the Soviet East was particularly easy, of course, especially during the winter, but here another factor comes into play that allowed missing Germans greater chances of surviving to go into captivity: the different nature of the wars in question. World War II in Europe was a conventional conflict fought primarily on the standard Western model, with large armies maneuvering against one another across the European continent. As a result, German MIAs tended to go missing in areas where those armies operated and had correspondingly better chances of being located by one side or the other. Of course, the genocidal behavior of German armed forces made capture that much riskier for their soldiers, particularly if they fell into partisan hands, but this was a risk that American fliers ran as well, with any number being killed upon reaching the ground either by NVA or NLF troops or by enraged Vietnamese civilians.[6] Unlike their German counterparts, however, those American fliers were much less likely to be found in the first place, as they fought their war for the most part in the remote, heavily jungled regions of Southeast Asia, with much sparser populations and fewer, if any, regular military formations in operation.

Of course, none of this would have mattered if not for one of the most important similarities shared by the two examples: for both the United States and Germany, their wars were nationally traumatic defeats. What is more, both wars did not create satisfactory war hero figures among their returning veterans. In the American example this was largely due to the unpopularity of the war within the shifting social narrative of America's tumultuous 1960s and early 1970s, and in the German case it was due to how the military was tarnished by its embrace of Nazism. This is not to say that the US military had not compromised its own image in Vietnam, of course. Massacres and atrocities marked its long engagement in Southeast Asia, of which My Lai is merely the most well-known. Indeed, Americans at the time even compared it, and by extension other such atrocities, to Nazi behavior. An eyewitness described part of that incident as "They had them in a group standing over a ditch—just like a Nazi-type thing. . . . One officer ordered a kid to machine-gun everybody down, but the kid just couldn't do it. He threw the machine gun down and the officer picked it up," clearly echoing the style of mass killings practiced by SS-Einsatzgruppen and others on the Eastern Front.[7]

Though much more common than most contemporary accounts of the war are willing to admit, atrocities in Vietnam were not official policy, though they may have been the inevitable consequences of official policy, as they were for the German military on the Eastern Front, and there is no American equivalent of Generalplan Ost. Nevertheless, such crimes left irreparable stains on both militaries, making returning veterans unsuitable figures for national veneration, regardless of personal complicity. As a result, civilians in both nations turned to POWs and MIAs to find suitable substitutes for the traditional war hero. Recasting such men as hero-victims allowed their advocates to reconceptualize the larger meaning of the wars and so by proxy move themselves from the ranks of the perpetrators to those of the victims.

POW returnees and the alleged live MIAs also shared another important characteristic that made their transformation that much easier in both examples. Unlike the traditional war hero, who won acclaim via daring deeds and heroic achievement, advocates considered POWs and MIAs heroic not for what they did but for what they endured. Their suffering and passive resistance redeemed not only whatever wartime sins they might have committed but also those of their larger nation. Ideology undeniably played a role in this as well, as both Americans and West Germans lauded their POW returnees for holding strong and not falling prey to insidious communism while behind the wire. The American case demonstrates this ideological angle in how the POWs themselves were on guard during their captivity against "rat finks" selling out their comrades to the North Vietnamese in exchange for lighter treatment.[8] West Germans went even further in both celebrating POWs' resistance to enemy ideology and punishing those thought to have violated acceptable norms of prisoner behavior via the Kameradenschinder trials in the late 1940s.[9]

Both examples demonstrate the conceptual transformation of POWs/MIAs into war heroes in how each nation treated its returning POWs as opposed to other veterans. In both examples, POW returnees experienced celebrations upon their repatriation, although in the German case this only applied to later returnees. Such behavior manifested itself in legislative efforts such as the 1950 Heimkehrergesetz that granted economic and transitional assistance to returnees. Since it was passed after veterans and POWs had come home from all other theaters, as well as after the end of regular repatriations from the USSR, that law clearly targeted those remaining prisoners in Soviet custody, including the live MIAs supposedly surviving in the silent camps.[10] Similarly, Operation Homecoming lavished benefits and reintegration assistance upon 591 returnees far beyond anything offered to ordinary Vietnam veterans.[11]

Despite such managing and glad-handing of returning POWs, both West Germans and Americans found those men to be occasionally inconvenient or imperfectly suited to their prescribed roles as redemptive figures. Even though these men had successfully resisted political contamination for the most part, on occasion they displayed other behavior incompatible with what was expected of them. Not for nothing had Operation Homecoming officers gone out of their way to spin returnee press appearances and to warn family members not to push too hard about what their man had actually gone through, thus to keep inconvenient realities from intruding upon the constructed triumph of POW repatriation.[12] Similarly, West Germans feared the dystrophic effects of prolonged imprisonment on their returnees, from whom they expected a restoration of traditional morals, and sought to minimize exposure of any potentially embarrassing behavior on the part of returned POWs.[13]

POW returnees did serve the purposes laid out for them despite these potential handicaps, but both Americans and West Germans considered MIAs to be better figures for heroic transformation. The very ambiguity of their missing status made them blank canvases, ideal for crafting this new heroic archetype. Presumed alive in the secret camps, surely their suffering was worse than even the known POWs, which served a redemptive role in advocates' telling. However, unlike POWs they never came home, never revealed personal shortcomings or contrary political opinions, never forced any uncomfortable confrontations with the realities of war.

The American example of this sort of behavior went much further than the German one, though, as indeed did belief in the secret camps overall. The German secret camp myth helped West Germans think of themselves as victims of World War II, but the American version took such a belief to its logical extreme and instead denied the very reality of defeat. By the time the American myth reached its apex in the late 1980s, it treated the return of the missing as the symbolic refighting of the war itself, only with America "being allowed to win this time," to paraphrase the myth's most prominent cinematic avatar.[14] Moving beyond snappy action movie one-liners, President Reagan allegedly said he would "start World War III" to bring out any live prisoners, if anyone could prove their actual existence.[15] The source of this alleged statement is admittedly less than reliable, but it speaks to sentiments among American secret camp advocates regardless by demonstrating how they viewed POW rescue as a way to win "a war someone else lost."[16]

Unlike the German myth, the American secret camp myth and indeed American POW/MIA activism generally had always carried within it the idea of prisoner repatriation as a marker of victory. The actual POW return in 1973 was tailor-made to encourage feelings of accomplishment and triumph. It built upon the Nixon administration's careful work that treated POW return and MIA accounting as the justification for continued US involvement in the war itself. Operation Homecoming attempted to take this justification to its conclusion and treat the 1973 repatriation as a victorious moment, signaling the culmination of Nixon's "peace with honor" and thus engineering a triumphant exit from the quagmire of Vietnam. Since that manufactured victory was short-lived, with Nixon shortly thereafter exiting the White House in disgrace and South Vietnam collapsing a mere two years later, those who sought to redeem the war turned to the remaining MIAs. Going further than German secret camp advocates ever had, American advocates equated the return of those men, whom they argued were alive in secret camps, with symbolically winning the lost war.

The manner in which each nation's POW/MIA movement developed also contributed to the differences in each myth. In Germany, POW/MIA activism did not emerge until very late in the war, and relatives of the missing were unable to act collectively until afterward. German civilians lacked the social and political space to seek information on the missing during the war, and they were hardly encouraged so to do by a totalitarian regime that considered living German POWs in the East contrary to Nazi hero cult ideology.[17] Even if they had enjoyed the political freedom to act, Germany was increasingly under direct attack from strategic bombing and advancing fronts as the war went on, and as a result personal survival became more and more a concern for civilians, further inhibiting the development of German POW/MIA activism during the war. This did not prevent individuals from doing what they could to discover what had happened to their missing relatives, but it severely restricted their avenues to do so and entirely inhibited the creation of advocacy groups. By contrast, American civilians enjoyed the twin luxuries of First Amendment freedoms and an inviolate home front during the Vietnam War. Unlike their German counterparts, those Americans were able to organize well before the end of that war, as indeed they did with the formation of the organization eventually known as the National League of Families of American Prisoners and Missing in Southeast Asia.

Though beginning at different times, both examples of POW/MIA activism have a common starting motivation. In both cases, early activism was informational and centered mainly on discovering the actual status of the missing. Whether furtively and individually as in the German case, or openly and collectively as in the women of the League of Wives of American Prisoners in Vietnam, relatives of the missing sought to discover their fates. In both cases, they at least initially received little, if any, assistance from official sources. German family members had to contest with WASt's intentional obstruction and obfuscation during the war, which was designed to get around the ideological problem of live POWs by denying their existence, as well as with the chaos of defeat and occupation afterward. American family members had similar though less trying difficulties dealing with US military sources who kept them at arms' length, due both to the Johnson administration's decision to downplay POW/MIA issues and to a traditional military culture that tied officers wives' status to that of their husbands.

As MIAs existed in an ambiguous nonspace somewhere between KIAs and known POWs, those wives were therefore both starved of information on their missing husbands and socially isolated. Unlike their German counterparts, however, they had the social space and resources necessary to organize on their own initiative.

The ambiguity that lies at the heart of the MIA status is another key commonality that motivated proponents of both secret camp myths. Specifically, both German and American relatives of the missing found themselves trapped by a "refusal to mourn."[18] Caught in the no-man's land of grief, these family members endured incredible stress and, in some instances, embraced any possible justification to keep hope alive. The pleading nature of information requests sent to the BMVT after the war and the well-publicized accounts of their American equivalents demonstrate how traumatic this could be. As *Life* magazine reporter Loudon Wainwright perceptively commented, "'The Grief Cycle' can only end for many of them with *knowing what happened*, and that information is often tragically elusive. The slightest glimmer of hope sets off the Yo-Yo of anguish and expectation."[19] Many of those so trapped found the possibility of secret camps almost irresistibly alluring, as they allowed believers to avoid having to face the unendurable: mourning a loss they could not accept as real.

In both examples as well, the POW/MIA activism that spawned secret camp advocacy only really gained national significance when prominent political figures embraced them, and in both cases the relevant figures did so as a way to harness those movements' potential to their own causes. In West Germany, Chancellor Konrad Adenauer found POW/MIA activism a useful tool in cementing the legitimacy of the Christian Democratic Union in the political landscape of his new country, as well as in service of his foreign policy toward the Soviet Union. In the United States, President Richard Nixon found in the league a way to peel support away from the antiwar movement, and also a sympathetic bloc whose POW/MIA interests could be seconded to his war plans. In trumpeting as loudly and frequently as possible how important POW return and MIA accounting were, Nixon perceived a "safe" way to prolong the war he was determined not to end on peacenik terms.

However, only one of the examples persisted well beyond the end of its war. The crucial difference lies in how the politicizations of both myths reached their natural conclusions: one was able to satisfy its constituency while the other was not. West Germans always knew that there were some live prisoners in Soviet custody, if for no other reason than that the Soviets openly admitted to retaining convicted war criminals after the end of repatriations in 1949. What they did not know was how many MIAs were among them, as well as who all these prisoners were, and where they were kept. The "secret" of the Soviet secret camps lay in the silence about their number and population, not in their existence. Even though the hoped-for hundreds of thousands of live MIAs never materialized, substantial numbers of these remaining prisoners did come home in 1953–1954 and 1955–1956.[20] The return of these men appeared to confirm the basic premise of the German secret camp myth, satisfied its adherents that they had done their bit for suffering heroes, and by so doing validated what could be redeemed from the war experience for Germany itself. Coupled with the larger economic recovery of West Germany and readmittance of the state into the community of Western Europe, such a success allowed for any remaining question of MIAs and indeed the war itself to slide quietly from the forefront of German national consciousness, not to reappear until the cultural clashes of the 1960s and again with the Wehrmachtsausstellung of the early 1990s. Even with those later reexaminations of the war and the role of Germany's military in the Nazi state, discussions of secret camps and MIAs did not revive, as prior late repatriation had allowed West Germans to stop hoping for impossible resurrections, admit that remaining MIAs were indeed dead, and move on to mourn at last.

Contrarily, the American secret camp myth did not find a satisfactory conclusion. Operation Homecoming only returned a comparative handful of the thousands of MIAs whom POW/MIA activists believed potentially still alive, due to manipulation of casualty reporting and overrepresentation of the missing by the Nixon administration. Evidence from Watergate revealed how that administration had inflated the number of potential live POWs and lied about where and when servicemen had been lost, but this did not convince POW/MIA activists that the core idea of large-scale MIA survival was a hoax. Rather, they concluded that the men were clearly still alive and that Nixon had just been lying to them about his desires to bring them home, not about their actual existence. This entrenchment of distrust came precisely at the moment that the more reasonable among American POW/MIA activists, who might have moderated such paranoia, were leaving the cause. Those who got their men back during Operation Homecoming, or who were able to accept that the missing were likely dead, largely departed the league and other advocacy groups just as those who were too desperate or self-interested to accept the likelihood of MIA death came to the forefront. Supported in such beliefs by opportunistic politicians, parasitic conmen, and Hollywood hysteria, secret camp advocates survived not one but two congressional inquiries that found no reason to believe there were any live prisoners left in Southeast Asia. In spite of what should have been decisive conclusions for the American secret camp myth, *that myth persists,* if perhaps less stridently than it once did, as the Vietnam generation ages and the American population moves on to new wars and new mythologies.

Nevertheless, the black POW/MIA flag still flies prominently in many American communities, a reminder of how fully POWs and MIAs dominate the American national consciousness and memory of the war in Vietnam. Indeed, by law it is required so to do over US post offices and Veterans Affairs facilities.[21] Many state laws also require its presence in or near governmental buildings, and many privately owned businesses choose to fly it voluntarily. No German equivalent has appeared outside of museums for over half a century. Ultimately, then, these two parallel cases of national trauma over prisoners and the missing demonstrate how wars can breed mythologies that, if not satisfied, can take on lives of their own and come to dominate national conversations on the history of warfare, aftermath, and defeat.

Notes

Introduction

1. H. Bruce Franklin, *Vietnam and Other American Fantasies* (Amherst: University of Massachusetts Press, 2000), 188.

2. H. Bruce Franklin, *MIA, or, Mythmaking in America* (New York: Lawrence Hill, 1992), 5–6.

3. Rüdiger Overmans, *Deutsche militärische Verluste im Zweiten Weltkrieg* (Munich: Oldenbourg, 2004), 288–289.

4. Franklin, *MIA, or, Mythmaking in America*, 11.

5. Nick Turse, *Kill Anything That Moves: The Real American War in Vietnam* (New York: Picador Books, 2013), 13–14.

6. Franklin, *Vietnam and Other American Fantasies*, 62.

7. Samuel Hynes, *The Soldiers' Tale: Bearing Witness to Modern War* (New York: Penguin Books, 1998), 277.

8. James Diehl, *The Thanks of the Fatherland: German Veterans after the Second World War* (Chapel Hill: University of North Carolina Press, 1993), 179.

9. Frank Biess, *Homecomings: Returning POWs and the Legacies of Defeat in Postwar Germany* (Princeton, NJ: Princeton University Press, 2006), 181–182.

10. Ibid., 194–195.

11. Nicholas Stargardt, *The German War: A Nation under Arms 1939–45* (New York: Basic Books, 2015), 4–5.

12. Bettina Greiner's *Suppressed Terror: History and Perception of Soviet Special Camps in Germany* examines a subject of related interest to this study: those German civilians accused of Nazi crimes who disappeared into Soviet prison camps

in East Germany between 1945 and 1955. Though there are interesting parallels between these camps and the alleged "silent camps" inside the USSR, Greiner's work does not directly relate to POW/MIA issues.

13. Franklin, *MIA, or, Mythmaking in America*, 4–5.

14. Ibid., 34.

15. Michael Allen, *Until the Last Man Comes Home: POWs, MIAs, and the Unending Vietnam War* (Chapel Hill: University of North Carolina Press, 2009), 15–16.

16. Ibid., 159.

17. Jean-Yves Le Naour, *The Living Unknown Soldier: A Story of Grief and the Great War* (New York: Metropolitan Books, 2002), 135.

18. Le Naour identifies unsubstantiated reports beginning in 1915 in the *Bulletin des réfugiés du Nord* of French POWs being forced to secretly dig German trenches and, later, of there being secret camps containing live MIAs. Unlike the German and American examples, however, he does not indicate that this belief continued beyond the end of hostilities in 1918. Ibid., 66.

19. Drew Gilpin Faust, *This Republic of Suffering: Death and the American Civil War* (New York: Vintage Books, 2008), xvii–xviii.

20. Ibid., 170.

21. Jay Winter, *Sites of Memory, Sites of Mourning: The Great War in European Cultural History* (Cambridge: Cambridge University Press, 1995), 5.

22. Ibid., 41.

23. Franklin, *MIA, or, Mythmaking in America*, 4–5.

Chapter One. Germany's War on the Eastern Front and
the Origins of Its Secret Camp Myth

1. Mark Mazower, *Hitler's Empire: How the Nazis Ruled Europe* (New York: Penguin Press, 2008), 42–43.

2. Adolf Hitler, *Mein Kampf* (Boston: Houghton Mifflin, 1943), 652.

3. Ibid., 655.

4. Franz Halder, *The Halder Diaries: The Private War Journals of Colonel General Franz Halder, Chief of the General Staff, Supreme Command of the German Army (OKH) 14 August 1939 to 24 September 1942* (Boulder, CO: Westview Press, 1976), vol. 2, 846–847.

5. "Guidelines for the Behavior of the Fighting Force in Russia," in Chris Bellamy, *Absolute War—Soviet Russia in the Second World War: A Modern History* (London: Macmillan, 2007), 25.

6. Omer Bartov, *Hitler's Army: Soldiers, Nazis, and War in the Third Reich* (New York: Oxford University Press, 1991), 104.

7. Nicholas Stargardt, *The German War: A Nation under Arms 1939–45* (New York: Basic Books, 2015), 472.

8. Wolfram Wette, *The Wehrmacht: History, Myth, Reality* (Cambridge, MA: Harvard University Press, 2006), 156.

9. Wolfgang Benz, *A Concise History of the Third Reich* (Berkeley: University of California Press, 2006), 180.

10. David M. Glantz and Jonathan M. House, *When Titans Clashed: How the Red Army Stopped Hitler* (Lawrence: University Press of Kansas, 1995), 256.

11. Among POWs, occupations were 20 percent agricultural, 44.8 percent industrial, 16.9 percent metal workers (which included skilled trades like electricians and chemical workers), and 5.2 percent unskilled laborers. For MIAs, it was 20.1, 41.7, 14.1, and 6.3 percent respectively. Dr. Pflüger, Ausschuss für KGfragen in den Ländern der US-Zone 1947, "Die Registrierung der Kriegsgefangenen und Vermissten in den Ländern der US-Zone" (stand mitte 1947), 6–7, in Bundesarchiv-Koblenz, B150–Bundesministerium für Vertriebene, Flüchtlinge, und Kriegsgeschädigte, 322–Kriegsgefangene–Registrierung in den Ländrern der US-Zone 1947.

12. Ibid., 5.

13. Officers and career rankers amounted to, perhaps, 5–10 percent overall. Wette, *The Wehrmacht,* 158.

14. Peter Fritzsche, *Life and Death in the Third Reich* (London: Belknap Press, 2008), 3–4.

15. Shelley Baranowski, *Strength through Joy: Consumerism and Mass Tourism in the Third Reich* (New York: Cambridge University Press, 2004), 45.

16. Stephen Fritz's excellent *Frontsoldaten: The German Soldier in World War II* (Lexington: University Press of Kentucky, 2010) stands as a notable exception to this rule.

17. "Department Military Archives (Department MA)," viewed 4 May 2015, at https://www.bundesarchiv.de/bundesarchiv/organisation/abteilung_ma/index.html.

18. Bartov, *Hitler's Army,* 30–31.

19. Ibid., 38–39.

20. Ibid., 134–135.

21. Antony Beevor, *Stalingrad: The Fateful Siege 1942–1943* (New York: Penguin, 1999), 23.

22. William Shirer, *The Rise and Fall of the Third Reich: A History of Nazi Germany* (New York: Simon & Schuster, 1960), 856.

23. Bartov, *Hitler's Army,* 12.

24. Beevor, *Stalingrad,* 24–25.

25. Rüdiger Overmans, *Soldaten hinter Stacheldraht: Deutsche Kriegsgefangene des Zweiten Weltkriegs* (Berlin: Ullstein, 2000), 272.

26. Bellamy, *Absolute War,* 22.

27. Bartov, *Hitler's Army,* 25.

28. Frank Biess, *Homecomings: Returning POWs and the Legacies of Defeat in Postwar Germany* (Princeton, NJ: Princeton University Press, 2006), 25.

29. Fritzsche, *Life and Death in the Third Reich,* 85.

30. Biess, *Homecomings,* 26–27.

31. Fritzsche, *Life and Death in the Third Reich,* 113.

32. Bellamy, *Absolute War,* 21–22.

33. Ibid.

34. Fritzsche, *Life and Death in the Third Reich*, 286.

35. Stephen G. Fritz, *Endkampf: Soldiers, Civilians, and the Death of the Third Reich* (Lexington: University Press of Kentucky, 2004), 33.

36. Halder, *The Halder Diaries*, 1477.

37. Beevor, *Stalingrad*, 75.

38. Georgi Zhukov, *Marshal Zhukov's Greatest Battles* (New York: Harper Row, 1969), 177.

39. David M. Glantz and Jonathan M. House, *Endgame at Stalingrad: December 1941–September 1943* (Lawrence: University Press of Kansas, 2009), 5.

40. Hitler, quoted in ibid., 564.

41. Bellamy, *Absolute War*, 549.

42. Hitler, in Felix Gilbert (trans.), *Hitler Directs His War: The Secret Records of His Daily Military Conferences* (New York: Ishi Press, 2011), 17–22.

43. Biess, *Homecomings*, 25.

44. Glantz and House, *Endgame at Stalingrad*, 581.

45. Michael Clodfelter, *Warfare and Armed Conflicts: A Statistical Reference to Casualties and Other Figures, 1500–2000* (Jefferson, NC: McFarland, 2002), 505–506.

46. Biess, *Homecomings*, 34–35.

47. Ibid., 34.

48. S. P. MacKenzie, "The Treatment of Prisoners of War in World War II," *Journal of Modern History* 66, 3 (September 1994): 510–511.

49. Shirer, *The Rise and Fall of the Third Reich*, 933.

50. Fritzsche, *Life and Death in the Third Reich*, 280–281.

51. Joseph Göbbels, "Nation, Rise Up, and Let the Storm Break Loose," viewed 19 May 2015, at http://research.calvin.edu/german-propaganda-archive/goeb36.htm.

52. Stephen Fritz, *Ostkrieg: Hitler's War of Extermination in the East* (Lexington: University Press of Kentucky, 2011), 323–324.

53. Karl-Heinz Frieser et al., *Das Deutsche Reich und der Zweite Weltkrieg, Vol. 8: Die Ostfront 1943–44—Den Krieg im Osten und an den Nebenfront* (Munich: Deutsche Verlags-Anstalt, 2007), 207.

54. Clodfelter, *Warfare and Armed Conflicts*, 515.

55. Glantz and House, *When Titans Clashed*, 191.

56. Fritz, *Ostkrieg*, 398.

57. Erich Gröner, *Die deutschen Kriegschiffe 1815–1945, Band 8/1: Flußfahrzeuge, Ujäger, Vorpostenboote, Hilfsminensucher, Küstenschutzverbände (Teil 1)*, (Bonn: Bernard & Graefe Verlag, 1993), 119.

58. Glantz and House, *When Titans Clashed*, 191.

59. Earl Ziemke, *From Stalingrad to Berlin: The German Defeat in the East* (Washington, DC: US Army Center for Military History, 1968), 294–295.

60. Clodfelter, *Warfare and Armed Conflicts*, 510.

61. Frieser et al., *Das Deutsche Reich*, 552.

62. Clodfelter, *Warfare and Armed Conflicts*, 511.

63. Bellamy, *Absolute War,* 614–615.

64. David M. House and Harold Orienstein, eds., *The Battle for L'vov: The So-viet General Staff Study* (New York: Routledge, 2007), 176.

65. Frieser et al., *Das Deutsche Reich,* 593–594.

66. Fritz, *Ostkrieg,* 355.

67. Clodfelter, *Warfare and Armed Conflicts,* 512–513.

68. "May 13rd, 1945 from the Soviet Information Bureau," viewed 31 May 2015, at http://eng.9may.ru/09.05.1945/eng_inform/m9004263.

69. Mazower, *Hitler's Empire,* 541–542.

70. Clodfelter, *Warfare and Armed Conflicts,* 513.

71. Anthony Beevor, *The Fall of Berlin 1945* (New York: Penguin, 2002), 284.

72. Frieser et al., *Das Deutsche Reich,* 922.

73. Mazower, *Hitler's Empire,* 526.

74. Beevor, *The Fall of Berlin,* 193.

75. Fritz, *Endkampf,* 116–117.

76. Clodfelter, *Warfare and Armed Conflicts,* 514.

77. Beevor, *The Fall of Berlin,* 378.

78. Ibid., 386–387.

79. Ibid., 404–405.

80. Stargardt, *The German War,* 549.

81. Clodfelter, *Warfare and Armed Conflicts,* 515.

Chapter Two. The Short-Lived German Secret Camp Myth

1. James Diehl, *Paramilitary Politics in Weimar Germany* (Bloomington: Indiana University Press, 1977), 29.

2. Dirk Schumann, *Political Violence in the Weimar Republic 1918–1933: Fight for the Streets and Fear of Civil War* (New York: Berghahn Books, 2009), xxi.

3. Diehl, *Paramilitary Politics in Weimar Germany,* 55.

4. James Diehl, *The Thanks of the Fatherland: German Veterans after the Second World War* (Chapel Hill: University of North Carolina Press, 1993), 232.

5. Nicholas Stargardt, *The German War: A Nation under Arms 1939–45* (New York: Basic Books, 2015), 565.

6. Edward N. Peterson, *The Many Faces of Defeat: The German People's Experience in 1945* (New York: Peter Lang , 1990), 87.

7. Peter Longerich, *Heinrich Himmler: A Life* (New York: Oxford University Press, 2012), 736.

8. Diehl, *Thanks of the Fatherland,* 66.

9. This is not to say that repatriation and reintegration in the West was effort-less or without controversy. Most notably novelist James Bacque in his book *Other Losses* has long alleged that the Western Allies systematically starved just under a million German POWs to death in the immediate aftermath of the war. His argument has not achieved significant agreement among historians, but here too there is a lack of consensus, as criticism of Bacque cannot avoid dealing with the tarnished legacy of Bacque's chief initial (though certainly not only) critic, Stephen Ambrose. "HNN

Debate: Was Ike Responsible for the Deaths of Hundreds of Thousands of German POWs? Pro and Con," 24 July 2017, http://historynewsnetwork.org/article/1266.

10. Reporting on the sluggish nature of POW repatriation in 1950, the BMVT reported that of their original estimate of 2 million POWs and 1.7 million MIAs, 1.76 million Germans in total had returned from the USSR, with at least 290,000 known POWs remaining, and 1.5 million MIAs still unaccounted for. Bundesministerium für Angelegenheiten der Vertriebenen to Dr. Reichling, 26 January 1950, in Bundesarchiv-Koblenz, B150–Bundesministerium für Vertriebene, Flüchtlinge, und Kriegsgeschädigte, 286A Arbeitsgemeinschaft der westdeutschen Länder fur Kriegsgefangenen- und Heimkehrerfragen-Errichtung, Organisation, sitzung protokolle, Finanzierung.

11. Lothar Wieland, *Das Bundesministerium für Vertriebene, Flüchtlinge und Kriegsgeschädigte* (Frankfurt: Athenäum Verlaug, 1968), 19.

12. Ibid., 22.

13. Liste der Kriegsgefangenenlager in Russland (Abschrift nur zur Verteilung an "Suchdienst"—Stellen und mit Quellenangabe gestattet), in Bundesarchiv-Koblenz, B150–Bundesministerium für Vertriebene, Flüchtlinge, und Kriegsgeschädigte, 344A–Kriegsgefangenen in sowjetischen Lagern.

14. Bundesarchiv-Koblenz, B150–Bundesministerium für Vertriebene, Flüchtlinge, und Kriegsgeschädigte, 322–Kriegsgefangene–Registrierung in den Ländrern der US-Zone 1947.

15. "Schweigelager in Russland," *Stuttgarter Zeitung* 22 July 1949 No. 135, in Bundesarchiv-Koblenz, B150–Bundesministerium für Vertriebene, Flüchtlinge, und Kriegsgeschädigte, 344A–Kriegsgefangenen in sowjetischen Lagern.

16. Robert Moeller, *War Stories: The Search for a Usable Past in the Federal Republic of Germany* (Berkeley: University of California Press, 2001), 40.

17. "Erneute deutsche Protestnote in der Kriegsgefangenenfrage," *Der Tagesspeigel*, 1 July 1949, 2.

18. Frank Biess, *Homecomings: Returning POWs and the Legacies of Defeat in Postwar Germany* (Princeton, NJ: Princeton University Press, 2006), 43–44.

19. Diehl, *The Thanks of the Fatherland*, 70.

20. Walter Schulte, *Hirnorganische Dauerschäden nach schwerer Dystrophie* (Munich: Urban & Schwarzenberg, 1953), 45–46.

21. Biess, *Homecomings*, 23–24.

22. Arnold Krammer, "Soviet Propaganda among German and Austro-Hungarian Prisoners of War in Russia, 1917–1921," in Samuel R. Williamson Jr. and Peter Pastor, eds., *War and Society in East Central Europe, Vol. V—Essays on World War I: Origins and Prisoners of War* (New York: Brooklyn College Press, 1983), 241–242.

23. Krammer, in ibid., 250–251.

24. Ibid., 256.

25. Biess, *Homecomings*, 154.

26. Moeller, *War Stories*, 114.

27. Dieter Riesenberger, ed., *Das Deutsche Rote Kreuz, Konrad Adenauer und*

das Kreigsgefangenenproblem: Die Rückführung der Deutschen Kreigsgefangenen aus der Sowjetunion (1952–1955) (Bremen: Donat Verlaug, 1994), 10.

28. Biess, *Homecomings*, 179.

29. Ibid., 219.

30. Norbert Frei, *Adenauer's Germany and the Nazi Past: The Politics of Amnesty and Integration* (New York: Columbia University Press, 2002), 177–178.

31. Karl Lewke to KPD, 2 December 1945, viewed 5 January 2016, at http://germanhistorydocs.ghi-dc.org/docpage.cfm?docpage_id=5679.

32. Frank Biess, "Pioneers of a New Germany: Returning POWs from the Soviet Union and the Making of East German Citizens, 1945–50," *Central European History* 32, 2 (1999): 144.

33. Christina Morina, "Instructed Silence, Constructed Memory: The SED and Return of German Prisoners of War as 'War Criminals' from the Soviet Union to East Germany, 1950–56," *Contemporary European History* 13, 3 (August 2004): 324.

34. Ibid., 325.

35. Biess, *Homecomings*, 180.

36. "Gefangene, die nicht heimkehren," *Die Zeit,* 19 May 1950, 1.

37. "Erkärung Zur Kriegsgefangene," 27 June 1949, in Bundesarchiv-Koblenz, B150–Bundesministerium für Vertriebene, Flüchtlinge, und Kriegsgeschädigte, 344A–Kriegsgefangenen in sowjetischen Lagern.

38. "Zwei Millionen kriegsgefangenen in der USSR," *Stuttgarter Nachrichten,* No. 131, 18 July 1949.

39. Frei, *Adenauer's Germany,* 136–137.

40. Sozialdemokratische Partei Deutschlands—"500000 fehlen, gebt sie frei!" in Bundesarchiv, Plak 004-007-001.

41. H. Blattman to Frau Wurst, 13 June 1949, in Bundesarchiv-Koblenz, B150–Bundesministerium für Vertriebene, Flüchtlinge, und Kriegsgeschädigte, 344A–Kriegsgefangenen in sowjetischen Lagern.

42. E. Bach to Odo Stoellger, 12 January 1949, in Bundesarchiv-Koblenz, B150–Bundesministerium für Vertriebene, Flüchtlinge, und Kriegsgeschädigte, 344A–Kriegsgefangenen in sowjetischen Lagern.

43. Lucy Ash, "Digging for Their Lives: Russia's Volunteer Body Hunters," viewed 18 August 2015, at http://www.bbc.com/news/magazine-25589709.

44. Riesenberger, *Das Deutsche Rote Kreuz,* 11.

45. Ibid., 9.

46. Ibid., 12.

47. "Präsidiumssitzung des DRK, Bonn, etwa Juni 1952" in ibid., 27.

48. Riesenberger, *Das Deutsche Rote Kreuz,* 28.

49. Charles Williams, *Adenauer: The Father of the New Germany* (New York: John Wiley and Sons, 2000), 430.

50. Thomas Maulucci, *Adenauer's Foreign Office: West German Diplomacy in the Shadow of the Third Reich* (DeKalb: Northern Illinois University Press, 2012), 189.

51. Konrad Adenauer to Heinrich Weitz, 23 January 1953, in Riesenberger, *Das Deutsche Rote Kreuz*, 63–64.

52. Lewis Edinger, *Kurt Schumacher: A Study in Personality and Political Behavior* (London: Oxford University Press, 1965), 334.

53. These two groups were the Central Association of Returnees (Zentralverband der Heimkehrer) and the Federal Association of Returnees (Bundesverband der Heimkehrer). Other smaller organizations were quick to follow suit and join with the VdH. Diehl, *Thanks of the Fatherland*, 93.

54. R. Weinmann, "Russland, wie ich es gesehan habe," *Frankfurter Allegemeine Zeitung*, 8 March 1952.

55. Christiane Wienand, *Returning Memories: Former Prisoners of War in Divided and Reunited Germany* (Rochester, NY: Camden Books, 2015), 65–66.

56. Moeller, *War Stories*, 40.

57. Ibid., 40–41.

58. VdH, "Unsere Kriegsgefangenen und die Verschleppten als Sowjetterrors klagen an," in Bundesarchiv–Plak 005-047-049.

59. Konrad Adenauer, in Stargardt, *The German War*, 556.

60. Morina, "Instructed Silence, Constructed Memory," 326–327.

61. Biess, *Homecomings*, 114.

62. Robert Moeller, "'The Last Soldiers of the Great War,' and Tales of Family Reunion in the Federal Republic of Germany," *Signs* 24, 1 (Autumn 1998): 130.

63. Michael Borchard, *Die Deutschen Kriegsgefangenen in der Sowjetunion: Zur politischen Bedeutung der Kriegsgefangenenfrage, 1949–1955* (Düsseldorf: Droste, 2000), 169–170.

64. Williams, *Adenauer*, 430.

65. Eberhard Stammler, "Busstag," *Westdeutchse Allgemeine Zeitung*, 16 November 1955.

66. "Erlebnis der Heimkehr," *Rhein Neckar Zeitung*, 10 October 1955.

67. Diehl, *The Thanks of the Fatherland*, 101–102.

68. Verband der Heimkehrer, "Entwurf zum Gesetz über die Entschädigung der deutschen Kriegsgefangenen," in Biess, *Homecomings*, 111.

69. Frei, *Adenauer's Germany*, 225.

70. Stargardt, *The German War*, 557–558.

71. Riesenberger, *Das Deutsche Rote Kreuz*, 20–21.

72. Michael Hughes, *Shouldering the Burdens of Defeat: West Germany and the Reconstruction of Social Justice* (Chapel Hill: University of North Carolina Press, 1999), 172.

73. Moeller, "'The Last Soldiers of the Great War,'" 143–144.

74. Diehl, *The Thanks of the Fatherland*, 177.

Chapter Three. Missing Americans in Southeast Asia and the Origins of POW/MIA Activism

1. Kathryn Statler, *Replacing France: The Origins of American Intervention in Vietnam* (Lexington: University Press of Kentucky, 2007), 196.

2. Fredrik Logevall, *Choosing War: The Lost Chance for Peace and the Escalation of War in Vietnam* (Berkeley: University of California Press, 1999), 2.

3. "Defense Prisoner of War/Missing Personnel Office US Unaccounted-For from the Vietnam War," 27 March 2013, http://www.dtic.mil/dpmo/vietnam/reports/documents/pmsea_una_p_name.pdf.

4. Michael Allen, *Until the Last Man Comes Home: POWs, MIAs, and the Unending Vietnam War* (Chapel Hill: University of North Carolina Press, 2009), 210.

5. Anne Leland and Mari-Jana "M-J" Oboroceanu, "American War and Military Operations Casualties: Lists and Statistics," 17 March 2014, http://www.fas.org/sgp/crs/natsec/RL32492.pdf.

6. "Defense Prisoner of War/Missing Personnel Office—About Us," 25 April 2013, http://www.dtic.mil/dpmo/about_us/.

7. Allen, *Until the Last Man Comes Home*, 180.

8. "Defense Prisoner of War/Missing Personnel Office US Unaccounted-For from the Vietnam War," 27 March 2013, http://www.dtic.mil/dpmo/vietnam/reports/documents/pmsea_una_p_name.pdf.

9. "Defense Prisoner of War/Missing Personnel Office US Accounted-For from the Vietnam War: Prisoners of War, Escapees, Returnees and Remains Recovered Report for: United States Air Force," 22 April 2103, http://www.dtic.mil/dpmo/vietnam/reports/documents/pmsea_acc_p_usaf.pdf.

10. "Vietnam-Era Statistical Report: Americans Unaccounted-For in Southeast Asia," 18 April 2013, http://www.dtic.mil/dpmo/vietnam/statistics/2013/Stats20130418.pdf.

11. "Defense Prisoner of War/Missing Personnel Office US Unaccounted-For from the Vietnam War," 11 March 2014, http://www.dtic.mil/dpmo/vietnam/reports/documents/pmsea_una_p_name.pdf.

12. Officer Candidate School, the main path for promising recruits (draftee or otherwise) to become officers, generally had a degree prerequisite, and the Reserve Officer Training Corps and service academies were by definition part of higher education. James Westheider, *Fighting on Two Fronts: African Americans in the Vietnam War* (New York: New York University Press, 1997), 123.

13. Those who failed to even make it into Category IV were usually released from service. Ibid., 38.

14. Ibid., 38–39.

15. John Darrell Sherwood, *Black Sailor, White Navy: Racial Unrest in the Fleet during the Vietnam War Era* (New York: New York University Press, 2007), 53–54.

16. There are a few notable exceptions here. Most prominent among them is Air Force Colonel Fred V. Cherry, an African American pilot shot down and taken prisoner in 1965. Fred V. Cherry in Wallace Terry, *Bloods: An Oral History of the Vietnam War by Black Veterans* (New York: Random House, 1984), 278–279.

17. This policy would remain in place until 1981, when medical testimony and congressional pressure finally convinced the Department of Defense to lift the ban, which frankly had never been about the actual science of the disease traits in question. Roland B. Scott, "US Air Force Revises Policy for Flying Personnel

with Sickle Cell Trait," *Journal of the National Medical Association* 72, 9 (1982): 835–836.

18. John Prados, *The Blood Road: The Ho Chi Minh Trail and the Vietnam War* (New York: John Wiley & Sons, 1999), 92.

19. This number includes those aircraft lost during Steel Tiger as well. Perry L. Lamy, *Barrel Roll 1968–1973: An Air Campaign in Support of National Policy* (Maxwell, AL: Air University Press, 1995), 48.

20. Earl Tilford, *Crosswinds: The Air Force's Setup in Vietnam* (College Station: Texas A&M University Press, 1993), 67.

21. Ibid., 152–153.

22. Lamy, *Barrel Roll,* 1.

23. H. Bruce Franklin, *MIA, or, Mythmaking in America* (New York: Lawrence Hill, 1992), 86.

24. William Shawcross, *Sideshow: Kissinger, Nixon and the Destruction of Cambodia* (New York: Simon & Schuster, 1979), 64.

25. Ibid., 19–20.

26. Ibid., 23.

27. Ibid., 25–26.

28. Tilford, *Crosswinds,* 196.

29. Shawcross, *Sideshow,* 28.

30. "Defense Prisoner of War/Missing Personnel Office US Accounted-For from the Vietnam War: Progress in Cambodia as of May 1, 2013," 11 June 2013, http://www.dtic.mil/dpmo/news/factsheets/documents/cambodia_factsheet.pdf.

31. Shawcross, *Sideshow,* 152.

32. Tilford, *Crosswinds,* 121–122.

33. Prados, *The Blood Road,* 126.

34. Tilford, *Crosswinds,* 245.

35. Herman Gilster, *The Air War in Southeast Asia: Case Studies of Selected Campaigns* (Maxwell, AL: Air University Press, 1993), 75.

36. James McCarthy, *Linebacker II: A View from the Rock* (Washington, DC: Office of Air Force History, 1985), 172.

37. "Joint Peace Proposal: Proposal of the Republic of Vietnam and the United States for a Negotiated Settlement of the Indochina Conflict, Made Public January 25, 1972," in Richard P. Stebbins and Elaine P. Adam, eds., *American Foreign Relations 1972: A Documentary Record* (New York: New York University Press, 1976), 245.

38. Franklin, *MIA, or, Mythmaking in America,* 97.

39. H. Bruce Franklin, "Missing in Action in the Twenty-First Century," in Scott Laderman and Edwin A. Martini, eds., *Four Decades On: Vietnam, the United States, and the Legacies of the Second Indochina War* (Durham, NC: Duke University Press, 2013), 261.

40. James and Sybil Stockdale, *In Love and War: The Story of a Family's Ordeal and Sacrifice during the Vietnam War* (New York: Harper & Row, 1984), 225–226.

41. Allen, *Until the Last Man Comes Home,* 25–26.

42. Donna Moreau, *Waiting Wives: The Story of Schilling Manor, Home Front to the Vietnam War* (New York: Simon & Schuster, 2010), 50.

43. James and Sybil Stockdale, *In Love and War,* 145–146.

44. Ibid., 225–226.

45. Allen, *Until the Last Man Comes Home,* 41.

46. "Mission," 24 January 2015, at http://www.pow-miafamilies.org/mission/.

47. Eileen Cormier in Margery Byers, "At Home with the Prisoners' Families," *Life,* 20 October 1967, 34B.

48. Evelyn Grubb and Carol Jose, *You Are Not Forgotten: A Family's Quest for Truth and the Founding of the National League of Families* (St. Petersburg, FL: Vandamere Press, 2008), 295.

49. Patty Zuhoski in "Living with Uncertainty: The Families Who Wait Back Home," *Time,* 7 December 1971, 28.

50. Madeleine Pambrun in Jean-Yves Le Naour, *The Living Unknown Soldier: A Story of Grief and the Great War* (New York: Metropolitan Books, 2002), 66–67.

51. James and Sybil Stockdale, *In Love and War,* 207.

52. Moreau, *Waiting Wives,* xv.

53. Allen, *Until the Last Man Comes Home,* 28–29.

54. Richard Nixon, *Richard Nixon Speaks Out: Major Speeches and Statements of Richard M. Nixon in the Presidential Campaign of 1968* (New York: Nixon-Agnew Campaign Committee, 1968), 281.

55. Daniel Moynihan to Richard Nixon, "First Year Goals of the Administration," 8 October 1969, in Bruce Oudes, ed., *From: The President—Richard Nixon's Secret Files* (New York: Harper & Row, 1989), 56–57.

56. Franklin, *MIA, or, Mythmaking in America,* 48–49.

57. Jeffrey Kimball, *Nixon's Vietnam War* (Lawrence: University Press of Kansas, 1998), 167.

58. Franklin, *MIA, or, Mythmaking in America,* 49.

59. William Beecher, "Laird Appeals to Enemy to Release US Captives," *New York Times,* 20 May 1969, 1.

60. Ibid., 3.

61. Secretary of Defense William Laird in Ted Sell, "Laird Asks Hanoi to Free GIs," *Washington Post,* 20 May 1969, A14.

62. Laird, in "Laird 'Shocked' by Rebuff from Hanoi on Prisoners," *New York Times,* 22 May 1969, 3.

63. Vernon Davis, *The Long Road Home: US Prisoner of War Policy and Planning in Southeast Asia* (Washington, DC: Office of the Secretary of Defense, 2000), 177.

64. Ibid., 198–199.

65. Franklin, *MIA, or, Mythmaking in America,* 49–50.

66. James and Sybil Stockdale, *In Love and War,* 361–362.

67. Sybil Stockdale to Richard Nixon, in Moreau, *Waiting Wives,* 123–124.

68. Richard Nixon, "12th Draft," 23 October 1968, in National Security Council Files—Vietnam Subject Files, Box 79, Drafts of President's Nov. 3 1969 Speech Folder (1 of 2).

69. Ibid.

70. Richard Nixon, "Final Draft," in ibid.

71. "Gallup Telephone Poll—The President's Speech," 4 November 1969, in National Security Council Files—Vietnam Subject Files, Box 79, Memo's [sic], Letters of Exchange and Reaction to the President's Nov. 3 1969 Speech Folder (1 of 2).

72. Talking Paper—Image of the President, in National Security Council Files—Vietnam Subject Files, Box 79, Notes of President's Nov. 3 1969 Speech Folder.

73. Talking Paper—November 15th Gameplan, in National Security Council Files—Vietnam Subject Files, Box 79, Notes of President's Nov. 3 1969 Speech Folder.

74. Ken Cole to Haldeman, 22 September 1969, in National Security Council Files—Vietnam Subject Files, Box 94, December 1970 US POWs in NVN Folder (1 of 3).

75. Haldeman to Kissinger, 23 September 1969, in National Security Council Files—Vietnam Subject Files, Box 94, December 1970 US POWs in NVN Folder (1 of 3).

76. Moreau, *Waiting Wives*, 364.

77. Alexander P. Butterfield to Nixon, "Game Plan for the President's Pursuit of Peace Speech," 12 November 1969, in Bruce Oudes, ed., *From: The President—Richard Nixon's Secret Files* (New York: Harper & Row, 1989), 69.

78. James and Sybil Stockdale, *In Love and War*, 367–368.

79. Mrs. J. K. Hardy in Danforth Austin, Jack Kramer, and Eric Morgenthaler, "Missing—or Dead? Some Relatives of POWs Say US Misleads Them," *Wall Street Journal*, 20 September 1971, 1.

80. These ads and mailings all contained a returnable section where the recipient could sign and mail back to affirm their support of Nixon's policies. Davis, *The Long Road Home*, 222.

81. Each bracelet retailed for either $2.50 or $3, depending on whether it was nickel-plated or made of copper. Franklin, *MIA, or, Mythmaking in America*, 56.

82. Ibid., 57.

83. Richard Nixon, "The Withdrawal Program," 15 December 1969, in Richard Wilson, ed., *Setting the Course the First Year: Major Policy Statements by President Richard Nixon* (New York: Funk & Wagnalls, 1970), 31.

84. Henry Kissinger to Richard Nixon, 20 September 1969, in Nixon Presidential Materials Staff, National Security Council Files—POW/MIA, Box 1—Presidential Daily Briefs, September 1–22 1969 Folder.

85. Kissinger to Nixon, 11 October 1969, in Nixon Presidential Materials Staff, National Security Council Files—POW/MIA, Box 1—Presidential Daily Briefs, October 11–21 1969 Folder.

86. Ibid.

87. Moreau, *Waiting Wives*, 153.

88. James Fazio to Henry Kissinger, 13 September 1972, in Nixon Presidential Materials Staff, National Security Council Files—POW/MIA, Box 1—Presidential Daily Briefs, September 1972 Folder.

89. Kissinger to Nixon, 22 September 1972, in ibid.

90. H. R. Haldeman, "Abandoning American Prisoners," in White House Special Files, Special Material Office Files—H. R. Haldeman Chronological Files, Box 201, Assault Book Folder.

91. Ibid.

92. Pat Buchanan and Ken Khachigian, "Assault Strategy," 8 June 1972, in Oudes, *From: The President,* 472.

93. Nixon, "United States Foreign Policy for the 1970s: A New Strategy for Peace—A Report to Congress," 18 February 1970, in Wilson, *Setting the Course the First Year,* 439.

94. Nixon, in Kissinger to Nixon, 27 February 1970, Nixon Presidential Materials Staff, National Security Council Files—POW/MIA, Box 1—Presidential Daily Briefs, February 20–28 1970 Folder.

95. Allen, *Until the Last Man Comes Home,* 36–37.

96. Ibid., 52.

97. Mrs. Samuel Beecher in Austin, Kramer, and Morgenthaler, "Missing—or Dead?" 1.

98. Mrs. Louis Jones in ibid.

99. Mrs. Randolf Ford in ibid.

100. Mrs. James Werner in ibid.

101. Walter Heynowski and Gerhard Schuemann, "US Prisoners in North Vietnam," *Life,* 20 October 1967, 26–27.

102. Ibid., 27.

103. Stuart Rochester and Frederick Kiley, *Honor Bound: The History of American Prisoners of War in Southeast Asia* (Washington, DC: Office of the Secretary of Defense, 1998), 345–446.

104. Allen, *Until the Last Man Comes Home,* 19.

105. National League of Families of American Prisoners and Missing in Southeast Asia, advertisement, "One side of the POW question is not complicated. That's the *human* side," Records of the United States Senate, 102nd Senate, Select Committee on POW/MIA Affairs, Records Received: Department of Defense, Office of the Secretary of Defense, Policy Files, Box 8.

106. Ibid.

107. Franklin, *MIA, or, Mythmaking in America,* 48–49.

108. Pulo Condore was the older, colonial-era name of Con Son prison. Pham Van Dong to William Fullbright, 14 December 1970, in Records of the United States Senate, 102nd Senate, Select Committee on POW/MIA Affairs, Records Received: Department of Defense, Office of the Secretary of Defense, Policy Files, Box 1.

109. Don Luce, "Behind Vietnam's Prison Walls," *Christian Century,* 19 February 1969, 261–262.

110. "How They Unearthed the Tiger Cages," *Life,* 17 July 1970, 2A.

111. "The Tiger Cages of Con Son," *Life*, 17 July 1970, 27.

112. Frank Walton in ibid., 29.

113. Ibid., 29.

114. National League of Families of American Prisoners and Missing in Southeast Asia, advertisement, "One side of the POW question is not complicated. That's the *human* side," Records of the United States Senate, 102nd Senate, Select Committee on POW/MIA Affairs, Records Received: Department of Defense, Office of the Secretary of Defense, Policy Files, Box 8.

115. Ambassador Philip Habib, "Text of the Opening Remarks by Ambassador Philip C. Habib at the Seventy-Sixth Plenary Session of the New Paris Meetings on Viet-Nam," 23 July 1970, in Records of the United States Senate, 102nd Senate, Select Committee on POW/MIA Affairs, Records Received: Department of Defense, Office of the Secretary of Defense, Policy Files, Box 9.

116. Ibid.

117. Heyward Isham in ibid.

118. Lieutenant Colonel Pat Caruthers in Austin, Kramer, and Morganthaler, "Missing—or Dead?" 4.

119. William Garoudy, "Statement of William R. Garoudy, Jr., Casualty Resolution Specialist, Laos Joint Casualty Resolution Center," 6 November 1991, in *Hearings before the Senate Committee on POW/MIA Affairs*, Part I (Washington, DC: Government Printing Office, 1992), 228–229.

120. Garoudy, 4 December 1992 "Committee Hearings on POW/MIA Affairs," viewed 1 April 2014, at http://www.c-span.org/video/?35600-1/powmia-affairs.

121. Roger Shields, "Statement of Dr. Roger Shields, Assistant to the Assistant Secretary of Defense (International Security Affairs) before the Armed Services Committee, House of Representatives," 10 October 1972, viewed 15 April 2014, at http://digitalcollections.library.cmu.edu/awweb/awarchive?type=file&item=400297.

122. Davis, *The Long Road Home*, 184.

123. Secretary of Defense Charles Wilson in *The US Fighting Man's Code of Conduct* (Washington, DC: Office of Armed Forces Information and Education, 1955), iv–v.

124. Davis, *The Long Road Home*, 12–13.

125. Executive Order 10631—Code of Conduct for members of the Armed Forces of the United States, 17 August 1955, viewed 24 July 2013, at http://www.archives.gov/federal-register/codification/executive-order/10631.html.

126. Stockdale described this as "Unity over Self," unaware perhaps of the irony of resisting communism via collective action. Jim and Sybil Stockdale, *In Love and War*, 252.

127. Ibid., 254.

128. Colonel Robinson Risner in "POWs Studied, Exercised," *Washington Post*, 16 February 1973, A21.

129. Lieutenant Commander Everett Alvarex in "1st Downed Flier among 60 Returnees," *Washington Post*, 16 February 1973, A1.

130. Henry Kissinger, *Ending the Vietnam War: A History of America's Involvement in and Extrication from the Vietnam War* (New York: Simon & Schuster, 2003), 224–225.

131. "Home at Last!" *Newsweek*, 26 February 1973, 18.

132. Haldeman to Steven Bull, 15 March 1973, in White House Special Files, Special Material Office Files—H. R. Haldeman Chronological Files, Box 202, March 1973 (A–I) Folder.

133. Allen, *Until the Last Man Comes Home*, 65.

134. Memoranda of Conversation, Richard Nixon, Elliot Richardson, Joint Chiefs of Staff, Brent Scowcroft, 15 February 1973, viewed 16 April 2014, at http://www.fordlibrarymuseum.gov/library/document/0314/1552559.pdf.

135. Memoranda of Conversation, Richard Nixon, Roger Shields, Brent Scowcroft, 11 April 1973, viewed 16 April 2014, at http://www.fordlibrarymuseum.gov/library/document/0314/1552575.pdf.

136. "The Vets: Heroes as Orphans," *Newsweek*, 5 March 1971, 24.

137. Even the name of this article is telling of the role many wanted the returnees to fit. "A Celebration of Men Redeemed," *Time*, 19 February 1973, 19.

138. Memorandum of Conversation, Nixon, John Scali, Scowcroft, 13 February 1973, in National Security Council Files—Name Files, Box 1026, MemCon President/HAK May 71–Dec 72 Folder 22.

139. Shana Alexander, "Prisoners of Peace," *Newsweek*, 26 February 1973, 32.

140. Ibid., 32.

141. H. R. Haldeman to Pat Buchanan, 20 February 1973, in White House Special Files, Special Material Office Files—H. R. Haldeman Chronological Files, Box 202, February 1973 (A–I) Folder.

142. Catherine Helwig in Major C. Wells, "Relatives of MIAs Ask Congress for Aid in Seeking Return," *Washington Post*, 16 November 1973, A14.

Chapter Four. Radicalization of POW/MIA Advocacy and the Emergence of the Secret Camp Myth

1. "Tidings of Joy—and Heartbreak," *Newsweek*, 12 February 1973, 20.

2. Ibid.

3. Ibid.

4. E. W. Teague in Steven V. Roberts, "US Has Cautious Hope of Finding More POWs," *New York Times*, 26 February 1973, 4.

5. Lieutenant Commander George Coker to the Board of Directors of the National League of Families, 27 October 1973, in *Hearings before the House Select Committee on Missing Persons in Southeast Asia*, Ninety-Fourth Congress, First Session, Part 2 (Washington, DC: Government Printing Office, 1975), 109–110.

6. Ibid., 109.

7. Ibid.

8. Roberts, "US Has Cautious Hope," 1.

9. The league's message counted these missing men to be 53 rather than 54, for some unknown reason. Helene Knapp to Brent Scowcroft, 20 February 1973,

in Nixon Presidential Staff Materials, National Security Council Files—POW/MIA, Box 2—Vietnam Subject Files, Vol. VI Jan 1973 Folder (1 of 2).

10. Ibid.

11. Roberts, "US Has Cautious Hope," 5.

12. John Scott Albright in ibid., 4.

13. The Joint Casualty Resolution Center later found Dodge's remains among those prisoners who had died in captivity but had not been identified at the time. *Defense Prisoner of War/Missing Personnel Office: US Accounted-For from the Vietnam War Prisoners of War, Escapees, Returnees and Remains Recovered Report for: United States Navy,* 29 September 2013, available at http://www.dtic.mil/dpmo /vietnam/reports/documents/pmsea_acc_p_usn.pdf.

14. Advertisement, "Have You Forgotten Him?" *Washington Post,* 12 February 1973, A7.

15. Henry Kissinger, Memorandum of Conversation, "US Prisoners of War in Southeast Asia," 29 January 1973, in Nixon Presidential Staff Materials, National Security Council Files—POW/MIA, Box 2—Vietnam Subject Files, Vietnam (POW) Vol. VI, Jan 1973 Folder (2 of 2).

16. "Most of War Missing to Be Presumed Dead," *New York Times,* 8 October 1953, 5.

17. Helen Knapp in John Sarr, "Where Are These Men?" *Washington Post,* 4 June 1973, C1.

18. "League Representation," 29 April 1974, State Department Records—Frank Sieverts, Box 38, Records of the US Senate 102nd Congress, Select Committee on POW/MIA Issues, RG 46.

19. "Resolution No. 429," attached to memo F. P. Jones to Brent Scowcroft, 2 October 1973, in National Security Council Files—Subject Files, Box 833, Scowcroft, Brent 1973–1974 Folder.

20. Sarr, "Where Are These Men?" C1.

21. Defense POW/Missing Personnel Office, "Vietnam-Era Statistical Report," 11 March 2014, viewed 5 May 2014, at http://www.dtic.mil/dpmo/vietnam/statis tics/2014/Stats20140311.pdf.

22. Robert Sheetz, "'Dog Tags' Report," 1 July 1991, in Investigator Files—Hilton Foster, Box 4, Records of the US Senate 102nd Congress, Select Committee on POW/MIA Issues, RG 46.

23. Bill Codhina to Alex Greenfeld, 19 February 1992, in ibid.

24. Defense POW/Missing Personnel Office, "Live Sightings Investigations" January 2010, viewed 5 May 2014, at http://www.dtic.mil/dpmo/news/factsheets/docu ments/Live%20Sighting%20Investigations.pdf.

25. Lieutenant Colonel Paul Mathers in William Boyles, "The Road to Hill 10," *Atlantic Monthly,* 1 April 1985, viewed 4 June 2014, at http://www.theatlantic.com /magazine/archive/1985/04/the-road-to-hill-10/306463/6/.

26. William LeGro, "Memorandum for the Record: Henry Bush and Trung Hieu," 10 June 1992, in Records of the United States Senate, 102nd Senate, Select Committee on POW/MIA Affairs, Investigators' Case Files—William LeGro, Box 1.

27. Susan Katz Keating, *Prisoners of Hope* (New York: Random House, 1994), 68–69.

28. Sheetz, "'Dog Tags' Report."

29. Knapp in Donald Barker, "MIA Status Debated in Convention," *Washington Post*, 29 July 1973, B4.

30. Douglas Clarke, *The Missing Man: Politics and the MIA* (Washington, DC: Government Printing Office, 1979), 19–20.

31. Barker, "MIA Status Debated in Convention," B4.

32. Evelyn Grubb and Carol Jose, *You Are Not Forgotten: A Family's Quest for Truth and the Founding of the National League of Families* (St. Petersburg, FL: Vandamere Press, 2008), 293.

33. Barker, "MIA Status Debated in Convention," B4.

34. This policy is still in place, though now one needs to pay the full year's $60 up front rather than by the month. "You Can Help," 21 April 2014, http://www.pow-miafamilies.org/partners-and-supporters/you-can-help/.

35. H. Bruce Franklin, *MIA, or, Mythmaking in America* (New York: Lawrence Hill, 1992), 129.

36. Frank Santiago, "POW, MIA League Argues over Direction," *Omaha World Herald*, 29 June 1974, 17.

37. Michael Allen, *Until the Last Man Comes Home: POWs, MIAs, and the Unending Vietnam War* (Chapel Hill: University of North Carolina Press, 2009), 57.

38. Iris Powers in *Hearings before the House Select Committee on Missing Persons in Southeast Asia*, Ninety-Fourth Congress, First Session, Part 2, 43.

39. Keating, *Prisoners of Hope*, 50.

40. Allen, *Until the Last Man Comes Home*, 151.

41. "Have You Forgotten Him?" A7.

42. Valerie J. Nelson, "Newt Heisley Dies at 88; Veteran Designed POW/MIA Flag," *Los Angeles Times*, 20 May 2009, viewed 30 October 2013, at http://www.latimes.com/news/obituaries/la-me-newt-heisley20-2009may20,0,3075716.story#axzz2jEroUo7B.

43. Keating, *Prisoners of Hope*, 85.

44. Jack Kemp to Henry Kissinger, 1 February 1973, in National Security Files—Henry A. Kissinger Office Files—Country Files, Far East: Vietnam, Box 110, EC Reconstruction Folder (3 of 3).

45. Paris Agreement, in Henry Kissinger, *Ending the War in Vietnam: A History of America's Involvement in and Extrication from the Vietnam War* (New York: Simon & Schuster, 2003), 448.

46. "Protocol on Healing the Wounds of War and the Rehabilitation of Economy in North Vietnam," 10 January 1973, in National Security Files—Henry A. Kissinger Office Files—Country Files, Far East: Vietnam, Box 110, EC Reconstruction Folder (3 of 3).

47. Congress only learned of the letter and the unfulfilled secret promises it contained in 1975 when members of a House investigatory committee traveled to Hanoi and were confronted with its contents by the Vietnamese. Former Nixon administra-

tion officials hotly denied everything in the face of all evidence, and sympathizers in the state department refused to release the letter itself until 1977. Franklin, *MIA, or, Mythmaking in America*, 125–126.

48. Richard Nixon to Pham Van Dong, 1 February 1973, in "Text of Announcement by State Department and Two Nixon Letters," *New York Times*, 20 May 1977, 17.

49. Arnold Isaacs, *Without Honor: Defeat in Vietnam and Cambodia* (Baltimore: Johns Hopkins University Press, 1999), 132.

50. William Clements in "What About Those MIAs?" *Panama City News-Herald*, 5 August 1973, 38.

51. William Clements to Richard Nixon, 17 July 1973, in Nixon Presidential Staff Materials, National Security Council Files—POW/MIA, Box 2, Vietnam (POW) Vol. VI Jan 1973 Folder (2 of 2).

52. Ibid.

53. Ibid.

54. Michael Ross, "'Dismay' on Nixon's '73 POW Stance," *Los Angeles Times*, 26 June 1992, A6.

55. Phyllis Corbitt, "Rethinking Our Position on MIAs," *Washington Post*, 25 October 1976, A14.

56. "United States House of Representatives Select Committee on Missing Persons in Southeast Asia," *The Vietnam-Era Prisoner-of-War/Missing-in-Action Database*, viewed 8 November 2013, at http://lcweb2.loc.gov/frd/pow/senate_house/investigation_H.html.

57. *Americans Missing in Southeast Asia: Hearings before the House Select Committee on Missing Persons in Southeast Asia*, 94th Congress, First Session (Washington, DC: Government Printing Office, 1975) Part 1, ii.

58. William Clairborne and Bart Barnes, "1,200 Protestors Arrested at Capitol," *Washington Post*, 6 May 1971, A14.

59. Franklin, *MIA, or, Mythmaking in America*, 14–15.

60. Representative Richard Ottinger in *Americans Missing in Southeast Asia: Hearings before the House Select Committee on Missing Persons in Southeast Asia*, 12.

61. Memorandum of Conversation, Arnaud de Borchgrave and Pham Van Dong, 24 October 1972, in Nixon Presidential Staff Materials, National Security Council Files—POW/MIA, Box 3—Vietnam Subject Files, Backchannel Message—1972 Southeast Asia Folder.

62. Franklin, *MIA, or, Mythmaking in America*, 196.

63. Dr. Roger Shields in *Americans Missing in Southeast Asia: Hearings before the House Select Committee on Missing Persons in Southeast Asia*, Part 1, 33.

64. Ibid., 35.

65. Earl Hopper in *Americans Missing in Southeast Asia: Hearings before the House Select Committee on Missing Persons in Southeast Asia*, Part 4, 56.

66. E. C. "Bus" Mills in *Americans Missing in Southeast Asia: Hearings before the House Select Committee on Missing Persons in Southeast Asia*, Part 1, 66.

67. Ibid., 67.

68. Coker in *Americans Missing in Southeast Asia: Hearings before the House Select Committee on Missing Persons in Southeast Asia*, Part 2, 113–114.

69. Ibid., 115.

70. *Americans Missing in Southeast Asia: Final Report together with Additional and Separate Views of the Select Committee on Missing Persons in Southeast Asia, United States House of Representatives* (Washington, DC: Government Printing Office, 1976), 22.

71. Ibid., 51.

72. *Americans Missing in Southeast Asia: Final Report together with Additional and Separate Views of the Select Committee on Missing Persons in Southeast Asia, United States House of Representatives*, 229.

73. Ibid., 241.

74. Ibid., 247–248.

75. Franklin, *MIA, or, Mythmaking in America*, 15.

76. Clarke, *The Missing Man*, 99.

77. Ann Mills Griffiths in "House Panel Declares No American Is Still an Indochina War Prisoner," *New York Times*, 16 December 1976, 11.

78. Carol Bates in "No MIAs Still Alive, House Probers Say; Report Angers Families," *Chicago Tribune*, 16 December 1976, 8.

79. Bruce W. Most, "If We Sweep the MIA Issue under the Rug, a Lump Will Show," *Los Angeles Times*, 23 September 1977, E7.

80. G. V. Montgomery in Kathy Sawyer, "No Hope, MIA Families Told," *Washington Post*, 24 July 1976, A6.

81. Jo Ann Waller in "Ford Vows to Aid Search for G.I.'s, Assures Families of Missing Men in Indochina," *New York Times*, 26 July 1976, 6.

82. Sawyer, "No Hope, MIA Families Told," A6.

83. Allen, *Until the Last Man Comes Home*, 173.

84. Ronald Reagan in Kathy Sawyer, "A Father Charges MIA 'Cover-Up,'" *Washington Post*, 25 July 1976, B7.

85. Allen, *Until the Last Man Comes Home*, 176–177.

86. Gerald Ford in Sawyer, "A Father Charges MIA 'Cover-Up,'" B7.

87. Sawyer, "A Father Charges MIA 'Cover-Up," B7.

88. Barbara Parker in "Ford Vows to Aid Search for G.I.'s," *New York Times*, 26 July 1976, A6.

Chapter Five. High-Water Mark of the Secret Camp Myth

1. Steven Roberts, "The Year of the Hostage," *New York Times Magazine*, 2 November 1980, 26, 30.

2. Advertisement, "Have You Forgotten Him?" *Washington Post*, 12 February 1973, A7.

3. Ibid., 30.

4. Michael Allen, *Until the Last Man Comes Home: POWs, MIAs, and the Unending Vietnam War* (Chapel Hill: University of North Carolina Press, 2009), 49.

5. Kathleen Kennedy in Roberts, "The Year of the Hostage," 60, 63.

6. Frank Kennedy in ibid, 63.

7. Wallace S. Wiggins, "Missing in Action," *Los Angeles Times*, 13 February 1980, D6.

8. Gladys Brooks in Allen, *Until the Last Man Comes Home,* 205.

9. David Rogers, "Hostage Families Seek Hope in FLAG," *Boston Globe,* 20 March 1980, 13.

10. Ronald Reagan, *Public Papers of the Presidency* (Washington, DC: Government Printing Office, 1981), 27.

11. Michael Hirsley, "POW-MIA Kin Cling to New Hope," *Chicago Tribune,* 8 July 1980, 1.

12. Ibid., 4.

13. Ibid.

14. Carol Bates in Dan Lohwasser, "Refugees' Story Rekindles Hope of POW-MIA Families," *Los Angeles Times,* 5 April 1981, 3.

15. Ibid.

16. "Wolff Says Hanoi Holds Remains of Servicemen," *Washington Post,* 31 January 1980, A13.

17. Ibid.

18. "Story of POW Bodies in Hanoi," *San Francisco Chronicle,* 28 June 1980, 6.

19. Ibid.

20. Tran Vien Loc in Hirsley, "POW-MIA Kin Cling to New Hope," 4.

21. Ibid.

22. T. C. Pinckney in "Story of POW Bodies in Hanoi," 6.

23. Charles Walker in ibid.

24. C. W. Gittins and Warren Gray, "Information Paper on POW/MIA Source Khambang Sibounheuang," in Records of the United States Senate, 102nd Senate, Select Committee on POW/MIA Affairs, Investigator Files—Hilton Foster, Box 6.

25. Ibid.

26. *Uncommon Valor*, directed by Ted Kotcheff (1983; Los Angeles, CA: Paramount Pictures, 1984), VHS.

27. *Missing in Action*, directed by Joseph Zito (1984; Los Angeles, CA: MGM, 2000), DVD.

28. William Boyles, "The Road to Hill 10," *Atlantic Monthly*, 1 April 1985, viewed 4 June 2014, at http://www.theatlantic.com/magazine/archive/1985/04/the -road-to-hill-10/306463/6/.

29. *Rambo: First Blood, Part II*, directed by George Cosmatos (1985; Culver City, CA: TriStar Pictures, 2008), DVD.

30. Ibid.

31. Ibid.

32. *Missing in Action.*

33. James "Bo" Gritz in Charles Patterson and G. Lee Tippin, *Heroes Who Fell from Grace: The True Story of Operation Lazarus, the Attempt to Free American POWs from Laos in 1982* (Canton, OH: Daring Books, 1985), 152.

34. Mark Gladstone and Richard Meyer, "'82 Raid in Search of US POWs Reported," *Los Angeles Times,* 31 January 1983, Part 1, 4.

35. Ibid.

36. *New information on US MIA-POW's in Indochina?: Hearing before the Subcommittee on Asian and Pacific Affairs of the Committee on Foreign Affairs, House of Representatives*, Ninety-Eighth Congress, First Session, 22 March 1983 (Washington, DC: Government Printing Office, 1983), 71.

37. James "Bo" Gritz, "Rebuttal to unsigned, undated accusations on NSC letterhead," 12 December 1989, in Records of the United States Senate, 102nd Senate, Select Committee on POW/MIA Affairs, Minority Staff Files—Tracy Usery, Box 20, Bo Gritz File.

38. James "Bo" Gritz, in Bob Sector, "Gritz Says He's on New POW Mission in Laos," *Los Angeles Times*, 21 February 1983, Part 1, 6.

39. Gladstone and Meyer, "'82 Raid in Search of US POWs Reported,'" 4.

40. Patterson and Tippin, *Heroes Who Fell from Grace*, 206.

41. Richard Meyer and Mark Gladstone, "Eastwood Told Reagan of Planned POW Raid," *Los Angeles Times*, 25 February 1983, Part 1, 1.

42. Ronald Reagan in Toby Glenn Bates, *The Reagan Rhetoric: History and Memory in 1980s America* (Dekalb: Northern Illinois University Press, 2011), 47.

43. Allen, *Until the Last Man Comes Home*, 216–217.

44. Ronald Reagan in Ben A. Franklin, "President Accepts Vietnam Memorial," *New York Times*, 12 November 1984, A16.

45. Ronald Reagan, "Remarks at the Veterans Day Ceremony at the Vietnam Veterans Memorial, November 11, 1988," viewed 22 March 2016, at https://reaganlibrary.archives.gov/archives/speeches/1988/111188b.htm.

46. Reagan in Allen, *Until the Last Man Comes Home*, 217.

47. H. Bruce Franklin, *MIA, or, Mythmaking in America* (New York: Lawrence Hill, 1992), 133.

48. Jack Bailey, Untitled Letter, 1986 in Records of the United States Senate, 102nd Senate, Select Committee on POW/MIA Affairs, Investigator Files—Hilton Foster, Box 8.

49. Ibid.

50. Alan Pell Crawford, "Patriots and Pigbones: The POW/MIA Rescue Hustle," *Nation*, 31 October 1988, 412.

51. Arnold Isaacs, *Vietnam Shadows: The War, Its Ghosts, and Its Legacy* (Baltimore: Johns Hopkins University Press, 1997), 123.

52. Crawford, "Patriots and Pigbones," 412.

53. National League of Families of Prisoners and Missing in Southeast Asia, "Frequently Asked Questions/League Responses on the POW/MIA Issue," 5 July 1991, in Records of the United States Senate, 102nd Senate, Select Committee on POW/MIA Affairs, Investigator Files—Hilton Foster, Box 6.

54. *Rambo: First Blood, Part II*.

55. Lee Lescaze, "Nixon Note on Aid to Hanoi Disclosed," *Washington Post*, 20 May 1977, viewed 16 February 2016, at https://www.washingtonpost.com/archive/politics/1977/05/20/nixon-note-on-aid-to-hanoi-disclosed/88206081-016d-4e85-8d49-2c45faod9ad6/.

56. Charlton Heston in Bill Paul, "Actor Heston's Fiery Telephone Pitch Enlists Support to Save Vietnam POWs," *Wall Street Journal*, 27 December 1984, 19.

57. Ibid.

58. Ibid.

59. John LeBoutillier in Crawford, "Patriots and Pigbones," 413.

60. Lieutenant Colonel Loren Haffner to Senator Daniel Inouye, 22 January 1986, in Records of the United States Senate, 102nd Senate, Select Committee on POW/MIA Affairs, Investigators' Case Files—William LeGro, Box 1.

61. Unsigned letter attached to Memo Dan Perrin to Jesse Helms, 3 May 1990, in Records of the United States Senate, 102nd Senate, Select Committee on POW/MIA Affairs, Minority Staff Files—Tracy Usry, Box 7.

62. Robert Buck Jr. to Senator Jesse Helms, 1989, in Records of the United States Senate, 102nd Senate, Select Committee on POW/MIA Affairs, Minority Staff Files—Tracy Usry, Box 4.

63. *Congressional Record—House*, 100th Congress, Second Session 1988, Vol. 134 Pt. 17, 24301.

64. Bill Paul, "POWs Won't Be Found without Cost," *Wall Street Journal*, 24 April 1985, 30.

65. "US POWs May Remain—House Task Force Report Sent to Reagan," *Washington Post*, 2 August 1986, A10.

66. Ibid.

67. Ibid.

68. Representative Paul McCloskey in Tom Matthews, "MIAs: Lives in Limbo," *Newsweek*, 9 August 1976, 26.

69. Representative Leon Panetta in ibid.

70. *Bill Summary & Status, 100th Congress (1987–1988)—H.R. 5226*, viewed 6 November 2013, at http://thomas.loc.gov/cgi-bin/bdquery/z?d100:H.R.5226.

71. Representative Charlie Rose in *Congressional Record*, 100th Congress, Second Session, 1988, Vol. 134 Pt. 17, 24298.

72. Representative Robert Michel in ibid., 24299.

73. Representative Bob Dornan in ibid., 24300.

74. "Minor Memos," *Wall Street Journal*, 2 August 1991, A1.

75. "'Road Map' to Renew Ties with Hanoi, Could Lead to Some Trade by Year End," *Wall Street Journal*, 15 April 1991, A10.

76. US Senate Committee on Foreign Relations Republican Staff, *Interim Report on the Southeast Asian POW/MIA Issue*, 29 October 1990, Folder 96, Box 27, Investigator Files—Hilton Foster, RG46.

77. US Senate Committee on Foreign Relations Republican Staff, *Examination of US Policy toward POW/MIAs*, 23 May 1991, viewed 18 November 2013, at http://www.nationalalliance.org/vietnam/overview.htm.

78. Carleton Bryant, "Helms Cleans House in Senate Panel," *Washington Times*, 8 January 1992, A3.

79. Deputy Assistant Secretary of Defense Carl Ford in *Hearings before the Senate Select Committee on POW/MIA Affairs*, 15 November 1991 (Washington, DC: Government Printing Office, 1992), Part I, 641.

80. Bryant, "Helms Cleans House in Senate Panel," A3.

81. *Congressional Record*, 102nd Congress, First Session, 2 August 1991 (Washington, DC: Government Printing Office, 1991), Vol. 137 Pt. 15, 21852–21853.

82. Bill Codhina to Alex Greenfeld, 31 March 1992, in "Select Committee on POW/MIA Issues," *Records of the US Senate*, 102nd Congress, Investigator Files—Hilton Foster, Box 4, RG46.

83. Senate Select Committee, *Report of the Senate Select Committee on POW/MIA Affairs* (Washington, DC: Government Printing Office, 1993), 198–199.

84. Senator John Kerry to Congresswoman Patsy Mink, 23 October 1992, in "Select Committee on POW/MIA Issues," *Records of the US Senate*, 102nd Congress, Investigator Files—William E. Le Gro, Box 1, Benge File, RG46.

85. Colonel Joseph Schlatter to Lousie Van Hoozer, 26 July 1988, in "Select Committee on POW/MIA Issues," *Records of the US Senate*, 102nd Congress, Foreign Relations Committee Minority Staff Files, Box 7, Bohica Folder, RG46.

86. "Senator Says Hanoi Sources Saw POWs in Secret Camp," *Chicago Tribune*, 5 August 1992, L4.

87. Ibid.

88. Allen, *Until the Last Man Comes Home*, 274–275.

89. Senator John Kerry in Senate Select Committee on POW/MIA Affairs, *Oversight Hearings: Department of Defense, POW/MIA Family Issues, and Private Sector Issues* (Washington, DC: Government Printing Office, 1992), 1282–1284.

90. Ibid.

91. Senate Select Committee, *Report of the Senate Select Committee on POW/MIA Affairs*, 7.

92. Ibid., 9.

93. Robert Smith in Thomas E. Ricks, "Senate Study on Vietnam-War Captives Concludes No US POWs Remain Alive," *Wall Street Journal*, 14 January 1993, A6.

94. Adam Clymer, "Claim of POW Cover-Up Rends Senate Decorum," *New York Times*, 8 September 1993, viewed 22 March 2016, at http://www.nytimes.com/1993/09/08/us/claim-of-pow-cover-up-rends-senate-decorum.html?pagewant ed=all.

95. Allen, *Until the Last Man Comes Home*, 277–278.

96. H. Bruce Franklin, "Missing in Action in the Twenty-First Century," in Scott Laderman and Edwin A. Martini, eds., *Four Decades On: Vietnam, the United States, and the Legacies of the Second Indochina War* (Durham, NC: Duke University Press, 2013), 285.

97. Ibid.

Conclusion

1. Dr. Pflüger, Ausschuss für KGfragen in den Ländern der US-Zone 1947, "Die Registrierung der Kriegsgefangenen und Vermissten in den Ländern der US-Zone" (stand mitte 1947), 6–7, in Bundesarchiv-Koblenz, B150–Bundesministrum für Vertriebene, Flüchtlinge, und Kriegsgeschädigte, 322–Kriegsgefangene–Registrierung in den Ländern der US-Zone 1947.

2. "Defense Prisoner of War/Missing Personnel Office US Unaccounted-For from the Vietnam War," 3 February 2016, http://www.dtic.mil/dpmo/vietnam/reports

/documents/pmsea_una_p_name.pdf; "Defense Prisoner of War/Missing Personnel Office US Accounted-For from the Vietnam War," 11 March 2014, http://www.dtic .mil/dpmo/vietnam/reports/documents/pmsea_acc_p_name.pdf.

3. Michael Allen, *Until the Last Man Comes Home: POWs, MIAs, and the Unending Vietnam War* (Chapel Hill: University of North Carolina Press, 2009), 210.

4. Michael Clodfelter, *Warfare and Armed Conflicts: A Statistical Reference to Casualties and Other Figures, 1500–2000* (Jefferson, NC: McFarland, 2002), 515.

5. Lieutenant Colonel Pat Caruthers in Danforth Austin, Jack Kramer, and Eric Morgenthaler, "Missing—or Dead? Some Relatives of POWs Say US Misleads Them," *Wall Street Journal*, 20 September 1971, 4.

6. Lieutenant Commander George Coker to the Board of Directors of the National League of Families, 27 October 1973, in *Hearings before the House Select Committee on Missing Persons in Southeast Asia*, Ninety-Fourth Congress, First Session, Part 2 (Washington, DC: Government Printing Office, 1975), 113–114.

7. "Hamlet Attack Called, 'Point-Blank Murder,'" *St. Louis Post-Dispatch*, 20 November 1969.

8. James and Sybil Stockdale, *In Love and War: The Story of a Family's Ordeal and Sacrifice during the Vietnam War* (New York: Harper & Row, 1984), 252.

9. Frank Biess, *Homecomings: Returning POWs and the Legacies of Defeat in Postwar Germany* (Princeton, NJ: Princeton University Press, 2006), 154.

10. James Diehl, *The Thanks of the Fatherland: German Veterans after the Second World War* (Chapel Hill: University of North Carolina Press, 1993), 101–102.

11. "Home at Last!" *Newsweek*, 26 February 1973, 18.

12. "The POW's Right-Hand Men," *Newsweek*, 19 February 1973, 20.

13. Walter Schulte, *Hirnorganische Dauerschäden nach schwerer Dystrophie* (Munich: Urban & Schwarzenberg, 1953), 45–46.

14. *Rambo: First Blood, Part II*, directed by George Cosmatos (1985; Culver City, CA: TriStar Pictures, 2008), DVD.

15. Charles Patterson and G. Lee Tippin, *Heroes Who Fell from Grace: The True Story of Operation Lazarus, the Attempt to Free American POWs from Laos in 1982* (Canton, OH: Daring Books, 1985), 206.

16. *Rambo: First Blood, Part II*.

17. Biess, *Homecomings*, 23.

18. Jean-Yves Le Naour, *The Living Unknown Soldier: A Story of Grief and the Great War* (New York: Metropolitan Books, 2002), 135.

19. Loudon Wainwright, "When Johnny Comes Marching Home—Or Doesn't," *Life*, 10 November 1972, 38.

20. Norbert Frei, *Adenauer's Germany and the Nazi Past: The Politics of Amnesty and Integration* (New York: Columbia University Press, 2002), 225.

21. "36 US Code § 902—National League of Families POW/MIA flag," viewed 12 September 2017, at https://www.law.cornell.edu/uscode/text/36/902.

Bibliography

Archives

Bundesarchiv, Koblenz
B136 – Bundeskanzleramt
B150 – Bundesministerium für Vertriebene, Flüchtlinge und Kriegsgeschädigte
199 – Suchdienst Zusammenarbeit der WASt mit dem DRK
203 – Registrierung der Kriegsgefangenen und Vermisste
245 – Zivilinternierte in der UdSSR: Dokumentation, Berichte von Heimkehrern
286A – Arbeitsgemeinschaft der westdeutschen Länder fur Kriegsgefangenen- und
  Heimkehrerfragen- Errichtung, Organisation, sitzung protokolle, Finanzierung
322 – Kriegsgefangene: Registrierung in den Ländrern der US-Zone 1947
344A – Kriegsgefangenen in sowjetischen Lagern
344B – Kriegsgefangenen in polishischen Lagern
344C – Kriegsgefangenen in jugoslavischen Lagern

National Archives, Washington, DC
Investigator Files: Hilton Foster
Investigator Files: William LeGro
Minority Staff Files: Tracy Usry
Policy Files of the Secretary of Defense
Record Group 46: Records of the United States Senate
Records of the Senate Select Committee on POW/MIA Affairs, 1991–1993
Records Received: Department of Defense
State Department Records: Frank Sieverts

Richard Nixon Library, Yorba Linda, CA
Henry A. Kissinger Office Files
National Security Council Files
Nixon Presidential Materials Staff
POW/MIA Files
Special Material Files: H. R. Haldeman Chronological Files
Subject Files
Vietnam Country Files
Vietnam Subject Files
White House Special Files

Department of Defense POW/Missing Personnel Office
Gerald Ford Library, Ann Arbor, MI
Ronald Reagan Library, Simi Valley, CA

Newspapers and Magazines

Atlantic Monthly
Boston Globe
Chicago Tribune
Christian Century
Der Tagespiegel
Die Zeit
Frankfurter Allegemeine Zeitung
Life
Los Angeles Times
The Nation
Newsweek
New York Times
Omaha World Herald
Panama City News-Herald (FL)
Parade
Rhein Neckar Zeitung
San Francisco Chronicle
St. Louis Post-Dispatch
Stuttgarter Nachrichten
Stuttgarter Zeitung
Time
Wall Street Journal
Washington Post
Washington Times
Westdeutsche Allgemeine Zeitung

Government Publications

US Congress. House Select Committee on Missing Persons in Southeast Asia. *Americans Missing in Southeast Asia: Final Report together with Additional and Separate Views.* 94th Congress, 2nd Session. Washington, DC: Government Printing Office, 1976.

———. *Americans Missing in Southeast Asia: Hearings before the House Select Committee on Missing Persons in Southeast Asia.* 94th Congress, 1st Session, Part 1. Washington, DC: Government Printing Office, 1976.

———. *Americans Missing in Southeast Asia: Hearings before the House Select Committee on Missing Persons in Southeast Asia.* 94th Congress, 1st Session, Part 2. Washington, DC: Government Printing Office, 1975.

———. *New information on US MIA-POW's in Indochina?: Hearing before the Subcommittee on Asian and Pacific Affairs of the Committee on Foreign Affairs, House of Representatives.* 98th Congress, 1st Session. Washington, DC: Government Printing Office, 1983.

US Congress. *Oversight Hearings: Department of Defense, POW/MIA Family Issues, and Private Sector Issues.* 102nd Congress, 1st Session, Part 1. Washington, DC: Government Printing Office, 1992.

———. *Report of the Senate Select Committee on POW/MIA Affairs.* 103rd Congress, 1st Session. Washington, DC: Government Printing Office, 1993.

———. Senate Select Committee on POW/MIA Affairs. *US MIAs in Southeast Asia: Hearings before the Senate Select Committee on POW/MIA Affairs.* Washington, DC: Government Printing Office, 1992.

US Department of Defense. *The US Fighting Man's Code of Conduct.* Washington, DC: Office of Armed Forces Information and Education, 1955.

Published Sources

Allen, Michael. *Until the Last Man Comes Home: POWs, MIAs, and the Unending Vietnam War.* Chapel Hill: University of North Carolina Press, 2009.

Baranowski, Shelley. *Strength through Joy: Consumerism and Mass Tourism in the Third Reich.* New York: Cambridge University Press, 2004.

Bartov, Omer. *Hitler's Army: Soldiers, Nazis, and War in the Third Reich.* New York: Oxford University Press, 1991.

Bates, Toby Glenn. *The Reagan Rhetoric: History and Memory in 1980s America.* Dekalb: Northern Illinois University Press, 2011.

Beevor, Anthony. *The Fall of Berlin 1945.* New York: Penguin Books, 2003.

———. *Stalingrad: The Fateful Siege 1942–1943.* New York: Penguin, 1999.

Bellamy, Chris. *Absolute War—Soviet Russia in the Second World War: A Modern History.* London: Macmillan, 2007.

Benz, Wolfgang. *A Concise History of the Third Reich.* Berkeley: University of California Press, 2006.

Biess, Frank. *Homecomings: Returning POWs and the Legacies of Defeat in Postwar Germany.* Princeton, NJ: Princeton University Press, 2006.

———. "Pioneers of a New Germany: Returning POWs from the Soviet Union and the Making of East German Citizens, 1945–50." *Central European History* 32, 2 (1999).

Borchard, Michael. *Die Deutschen Kriegsgefangenen in der Sowjetunion: Zur politischen Bedeutung der Kriegsgefangenenfrage, 1949–1955*. Düsseldorf: Droste, 2000.

Clarke, Douglas. *The Missing Man: Politics and the MIA*. Washington, DC: National Defense University Press, 1979.

Clodfelter, Michael. *Warfare and Armed Conflicts: A Statistical Reference to Casualties and Other Figures, 1500–2000*. Jefferson, NC: McFarland, 2002.

Dalloz, Jacques. *The War in Indochina 1945–54*. London: Gill & Macmillan, 1990.

Davis, Vernon. *The Long Road Home: US Prisoner of War Policy and Planning in Southeast Asia*. Washington, DC: Office of the Secretary of Defense, 2000.

Diehl, James. *Paramilitary Politics in Weimar Germany*. Bloomington: Indiana University Press, 1977.

——. *The Thanks of the Fatherland: German Veterans after the Second World War*. Chapel Hill: University of North Carolina Press, 1993.

Duiker, William J. *Ho Chi Minh*. New York: Hyperion, 2000.

Edinger, Lewis. *Kurt Schumacher: A Study in Personality and Political Behavior*. London: Oxford University Press, 1965.

Faust, Drew Gilpin. *This Republic of Suffering: Death and the American Civil War*. New York: Vintage Books, 2008.

Franklin, H. Bruce. *MIA, or, Mythmaking in America*. New York: Lawrence Hill, 1992.

——. *Vietnam and other American Fantasies*. Amherst: University of Massachusetts Press, 2000.

Frei, Norbert. *Adenauer's Germany and the Nazi Past: The Politics of Amnesty and Integration*. New York: Columbia University Press, 2002.

Frieser, Karl-Heinz, et al. *Das Deutsche Reich und der Zweite Weltkrieg—Vol. 8: Die Ostfront 1943–44—Den Krieg im Osten und an den Nebenfront*. Munich: Deutsche Verlags-Anstalt, 2007.

Fritz, Stephen G. *Endkampf: Soldiers, Civilians, and the Death of the Third Reich*. Lexington: University of Kentucky Press, 2004.

——. *Frontsoldaten: The German Soldier in World War II*. Lexington: University of Kentucky Press, 1995.

——. *Ostkrieg: Hitler's War of Extermination in the East*. Lexington: University of Kentucky Press, 2011.

Fritzsche, Peter. *Life and Death in the Third Reich*. London: Belknap Press, 2008.

Gilbert, Felix, trans. *Hitler Directs His War: The Secret Records of His Daily Military Conferences*. New York: Ishi Press, 2011.

Gilster, Herman. *The Air War in Southeast Asia: Case Studies of Selected Campaigns*. Maxwell, AL: Air University Press, 1993.

Glantz, David M., and Jonathan M. House. *Endgame at Stalingrad: December 1941–September 1943*. Lawrence: University Press of Kansas, 2009.

————. *When Titans Clashed: How the Red Army Stopped Hitler*. Lawrence: University Press of Kansas, 1995.

Glantz, David M., and Harold Orienstein, eds. *The Battle for L'vov: The Soviet General Staff Study*. New York: Routledge, 2007.

Greiner, Bettina. *Suppressed Terror: History and Perception of Soviet Special Camps in Germany*. Lanham, MD: Lexington Books, 2014.

Gröner, Erich. *Die deutschen Kriegschiffe 1815–1945, Band 8/1: Flu fahrzeuge, Ujäger, Vorpostenboote, Hilfsminensucher, Küstenschutzverbände, Teil 1*. Bonn: Bernard & Graefe Verlag, 1993.

Grubb, Evelyn, and Carol Jose. *You Are Not Forgotten: A Family's Quest for Truth and the Founding of the National League of Families*. St. Petersburg, FL: Vandamere Press, 2008.

Halder, Franz. *The Halder Diaries: The Private War Journals of Colonel General Franz Halder, Chief of the General Staff, Supreme Command of the German Army (OKH) 14 August 1939 to 24 September 1942*. Boulder, CO: Westview Press, 1976.

Hitler, Adolf. *Mein Kampf*. Boston: Houghton Mifflin, 1943.

Hughes, Michael. *Shouldering the Burdens of Defeat: West Germany and the Reconstruction of Social Justice*. Chapel Hill: University of North Carolina Press, 1999.

Hynes, Samuel. *The Soldiers' Tale: Bearing Witness to Modern War*. New York: Penguin Books, 1998.

Isaacs, Arnold. *Vietnam Shadows: The War, Its Ghosts, and Its Legacy*. Baltimore: Johns Hopkins University Press, 1997.

————. *Without Honor: Defeat in Vietnam and Cambodia*. Baltimore: Johns Hopkins University Press, 1999.

Keating, Susan Katz. *Prisoners of Hope*. New York: Random House, 1994.

Kimball, Jeffrey. *Nixon's Vietnam War*. Lawrence: University Press of Kansas, 1998.

Kissinger, Henry. *Ending the Vietnam War: A History of America's Involvement in and Extrication from the Vietnam War*. New York: Simon & Schuster, 2003.

Laderman, Scott, and Edwin A. Martini, eds. *Four Decades On: Vietnam, the United States, and the Legacies of the Second Indochina War*. Durham, NC: Duke University Press, 2013.

Lamy, Perry L. *Barrel Roll 1968–1973: An Air Campaign in Support of National Policy*. Maxwell, AL: Air University Press, 1995.

Lavalle, A. J. C., ed. *Air Power and the 1972 Spring Invasion*. Washington, DC: Office of Air Force History, 1985.

Lawrence, Mark Atwood. *Assuming the Burden: Europe and the American Commitment to War in Vietnam*. Berkeley: University of California Press, 2005.

Leland, Anne, and Mari-Jana Oboroceanu. *American War and Military Operations Casualties: Lists and Statistics*. Washington, DC: Congressional Research Service, 2010.

Le Naour, Jean-Yves. *The Living Unknown Soldier: A Story of Grief and the Great War*. New York: Metropolitan Books, 2002.

Logevall, Fredrik. *Choosing War: The Lost Chance for Peace and the Escalation of War in Vietnam*. Berkeley: University of California Press, 1999.

Longerich, Peter. *Heinrich Himmler: A Life*. New York: Oxford University Press, 2012.

MacKenzie, S. P. "The Treatment of Prisoners of War in World War II." *Journal of Modern History* 66, 3 (September 1994).

Maulucci, Thomas. *Adenauer's Foreign Office: West German Diplomacy in the Shadow of the Third Reich*. DeKalb: Northern Illinois University Press, 2012.

Mazower, Mark. *Hitler's Empire: How the Nazis Ruled Europe*. New York: Penguin Press, 2008.

McCarthy, James. *Linebacker II: A View from the Rock*. Washington, DC: Office of Air Force History, 1985.

Military History Institute of Vietnam and Merle Pribbenow, trans. *Victory in Vietnam: The Official History of the People's Army of Vietnam, 1954–1975*. Lawrence: University Press of Kansas, 2002.

Moeller, Robert. "'The Last Soldiers of the Great War,' and Tales of Family Reunion in the Federal Republic of Germany." *Signs* 24, 1 (Autumn 1998).

———. *War Stories: The Search for a Usable Past in the Federal Republic of Germany*. Berkeley: University of California Press, 2001.

Moreau, Donna. *Waiting Wives: The Story of Schilling Manor, Home Front to the Vietnam War*. New York: Simon & Schuster, 2010.

Morina, Christina. "Instructed Silence, Constructed Memory: The SED and Return of German Prisoners of War as 'War Criminals' from the Soviet Union to East Germany, 1950–56." *Contemporary European History* 13, 3 (August 2004).

Mrozek, Donald. *Air Power and the Ground War in Vietnam: Ideas and Actions*. Maxwell, AL: Air University Press, 1988.

Nixon, Richard. *Richard Nixon Speaks Out: Major Speeches and Statements of Richard M. Nixon in the Presidential Campaign of 1968*. New York: Nixon-Agnew Campaign Committee, 1968.

Oudes, Bruce, ed. *From: The President—Richard Nixon's Secret Files*. New York: Harper & Row, 1989.

Overmans, Rüdiger. *Deutsche militärische Verluste im Zweiten Weltkrieg*. Munich: Oldenbourg, 2004.

———. *Soldaten hinter Stacheldraht: Deutsche Kriegsgefangene des Zweiten Weltkriegs*. Berlin: Ullstein, 2000.

Patterson, Charles, and G. Lee Tippin. *Heroes Who Fell from Grace: The True Story of Operation Lazarus, the Attempt to Free American POWs from Laos in 1982*. Canton, OH: Daring Books, 1985.

Peterson, Edward N. *The Many Faces of Defeat: The German People's Experience in 1945*. New York: Peter Lang, 1990.

Prados, John. *The Blood Road: The Ho Chi Minh Trail and the Vietnam War*. New York: John Wiley & Sons, 1999.

Reagan, Ronald. *Public Papers of the Presidency*. Washington, DC: Government Printing Office, 1984.

Riesenberger, Dieter, ed. *Das Deutsche Rote Kreuz, Konrad Adenauer und das Kreigsgefangenenproblem: Die Rückführung der Deutschen Kreigsgefangenen aus der Sowjetunion (1952–1955)*. Bremen: Donat Verlaug, 1994.

Rochester, Stuart, and Frederick Kiley. *Honor Bound: The History of American Prisoners of War in Southeast Asia*. Washington, DC: Office of the Secretary of Defense, 1998.

Schulte, Walter. *Hirnorganische Dauerschäden nach schwerer Dystrophie*. Munich: Urban & Schwarzenberg, 1953.

Schumann, Dirk. *Political Violence in the Weimar Republic 1918–1933: Fight for the Streets and Fear of Civil War*. New York: Berghahn Books, 2009.

Scott, Roland B. "US Air Force Revises Policy for Flying Personnel with Sickle Cell Trait." *Journal of the National Medical Association* 72, 9 (1982): 835–836.

Shawcross, William. *Sideshow: Kissinger, Nixon and the Destruction of Cambodia*. New York: Simon & Schuster, 1979.

Sherwood, John Darrell. *Black Sailor, White Navy: Racial Unrest in the Fleet during the Vietnam War Era*. New York: New York University Press, 2007.

Shirer, William. *The Rise and Fall of the Third Reich: A History of Nazi Germany*. New York: Simon & Schuster, 1960.

Stargardt, Nicholas. *The German War: A Nation under Arms 1939–45*. New York: Basic Books, 2015.

Statler, Kathryn. *Replacing France: The Origins of American Intervention in Vietnam*. Lexington: University Press of Kentucky, 2007.

Stebbins, Richard P., and Elaine P. Adam, eds. *American Foreign Relations 1972: A Documentary Record*. New York: New York University Press, 1976.

Stockdale, James and Sybil. *In Love and War: The Story of a Family's Ordeal and Sacrifice during the Vietnam War*. New York: Harper & Row, 1984.

Terry, Wallace. *Bloods: An Oral History of the Vietnam War by Black Veterans*. New York: Random House, 1984.

Tilford, Earl. *Crosswinds: The Air Force's Setup in Vietnam*. College Station: Texas A&M Press, 1993.

Turse, Nick. *Kill Anything That Moves: The Real American War in Vietnam*. New York: Picador Books, 2013.

Van Staaveren, Jacob. *Interdiction in Southern Laos: 1960–1968*. Washington, DC: Center for Air Force History, 1993.

Westheider, James. *Fighting on Two Fronts: African Americans in the Vietnam War*. New York: New York University Press, 1997.

Wette, Wolfram. *The Wehrmacht: History, Myth, Reality*. Cambridge, MA: Harvard University Press, 2006.

Wieland, Lothar. *Das Bundesministerium für Vertriebene, Flüchtlinge und Kriegsgeschädigte*. Frankfurt: Athenäum Verlaug, 1968.

Wienand, Christiane. *Returning Memories: Former Prisoners of War in Divided and Reunited Germany*. Rochester, NY: Camden Books, 2015.

Williams, Charles. *Adenauer: The Father of the New Germany*. New York: John Wiley & Sons, 2000.

Williamson, Samuel R., Jr., and Peter Pastor, eds. *War and Society in East Central Europe, Vol. V—Essays on World War I: Origins and Prisoners of War.* New York: Brooklyn College Press, 1983.

Wilson, Richard, ed. *Setting the Course the First Year: Major Policy Statements by President Richard Nixon.* New York: Funk & Wagnalls, 1970.

Winter, Jay. *Sites of Memory, Sites of Mourning: The Great War in European Cultural History.* Cambridge: University of Cambridge Press, 1995.

Zhukov, Georgi. *Marshal Zhukov's Greatest Battles.* New York: Harper & Row, 1969.

Ziemke, Earl. *From Stalingrad to Berlin: The German Defeat in the East.* Washington, DC: US Army Center for Military History, 1968.

Index

hero-victim figure, 15, 32, 43–44, 46,
  51–54, 148, 150–151
Association of Returnees and, 51–54
compared to American activism, 153–154
controversy over prisoners in the USSR
  after repatriation's end, 45–56
final POW repatriations from the USSR
  and the end of, 56–57
German Red Cross and, 48–51, 54
origin of, 153
politics of, 5, 48–51, 154
postwar factors limiting, 35–37
secret camp myth and, 12, 33
German POWs/MIAs
chances for MIA survival, 149–150
chronological categories of losses in the
  East, 17
civilian difficulties in obtaining
  information about, 19–21
composition of, 15–17, 149
conflicting accounts of the total number
  of, 32–33
controversy over prisoners in the USSR
  after repatriation's end, 43–48
deteriorating ability of the Wehrmacht to
  keep records of, 26–27, 30, 32
East German view of, 44–45
elevation to hero status, 3–4
fears of physical and sexual disorders
  from imprisonment, 41
fears of political contamination from
  imprisonment, 41–42, 151, 152
final repatriations from the USSR, 54–57
German suppression of information
  about, 19, 24
held by the Soviets as war criminals, 35
incomplete return of from the USSR, 11,
  23–24, 37–43
lack of information about immediately
  following the war, 35–37
lack of international oversight, 20, 35
from the loss at Kursk, 26
from the loss at Sevastopol, 28
from the loss at Stalingrad, 21–23, 24, 25
from the loss of Army Group Courland, 29
from the loss of Budapest, 30
Nazi hero-cult and, 19, 23, 24
from Operation Bagration, 28–29
from Operation Barbarossa, 19, 21–22
as a problem for the Nazi state, 23

recast as hero-victims, 15, 32, 43–44, 46,
  51–54, 148, 150–151
reception and reintegration in West
  Germany, 40–43, 55–56, 151
returned from Allied captivity, 35, 37
returned from Yugoslavia, 39–40
total number of, 3, 149
treatment of in Soviet camps, 24–25
German Propaganda Ministry, 19
German Red Cross (DRK), 48–51, 54
German secret camp myth
ambiguity of the MIA status and, 154
Battle of Kursk and, 26
controversy over prisoners in the USSR
  after repatriation's end, 43–48
Eastern Front as a war of extermination
  and, 14–15
elevation of POWs/MIAs to hero status,
  3–4
final POW repatriations from the USSR
  and the decline of, 54–57
German appropriated suffering and
  creation of the hero-victim figure, 15,
  32, 43–44, 46, 51–54, 148
German attitudes toward veterans and, 3,
  4
historiography of, 4–6
iconography, 46, 52
key factors in the origin of, 2–4, 11–12,
  33, 34–35
loss of Army Group Courland and, 29
loss of German ships and, 27–28, 29–30
Operation Bagration and, 28–29
Operation Barbarossa and, 18
overview and comparison to the American
  myth, 2–4, 148–156
rumors of Soviet "silent camps" and,
  38–39, 50, 54, 57
short life and resolution of, 2–3, 12, 35,
  57, 154–155
Stalingrad and, 22
unreliable reports about casualties and, 17
German veterans, 3, 4, 36
German War, The (Stargadt), 6
Gerstenmaier, Eugen, 46
Gestapo, 19
Goebbels, Josef, 25
Go Public campaign
acceleration of the secret camp myth and,
  88, 96, 97

League of German Officers (BDO), 41

League of Wives of American Prisoners in Vietnam, 69, 71, 73–74, 95, 153. *See also* National League of Families of American Prisoners and Missing in Southeast Asia

LeBoutillier, John, 135

Le Naour, Jean-Yves, 7–8, 72

Lewke, Karl, 44–45

Life magazine, 84–85, 87–88, 154

Lindey, Albro, 142

"live sighting" witnesses, 104–105, 125–128, 142–143

Lodge, Henry Cabot, 80

Los Angeles Times, 119, 124–125

Luce, Don, 86–87

Lucier, James, 142

Maschke, Erich, 5

Mathers, Paul, 105

McCain, John, 142

McCloskey, Frank, 139

McCloskey, Paul, 140

McDaniel, Eugene "Red," 135

McGovern, George, 81, 82

MIA, or, Mythmaking in America and Vietnam (Franklin), 6, 7

MIAs (missing in action)
    chances for American MIA survival in Vietnam, 89–90, 114–117, 138, 149
    chances for German MIA survival on the Eastern Front, 149–150
    continuing American belief in MIA survival, 98–103, 133–134
    controversy over status changes in the United States, 106–107
    reclassification following the Korean War, 102–103
    See also American POWs/MIAs; German POWs/MIAs; POWs/MIAs

Military Assistance Advisory Group (MAAG), 60

Mills, E. C. "Bus," 115–116

Mills, James, 108

Minsk pocket, 28

Missing in Action (film), 7, 129–130, 131

Missing Persons Act (US), 106–107

Montgomery, G. V. "Sonny," 113–114, 118, 119–120

Montgomery Committee hearings, 113–120

Most, Bruce W., 119

Murphy, Barry, 66

My Lai massacre, 3, 150

Napier, Charles, 130

National Committee for a Free Germany (NKFD), 41

National Convention of the Veterans of Foreign Wars, 74th, 104

National Day of Prayer for POWs, 77

National Democratic Party (NPD), 51

National League of Families of American Prisoners and Missing in Southeast Asia
    changes in POW/MIA activism following Operation Homecoming and, 103–109, 112
    continued belief in MIA survival, 100–103
    criticism of Nixon's use of POWs/MIAs to continue the war, 84
    disengagement from public activism, 97
    Gerald Ford and, 121
    Go Public campaign and, 77–79
    importance of in POW/MIA activism, 69
    Iranian hostage crisis and, 124–125
    Montgomery Committee hearings and, 113, 115–116, 118, 119–120
    origin of, 153
    Paris peace talks and, 80–81
    Ronald Reagan and, 120–121
    Senate Select Committee hearings and, 144
    testimony of Tran Vien Loc and, 125–128
    See also American POW/MIA activism; American POW/MIA wives; League of Wives of American Prisoners in Vietnam

National Liberation Front (NLF), 63

National POW/MIA Recognition Day, 139

Nazi Germany
    Battle of Kursk and accelerating German casualty rates, 25–27
    collapse and surrender, 30–33
    collapse of the Eastern Front and encirclements of German forces, 27–30
    conventions on the treatment of prisoners and, 20
    invasion of the Soviet Union and German losses, 17–22
    losses at Stalingrad, 21–23, 24, 25
    postwar "Clean Hands" myth, 53–54